MW01092184

DOWN AND OUT IN SAIGON

DOWN AND OUT
IN SAIGON

STORIES OF THE POOR IN A COLONIAL CITY

Haydon Cherry

Studies of the Weatherhead East Asian Institute, Columbia University
The Studies of the Weatherhead East Asian Institute of Columbia
University were inaugurated in 1962 to bring to a wider public the results
of significant new research on modern and contemporary East Asia.

Yale
UNIVERSITY PRESS

New Haven & London

Published with assistance from the Louis Stern Memorial Fund and
from the Kingsley Trust Association Publication Fund established
by the Scroll and Key Society of Yale College.

Yale University Press books may be purchased in
quantity for educational, business, or promotional use.
For information, please e-mail sales.press@yale.edu
(U.S. office) or sales@yaleup.co.uk (U.K. office).

Set in MT Gentium type by Newgen North America.
Printed in the United States of America.

Library of Congress Control Number: 2018959651
ISBN 978-0-300-21825-1 (hardcover : alk. paper)

A catalogue record for this book is available from the British Library.

This paper meets the requirements of
ANSI/NISO Z39.48-1992 (Permanence of Paper).

10 9 8 7 6 5 4 3 2 1

For Tyler

Leben heißt für den Menschen: die Prozesse organisieren, denen er unterworfen ist.

For a human being, to live means: to organize the processes to which one is subjugated.

—Berthold Brecht

CONTENTS

CONTENTS

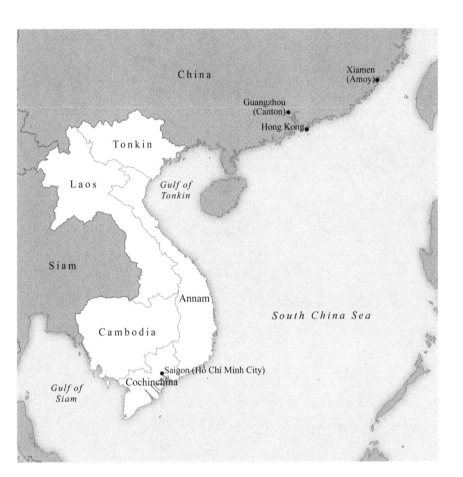

Saigon, French Indochina, and the South China Sea.
Map by Mapping Specialists.

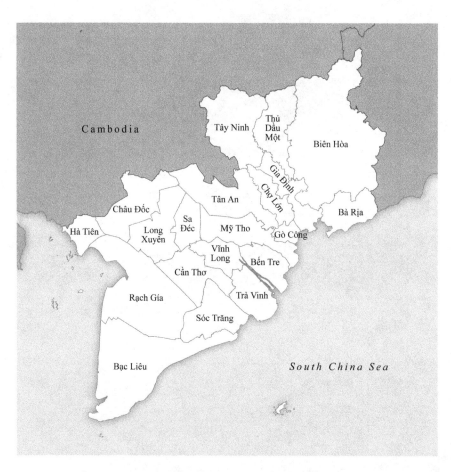

The Provinces of Cochinchina in the Early Twentieth Century.
Map by Mapping Specialists.

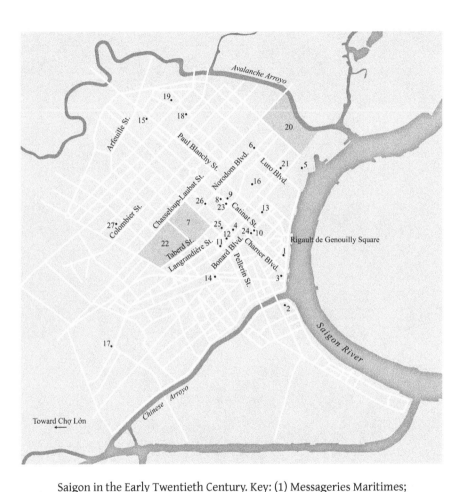

Saigon in the Early Twentieth Century. Key: (1) Messageries Maritimes;
(2) Messageries Fluviales; (3) Customs and Excise Building; (4) City Hall; (5) Arsenal;
(6) Barracks; (7) Palace of the Governor General; (8) Cathedral; (9) Post Office;
(10) Municipal Theater; (11) Central Prison; (12) Palace of the Lieutenant Governor
of Cochinchina; (13) Opium Refinery; (14) Central Market; (15) Tân Định Church;
(16) Military Hospital; (17) Camp des Mares; (18) European Cemetery; (19) Asian
Cemetery; (20) Botanical and Zoological Gardens; (21) Orphanage of the Holy
Childhood Association; (22) Municipal Garden; (23) Statue of Bishop Pigneau de
Béhaine and Prince Nguyễn Phúc Cảnh; (24) Statue of Francis Garnier; (25) Central
Police Station; (26) Statue of Léon Gambetta; (27) Municipal Dispensary.
Map by Mapping Specialists.

ACKNOWLEDGMENTS

I have incurred many debts while completing this book, which began as a doctoral dissertation submitted to the Department of History at Yale University. I am grateful to Benedict Kiernan, who directed the original dissertation, and to Jonathan Spence, Hue-Tam Ho Tai, Christopher Goscha, and Erik Harms, who provided additional guidance. I could not have hoped to learn from better teachers. Valerie Hansen deserves special thanks for her friendship, example, and encouragement over many years. My original training in Southeast Asian history began as an undergraduate at the National University of Singapore, supported by a scholarship from the Asia: NZ Foundation. During that time, I was fortunate to attend lectures and seminars given by Geoffrey Benjamin, Goh Beng Lan, Hong Lysa, Reynaldo Ileto, Paul Kratoska, John Miksic, Anthony Milner, Ng Chin-Keong, Niti Pawakapan, Thien Do, Wang Gungwu, and James Francis Warren. Michael Montesano first introduced me to the social history of modern Southeast Asia and Bruce Lockhart to the history of Vietnam. The enduring influence of their teaching cannot be measured.

The generous support of a number of institutions made the research and writing of this book possible. At Yale University I received funding from the John F. Enders Fellowship, the Charles Kao Fund, the MacMillan Center for International and Area Studies, the Council on Southeast East Asian Studies, the Smith-Richardson Foundation, the Fox International Fellowship, and the Mrs. Giles Whiting Foundation. A fellowship from the International Dissertation Research Fellowship Program of the Social Science Research Council, with funds provided by the Andrew W. Mellon Foundation, supported a year of research in Vietnam. A postdoctoral fellowship from the Mahindra Humanities Center at Harvard University furnished a congenial environment in which to begin revising the original dissertation. The College of Humanities and Social Sciences at North Carolina State University; the Center for Vietnamese Philosophy, Culture, and Society at Temple University; and the Weinberg College of Arts and Sciences at Northwestern University provided essential support during later stages of research and writing. I completed the penultimate draft while a fellow at the International Institute for Asian Studies in Leiden. I would like to thank its director, Philippe Peycam, and the fellowship coordinator, Sandra van der Horst, for making my stay in the Netherlands so productive.

The research for this book was carried out in several archives and libraries. In France, I would like to the staff of the Archives Nationales d'Outre-Mer in Aix-en-Provence, especially Olivia Pelletier and Marie-André Durand for their assistance. Noël Coulet and the Fondation Paul-Albert Février made several visits to Aix-en-Provence possible. I am grateful to the late Father Gérard Moussay at the Société des Missions Etrangères de Paris for allowing me use materials in the private archives of the society and to Brigitte Appavou for cheerfully helping me navigate my way through the collection. In Vietnam, I would like to thank the late Phan Huy Lê, director of the Institute for Vietnamese Studies and Development Sciences, and Đỗ Kiên at Hà Nội National University for sponsoring my preliminary research. I am particularly grateful to Nguyễn Văn Huệ, dean of the Faculty of Vietnamese Studies, as well as Nguyễn Duy Đoài and Đặng Thị Cẩm Tú for making my research in Hồ Chí Minh City possible. I would like to thank the directors and staffs of the Vietnam National Archives Center II in Hồ Chí Minh City and Center I in Hà Nội for allowing me access to their collections. I am also grateful to the staffs of the National Library of Vietnam in Hà Nội and the General Sciences Library and the library of the Museum of History in Hồ Chí Minh City for their assistance.

I would like to record my gratitude to the many colleagues and friends who answered my questions and queries, especially Susan Bayly, David Biggs, Pascal Bourdeaux, Pierre Brocheux, Nola Cooke, Bradley Davis, Erich deWald, Denis Duffy, Christina Firpo, Gilles de Gantès, Christopher Goscha, Andrew Hardy, Henrietta Harrison, Caroline Herbelin, Charles Keith, Nicolas Lainez, Li Tana, Bruce Lockhart, Hy Van Luong, David Marr, Shawn McHale, Edward Miller, Laurence Monnais, Michael Montesano, Cam Nguyen, Philippe Peycam, Brett Reilly, Paul Sager, Gerard Sasges, Michele Thompson, Nu-Anh Tran, Quang Phu Van, Benjamin Wilkinson, and Peter Zinoman. I also learned an enormous amount from discussions and correspondence with Michitake Aso, Sarah Grant, Claire Edington, Liam Kelley, Ann Marie Leshkowich, Martina Nguyen, Jason Picard, Natalie Porter, and Allen Tran. Jessica Biddlestone, Antoine Colonna d'Istria, Cécile Colonna d'Istria, Elizabeth Herman, Alec Holcombe, Annette Kim, Michelle Pinto, Brett Reilly, Erich deWald, and Benjamin Wilkinson all generously provided me with additional materials at crucial points.

Colleagues past and present commented thoughtfully on the manuscript in whole or in part. At North Carolina State University I would like to thank: David Ambaras, Daniel Bolger, Katherine Mellen Charron, Megan Cherry, Sandria Freitag, Craig Friend, David Gilmartin, Brent Sirota, and David Zonderman. I will be forever grateful to the late Jonathan Ocko for his early support of my work and for his wise example. At Northwestern University, Ken Alder, Michael Allen, Henry Binford, Peter Carroll, Caitlin Fitz, Laura Hein, Daniel Immerwahr, Rajeev Kinra, Melissa Macauley, Sarah Maza, Edward Muir, Scott Sowerby, Amy Stanley, Helen Tilley, and Jeffrey Winters all asked questions that I have tried to answer. Working with students at both institutions helped me consider how best to communicate the history of modern Vietnam and Southeast Asia. In that regard, Crosby Lupton and Amy Eisenstein merit special recognition.

I would like to give special thanks to Mara Caden, Amy Eisenstein, Charles Keith, Bruce Lockhart, Amy Stanley, and Peter Zinoman, who read the penultimate draft of this book, corrected many errors, and offered a number of suggestions that improved the final manuscript. Naturally, the remaining faults are my own. *Parturient montes, nascetur ridiculus mus.*

Jaya Aninda Chatterjee patiently shepherded the book through the editorial process at Yale University Press. I am further grateful to the press for permission to reproduce selections from *An Anthology of Vietnamese Poems* by Huỳnh Sanh Thông. Mapping Specialists, Ltd. in Fitchburg, Wisconsin, produced the maps. Annette Kim generously provided several of the images. Martin Schneider copyedited the final manuscript and Fred Kameny and Nguyễn Hồng Liên proofread the final draft. Arc Indexing prepared the index.

I could not have completed this project without the support of many friends. Mara Caden provided love and companionship during countless difficult times. I have learned more from Michael Montesano than from any other person. He has been a peerless source of friendship, guidance, and advice over many years. There are few more convivial companions than Brian Vivier, and his company has always been the most stimulating of distractions at home and abroad. Daniel Brückenhaus is an imaginative, humane, and sympathetic historian and an even more gifted friend. The Vietnamese Studies community knows Charles Keith to be a scholar of exceptional creativity, diligence, and integrity. He is also the most thoughtful of colleagues, genial of companions, and exemplary of friends. Van Ly welcomed me at Tân Sơn Nhất airport when I first arrived in Hồ Chí Minh City to do research and helped me to make the city my home. She then did it again and then again. I know of no one more generous and fierce.

My family often reminds me that I have now lived abroad longer than I have lived in my native New Zealand. Despite the long absence of their son, brother, and uncle they have continued to encourage my idiosyncratic labors with love and skeptical bemusement. This book is for my nephew, Tyler.

The author's royalties from this book are being given in support of the Saigon Children's Charity. Readers may make further donations online at: http://www.saigonchildren.com/.

DOWN AND OUT IN SAIGON

PROLOGUE

They leave rice fields to travel far and wide:
who doesn't count on them for sustenance?
Doffing their golden coats, they bask in sun;
displayed in every place, they shine like jade.
—*Phan Văn Trị, "Grains of Rice"*[1]

A vagrant limped onto the stage of modern Vietnamese history in early February 1913.

He entered upstage, far from the limelight; he did not have a speaking part, nor even a name.

The vagrant first appeared in a letter to the chief of the Saigon police. For more than a year and a half, the letter said, a vagrant had been hobbling through the streets of Saigon, leaning on a stick. Lame in one leg, he moved from street to street and stoop to stoop, seeking charity from shopkeepers, residents, and passersby. Every two weeks, the vagrant passed through Tân Định, a poor quarter located northwest of the city center. He made his way down Arfeuille Street, which traced a crooked line from Tân Định Market on Paul Blanchy Street to the intersection of Eyriaud des Vergnes and Mayer streets.[2] When he reached house number 92, the vagrant often lingered. Monsieur Chenieux, the French proprietor of number 92, thought that the vagrant was a leper and took pity on him; the

Frenchman allowed him to rest in the doorway and sometimes gave him alms. But soon the proprietor began to worry: in the heat of the day, itinerant merchants selling cakes and fruit rested in the same place. Fearing that they might contract leprosy from his stoop, he informed the local police post. When the vagrant arrived again two weeks later, Monsieur Chenieux wrote to the commissioner of police in Saigon. "Is there nothing to be done?" he asked. "I confess that I am a little ashamed of us French that such material and physical poverty cannot be helped in a city such as Saigon."

After one more foray onto the stage, the vagrant exited into the wings, never to appear again.

He made his final appearance in a letter to the governor of Cochinchina. The police had questioned the vagrant and learned that his name was Lê Văn Bội. He had arrived in Saigon two years earlier on a junk from Nha Trang in Annam, the French protectorate to the north. He carried no identity papers and had no record of having paid his taxes. The police took Lê Văn Bội to the municipal doctor, who declared: "The Vietnamese in question does not suffer from leprosy but from tertiary syphilis and is in a state of physical decline due to an addiction to opium. He refuses to go to the hospital." In his letter to the governor, the commissioner of police wrote: "I have the honor of asking you to kindly expel this individual."[3] And so the governor sent Lê Văn Bội back to Annam. What happened to him there? And after that? The documents do not say. They were pinned together and crammed with many other papers into a binder eventually labeled V.10/04.02. Lê Văn Bội was only one of the many poor migrants who came to Saigon during the colonial period looking for work or charity. His expulsion was a matter of simple routine.

The authorities in Saigon soon had to confront a much more serious problem. On March 22, 1913, just a few weeks after the authorities sent Lê Văn Bội back to Annam, a gendarme in Phan Thiết arrested a youth named Phan Phát Sanh. Phan Phát Sanh had arrived that morning on the train from Saigon, wearing jewelry and luxurious clothes of white silk. He carried a large sum of money but claimed to be a day laborer, which aroused the suspicion of the police. Searching his lodgings, they found elaborate costumes; manuscripts carrying magical invocations; large gilded jewels; a royal seal bearing the head of a dragon; an engraved sword; a bracelet with inscriptions, inside and out; and a pendant bearing the name "Phan Xích Long," or "Phan the Red Dragon." Two days later, the police discovered several bombs waiting to explode in key locations in Saigon and the neighboring city of Chợ Lớn. Flyers distributed in the two cities challenged French rule and proclaimed the arrival of a new emperor, Phan Xích Long. The flyers concluded with an exhortation: "Let us rise up and take back our country!" On March 28, six hundred cultivators marched on Saigon, dressed in white and wearing amulets, armed only with spears and swords. Colonial troops garrisoned in the city quickly defeated the uprising. The authorities tried its leader, Phan Phát Sanh—the self-proclaimed emperor—and the other rebels and imprisoned him along with more than sixty others.[4] The rebellion and subsequent trial scandalized the local press and generated hundreds of pages of official reports and correspondence.[5] Because of these many documents and the political significance of the rebellion, the story of Phan Xích Long is well known among historians of Vietnam, while the story of Lê Văn Bội has been almost completely forgotten.[6] Scholars have illuminated the political history of Vietnam, but much of its social history remains obscure.[7]

This book seeks, therefore, to illuminate the lives of those who, like Lê Văn Bội, numbered among the many poor in colonial Saigon.[8] It traces the itineraries of six poor individuals—a prostitute, a Chinese laborer, a rickshaw puller, an orphan, an untreatable invalid, and a poor Frenchman—who passed through the city during the first four decades of the twentieth century. They and their peers did not march in formation as members of a reserve army of labor down a narrow road toward revolution.[9] They cut their own paths as they navigated the changing fortunes of their native place, the vagaries and vicissitudes of the regional rice economy, and the institutional constraints of life under colonial rule.[10]

The ties of a native place, the town or village in which somebody was born, could not always hold them secure. Such a place might be well known for the excellence of its government, the tranquility of its people, and the wealth of its fields, or it might be notorious for the corruption of its officials, the rancor of its inhabitants, and the barrenness of its terrain. It might be flat and fertile so that the harvest was always abundant, like Vĩnh Long; or it might be hilly and sandy so that food crops struggled to grow there, as among the hills and valleys of eastern Biên Hòa. A native place might be protected from typhoons by mountains, like the seaside town of Nha Trang; or it could be more exposed to the turbulent weather of the South China Sea, like Cape St. Jacques. It could be close to Saigon with modern conveniences, like Mỹ Tho; or it might be remote and rustic, like the border town of Châu Đốc. For many Vietnamese, when life in their native place seemed especially arduous or marked by calamity, Saigon promised a life of relative ease and plenty.

The regional rice trade had made Saigon a prosperous city. After the French conquest of Cochinchina, the city had become increasingly tied to its rural hinterland and to a thriving regional rice market that spanned the South China Sea. The demand for rice, mainly from Hong Kong and southern China, kept ships moving in and out of the port of Saigon, the mills of neighboring Chợ Lớn turning; barges laden with paddy made their way through the waterways of Cochinchina, and the fields of the Mekong Delta were planted in rice. The flourishing rice trade attracted migrants from far and wide who sought opportunities in the city. While some found permanent paid employment and others amassed modest wealth trucking and trading in the commercial houses of the city, many did not. The less fortunate joined the ranks of the poor and performed countless petty labors: they pulled rickshaws, collected old newspapers, carried water, hauled bricks and lumber, repaired umbrellas, sharpened knives, sold soup, pedaled prognostications, and engaged in prostitution, among other makeshift work.[11]

The authorities in Saigon founded a number of new institutions to administer this burgeoning population of the urban poor. They imposed new taxes, legislated new crimes, and had new expectations of Vietnamese behavior. They also established orphanages, dispensaries, municipal clinics, hospitals, police posts, and prisons, each with a distinct set of rules, regulations, and standards of conduct and comportment. The poor needed knowledge and skill, if not cunning and guile, to find a place to sleep, a bowl of rice to eat, or care for an injury or illness.

This book draws on a wide variety of sources: published statistics, missionary letters, official reports, travelers' accounts, reportage, and colonial social scientific studies, among others. These documents record descriptions, measures, and observations of everyday life in colonial Saigon that range broadly in their comprehensiveness and exactitude. But read together, these documents shed light upon one another, because the individuals they describe, measure, and observe took part in one another's lives; they "grew old" together.[12] Such documents differ from the social scientist's survey, which yields facts of dubious certainty about supposed classes of people who are not otherwise related: Vietnamese laborers in Saigon earning less than $1.20—one piaster and twenty centimes—per day or all who could read romanized Vietnamese. By contrast, the stories of the urban poor crisscross and overlap in multiple ways. Orphans might become prostitutes; both rickshaw pullers and poor Frenchmen visited brothels; and all experienced illness of some kind. They came from different directions but traveled the same streets and lived in the same quarters of the city; they were buoyed together by periods of prosperity and burdened alike in times of privation; they were subject to the same laws and encountered the same institutions of authority.

The institution that the poor seem to have encountered most often was the municipal police. Many of the strategies that the poor used to get by— moving from place to place, begging, petty theft, tax avoidance, child abandonment, and clandestine prostitution—were crimes. If the poor were unlucky, the police arrested them, deposed them, and wrote a report. These reports followed common templates and were often spare, repetitive, and formulaic.[13] But from time to time—perhaps on orders from his superiors, perhaps out of curiosity or ambition—a policeman probed further and produced a more detailed deposition. These interviews, conducted in Vietnamese but transcribed in French, sometimes recorded direct speech, uniquely preserving the stories of the poor in their own words, as they talked about their origins, occupations, movements, habits, family, and acquaintances. Every so often, an industrious policeman tried to corroborate these details by interviewing neighbors, family members, employers, and other associates. Prejudice, fatigue, malice, and misinformation sometimes shaped the reports the policeman compiled, but charity, sympathy, and a sense of justice and fairness could help shape them too.[14]

The preservation of these reports, and the stories they tell of Saigon's poor, has almost been a matter of serendipity. The archives of the colonial police in Saigon seem to have been lost. But when the municipal authorities needed to expel a vagrant like Lê Văn Bội from the colony, or when they sought to recover the cost of confining a prostitute or treating an opium addict, they sent a copy of the relevant dossier to the Government of Co-chinchina. And the archives of the colonial government have been pre-served. The colonial administration began to safeguard its records in 1868, when it established the Direction of the Interior. Each office was respon-sible for conserving its own documents. In 1909, a newly founded archival service centralized the records of the Government of Cochinchina and or-ganized them alphabetically by subject, ranging from "Abonnements aux journaux (voir publications périodiques)" to "warrants agricoles." In the course of 1917 and 1918, the Government General reorganized the archives throughout French Indochina, making the records of Cochinchina part of a single administration, uniformly indexed and organized. For decades, the Central Library on Lagrandière Street with the later addition of a villa on Nguyễn Du Street housed the archives of Cochinchina, defending them from the ravages of war—but less successfully from humidity, mold, and insects. The archives remained in place under the Republic of Vietnam, until they were relocated and reorganized after the establishment of the Socialist Republic in 1976.[15] The colonial desire to discipline the urban poor and to order, classify, and preserve their documentary traces has left fragments of their stories for historians to piece together.

This book begins in 1904 on the eve of a typhoon that ruined the har-vest, threw the rice trade into disarray, and caused misery in Saigon and the provinces. Chapter 1 places the history of Saigon in the context of the regional rice trade. Each of the later chapters tells the story of one of six poor residents of Saigon and its environs: Lương Thị Lắm, a prostitute from the province of Biên Hòa who kept running away from home and from the colonial authorities; Trần Dưỡng, a Hakka laborer from southern China accused by his former employers of belonging to the illegal Heaven and Earth Society; Aimée Lahaye, a young woman who grew up in the or-phanage of the Holy Childhood Association, only to find herself orphaned once again later in life; a "human horse" calling himself Nguyễn Văn Thủ who pulled a rickshaw through the streets of the city; an incurable in-valid named Trần Văn Chinh who struggled against crippling disability; and Félix Colonna d'Istria, a poor Frenchman who was a constant victim of his own nonchalance. Their stories hinge on a series of small events: confinement in a municipal dispensary, a malicious letter to a provincial administrator, a trip abroad to convalesce, the need to register a place of residence, a chance epidemic, and the desire to secure a supply of opium. Such incidents might seem like trifles in the context of twentieth-century Vietnamese history—which was punctuated by the Nghệ Tĩnh Rebellion, the Second World War, the August Revolution, the Geneva Accords, the Tonkin Gulf Resolution, and the Paris Peace Agreement—but they were of fundamental and even mortal importance in the lives of the poor.[16] The stories in this book are sometimes melancholy and sorrowful and sometimes frustrating or despairing. But they are also testimony to the tenacity, resilience, and creativity of the urban poor as they sought to fashion their lives in colonial Saigon.

CHAPTER ONE

PAULATIM CRESCAM

For merit here below, who equals it?
To grind our rice, all call upon the mill.
Dauntless, it copes with storms of wind and dust;
unshaken, it will take a hundred spins.
To serve its lord, it must wear out its teeth.
Who made it so it chokes within its throat?
It cares not if its stones have both worn down:
because the foe's still there, it must fight on.
—*Phan Văn Trị, "The Rice Mill"*[1]

A typhoon struck Cochinchina on May 2, 1904. It made landfall after midnight and swept through the provinces of the colony. In the province of Bà Rịa, the fishing village of Long Hải lost thirty boats to the storm and almost two hundred residents perished. The typhoon overturned bridges, washed out roads, cut off the water supply, and left two government villas at Cape St. Jacques uninhabitable. The cape lost a number of residents: A French soldier drowned while saving two Vietnamese, and nineteen junks capsized or sank, killing at least fifty-two people. The French warship *Pascal* managed to save eighteen others who survived the wreck of their vessels. In the province of Gò Công, a tidal wave carried several coastal villages out to sea. The typhoon left many Vietnamese in the province of Mỹ Tho homeless. Even the sturdiest buildings, built from stone and brick, sustained significant damage. Several launches and two dredges that were anchored on the waterways sank. The storm destroyed the rice fields in Mỹ Tho and Gò Công. In both provinces, and in the provinces of Cần Thơ and Vĩnh Long further to the south, the drinking water became contaminated, leading to an outbreak of cholera. An unknown disease spread among the buffalo, which made the tasks of plowing and replanting doubly difficult. The typhoon injured many residents of Vĩnh Long and Bến Tre and left them homeless. Upriver in Cambodia, the storm toppled trees in Phnom Penh and damaged buildings both hardy and frail. It sank ships moored on the banks of the Mekong River and felled telegraph lines. The résident supérieur of Cambodia had to send his report overland to Saigon before it could be wired to the government in Hà Nội.[2]

The typhoon reached Saigon while the city slept. Ferocious winds uprooted trees and strewed them across the streets. In the palace gardens of the governor general, the storm knocked down trees, snapped branches, smashed flower pots, and blanketed the ground in berries. But it left the palace itself undamaged. Throughout the city, fallen trees and branches collapsed roofs and knocked down flimsy thatched dwellings. Several sampans, small boats that the Vietnamese called *tam bản,* and barges laden with merchandise sank or capsized. After the storm, the Office of the Public Prosecutor sought temporary accommodation in a thatched hut while workers repaired its building. Almost miraculously, the authorities did not record any deaths in the city.

The government came to the aid of the worst off. It raised funds publicly and privately so that money, clothes, rice, paddy, and materials for housing could be distributed to the needy. Schools in the most heavily affected areas closed for two months so that children could assist their parents with the tasks of rebuilding their homes and replanting their fields. The government delayed collecting taxes and in some places forgave them entirely.[3] Slowly, the residents of Cochinchina began to rebuild.

And then, a second typhoon swept across the colony in November. The Tiền Giang and Hậu Giang rivers, distributaries of the Mekong River, inundated Sa Đéc and spoiled the rice waiting to be harvested. The farmers there were ruined; many had to pawn the few items of value they possessed to survive. The government directed emergency funds to the province for aid and rebuilding.[4] The administrator of Sa Đéc recorded that "thanks to the measure that the local government was willing to take, in dedicating a sum of $20,000 to assist the poor, food is at least assured to most families. All of the people who come to the work sites are accepted, men, women, and children, each of whom is paid according to the work that they can do."[5] A drought followed in the wake of the flood.

Farmers everywhere struggled. Across Cochinchina, they abandoned their fields and headed for regions that had suffered less. Robberies increased in the provinces of Gia Định, Bến Tre, Trà Vinh, Cần Thơ, Châu Đốc, and Mỹ Tho, and cholera and smallpox began to spread in the countryside. Administrators estimated that the harvest in 1905 would be only half that of 1904. Confronted with widespread misery, the government again delayed collecting taxes and forgave them in the worst-affected areas. Vietnamese across the colony raised $36,000 to aid the worst off. In 1905, the Lunar New Year celebrations called Tết were muted, with few having money to spend on revelry or gaiety. After the farmers replanted their fields and readied another crop for harvest, great swarms of locusts attacked Cochinchina at the end of the year and threatened yet another harvest.[6]

Misery in the provinces caused misery in Saigon. The lieutenant governor wrote in 1905: "In Cochinchina, more than in any other country, all economic movement depends on the rice harvest. The past year having been poor, commerce and industry have been in decline."[7] This decline was everywhere evident in the capital of Cochinchina. With much of the crop ruined, there was little rice available for export. In 1905, the port of Saigon moved only 510,000 tons of paddy or rice in the husk, milled rice, and flour—a 42 percent decline from the previous year. Exports to Hong Kong fell by almost the same proportion. A slight increase in the price of rice could not compensate for the staggering drop in the volume available for export.[8] Saigon entered a slump. After the first typhoon in 1904, many Chinese left Cochinchina.[9] The Immigration and Identification Service recorded seven thousand fewer Chinese in the colony in the following year.[10] More than a thousand Europeans abandoned Saigon.[11] The number of Vietnamese taxpayers registered in the city fell from 6,185 in

1903 to 5,499 in 1905. As many as seven thousand people left Saigon in
1905: The population fell to 48,800. In 1906, it dropped slightly further to
48,700.[12] Many moved beyond the city limits where the taxes were lower.
Most of the workers at the Saigon arsenal, which built and repaired ships,
had moved to Gò Vấp in neighboring Gia Định. Factory workers in Khánh
Hội, near the port, went to live in the nearby province of Chợ Lớn. Many
other laborers—domestic servants, cooks, boys, coolies, and porters—left
the city.[13] Commenting on the Vietnamese retreat, the Apostolic Vicar of
the Catholic Church in Saigon observed that "what characterizes the Vietnamese in Cochinchina is . . . his vagrant temperament, his taste for moving, and the ease with which he leaves one part of the country to establish
himself temporarily in another. He abandons his thatched house as the
nomad of the desert folds his tent . . . nothing is so sad as to see him begin
an exodus from poverty once again."[14] At the end of 1906, the harvest was
strong, and in 1907 the port moved more rice than it had ever exported before. More than half of all the milled rice went to Hong Kong and the ports
of southern China.[15] As the economy recovered, migrants began to return
to the city, and with the incorporation of the villages of Khánh Hội and
Chánh Hưng into the city, the population reached fifty-three thousand.[16]
Once again, Saigon began to show signs of prosperity.

The residents of Saigon knew the city by many names: the Khmer called
it Prei Nokor; at different points in time the Vietnamese called it Gia Định,
Phiên An, Bến Nghé, and Sài Gòn; the Cantonese designated it Tai Ngon
(堤岸), while other Chinese speakers called it Xī Gòng (西貢); and the
French called it Saïgon after the conquest. The origins of the name *Saigon*
are obscure. In 1776, Lê Quý Đôn wrote the *Phủ Biên Tạp Lục* (撫邊雜錄),
the earliest surviving Vietnamese text to use the characters for Saigon
(柴棍), while referring to events that took place in 1674.[17] Catholic missionary documents from 1732 contain perhaps the earliest example of the
name in romanized form.[18] Western travelers to Cochinchina in the early
nineteenth century associated the name *Saigon* with the adjacent city that
became known as Chợ Lớn; they called Saigon *Bingeh* or *Pingeh,* a corruption of the Vietnamese vernacular name, Bến Nghé.[19] At the beginning of
the nineteenth century, both Bến Nghé and Saigon were vernacular names
for the area known administratively as Phiên An.[20] Saigon could refer to

many places, sometimes to only a market, at other times to a city, and at still other times to a whole canton.[21] The name *Saigon* may be related to the Khmer name of an earlier settlement, Prei Nokor, which means "forest of the realm," and possibly referred to the state-sponsored cultivation of groves of kapok that grew nearby.[22] It may also have denoted firewood cut from the same tree.[23] Whatever its etymology, by the beginning of the twentieth century "Saigon" had become the name of the prosperous capital of the French colony of Cochinchina.

The name *Cochinchina* itself has a complex history. It first appeared on a Portuguese map by the Genoese cartographer Albert Contino in 1502, as "Chinacochim," and named an area around the Red River delta in the north of Vietnam. At the time, the Portuguese had no direct knowledge of the Vietnamese coast and must have taken the name from Arab or Malay sources. Cochinchina first appeared in its current form in a letter, dated January 8, 1515, from Jorge de Albuqeurque in Malacca to King Manuel I of Portugal. Until 1615, Western writers and navigators used Cochinchina to refer to the Vietnamese kingdom, from the frontier with China in the north to the frontier with Champa in the south. After 1615, Cochinchina denoted the Vietnamese territory from Đồng Hới in the central province of Quảng Bình to its expanding frontier in the south of the peninsula. After the French occupation of the south began in 1861, the French sometimes referred to Lower Cochinchina or French Cochinchina. But by 1887, the French used the name *Cochinchina* to refer exclusively to their colony in the south of the peninsula. The name comes from the Chinese place name Jiaozhi (交阯), or Giao Chỉ in Vietnamese, which once denoted various provinces, commanderies, and prefectures in northern Vietnam before the tenth century. Transmitted in Arab, Malay, and Portuguese texts, "Giao Chỉ" eventually became "Cochin." The designation "Cochinchina" distinguished it from the port of Cochin on the distant Malabar coast of India.[24]

Most visitors to Cochinchina, at the beginning of the twentieth century, arrived in the colony through the Port of Saigon. A lighthouse on the island of Poulo Condore guided steamers from Singapore, Colombo, or Europe approaching from the south, and a light at Kê Gà on the coast of Annam aided ships from Hong Kong, Shanghai, or Japan arriving from the north. The ships entered Gành Rái Bay at Cape St. Jacques on the South

China Sea. Two lights at Cần Giờ marked the mouth of the Saigon River, itself a tributary of the Đồng Nai River. The ships followed the river inland for eighty kilometers, meandering past rice fields and colonial plantations. Several ships could traffic on the river at once: it was three hundred meters wide at its narrowest point and usually ranged between nine and twelve meters deep.[25] As the vessels made their way inland, the spires of Saigon Cathedral eventually came into view, followed by the municipal monuments and large trees that flanked the city's boulevards. The city of Saigon was the shape of an irregular quadrilateral, its sides formed by the waterways of the Saigon River, the Chinese Arroyo, the Belt Canal, and the Avalanche Arroyo. Its streets were typically straight and parallel and intersected one another at right angles. Wide boulevards cut through the city in all directions and connected its spacious squares.[26] Over time, the French inscribed the history of their presence in Saigon in the streets they named, the buildings they constructed, and the monuments they erected. Poor Vietnamese begged on those streets and took shelter from the sun in the buildings' shadows; rickshaws ferried the city's residents from one place to the next; and prostitutes went in furtive search of clients along its boulevards.

Having reached the port, ships anchored at the dock of the Messageries Maritimes, or Merchant Shipping Company, or at the Charner Pier that faced the boulevard of the same name. From the Messageries Maritimes, visitors could take a sampan and disembark near Charner Boulevard, or they could hire a carriage or rickshaw and travel across the bridge that spanned the Chinese Arroyo, the waterway that linked Saigon with the neighboring city of Chợ Lớn.[27]

Charner Boulevard had once been a brackish and foul-smelling canal, which the French filled and covered over to turn it into a street. The boulevard was lined with shops and houses and illuminated at night by electric arc lamps, as were its neighboring streets. The Municipal Council named the boulevard after Léonard Charner, the French admiral who ended the siege of Saigon at the Battle of Kỳ Hòa in 1861.[28] At one end of the boulevard, on the riverfront, stood the imposing Customs and Excise building; at the other end was the recently completed city hall. When it was established in 1869, the Municipal Council originally occupied premises on the riverfront in the Wang Tai Building, the property of a wealthy Chinese entrepreneur. Council members fought among themselves for decades over the location, design, cost, and construction materials of a new city hall. In 1896, the council finally commissioned the architect Paul Gardès to design the building and the artist Antoine-Justin Ruffier to produce the murals and sculptural ornamentation to adorn it. The decorative work proved extremely controversial, and the council eventually decided to end Ruffier's contract. When the building was completed after considerable delay and at great expense, some judged its baroque facade and Corinthian columns, pilasters, and sculptural figures stylish and original, while others thought the effect little short of grotesque.[29]

On the riverfront, the offices of the Chargeurs Réunis or United Shipping Company, the Messageries Fluviales or River Shipping Company, and other maritime transportation firms stood on the south side of Rigault de Genouilly Square. The square was named for Charles Rigault de Genouilly, the admiral who captured Saigon in 1859. In 1879, the city inaugurated a handsome bronze statue of the admiral in battle dress in the center of the square. Beside it the city later placed an obelisk to commemorate Ernest Doudart de Lagrée, the French naval officer and explorer who died in Yunnan in 1868 while leading an expedition up the Mekong River.[30]

Several streets fanned out from Rigault de Genouilly Square. The most important of these was Paul Blanchy Street. The street had previously been named Impériale Street, République Street, and finally Nationale Street before taking the name Paul Blanchy Street in 1901 to commemorate the death of the eponymous mayor. Paul Blanchy had arrived in Cochinchina in 1871 to plant coffee in the province of Biên Hòa. In 1873, he installed himself in Saigon and joined the Colonial Council, eventually becoming its president in 1882. In 1895, he became the mayor of the city. The street named in his honor extended northwest from Rigault de Genouilly Square through the city and into the province of Gia Định, linking Saigon with the surrounding countryside.[31]

On the other side of Rigault de Genouilly Square stood the naval stores and maintenance depots, the office of the Naval Commander, the Naval Artillery workshops, and, on Luro Boulevard, the Arsenal. The Arsenal was the largest and busiest industrial installation in Saigon. It employed French and Vietnamese civilian workers as well as sailors and soldiers stationed in the city to build and repair naval and merchant vessels. In the forge, thirty fires roared, while three steam hammers fell with a regular cadence upon molten metal, a rolling mill flattened sheets of iron, and two cranes moved heavy objects. In the foundry, four cupola furnaces, fueled with coke, melted cast iron for working; an oven with four furnaces, two series of crucibles, and an annealing oven aided the workers in repairing stricken vessels. There was a massive boiler works and a workshop for fitting and turning in which mechanical shafts and belts powered tools for milling, gearing, tapping screw threads, filing, clamping, and sharpening metal to a high degree of precision. There was also a floating dock, a small refitting basin, and a large basin that had been inaugurated in 1888 for large oceangoing vessels. By the beginning of the twentieth century, the large basin had become too small to repair the largest steamships that sometimes anchored in Saigon.[32]

A number of villas bordered Luro Boulevard, as did St. Joseph's Seminary, and the Orphanage of the Holy Childhood, run by the Sisters of Saint Paul de Chartres. The boulevard terminated before a vast square with manicured lawns in front of the Colonial Infantry Barracks. The barracks were built on the site of the former Vietnamese citadel, constructed in 1790 according to the design of the French military engineer Sébastien le Prestre de Vauban. Emperor Minh Mệnh had the first citadel dismantled in 1835 and replaced it with a smaller structure, which the French destroyed during the conquest of Saigon.[33] The barracks were made up of large and airy iron pavilions surrounded by verandahs on each floor. Trees flanked the pathways connecting the pavilions. Next to the barracks was a club for sailors and soldiers. It had a reading room with a library of fifteen hundred volumes, a bar that sold refreshments, and a hall in which a military theater company gave evening performances.[34]

Near the barracks, beside the Avalanche Arroyo, and among a forest of tall trees were the Botanical and Zoological Gardens. The gardens were almost as old as the French colony itself, having been established by Rear-Admiral Pierre-Paul de la Grandière in 1864.[35] Wide pathways crisscrossed the gardens, which contained countless varieties of trees and plants, from acacia and aloe to roses and violets.[36] There were also caged animals of all kinds, including deer, panthers, and elephants. A large pavilion served as an aviary, home to finches and waders. A forest kiosk displayed all the different species and varieties of wood in Cochinchina.

15

Extending in front of the gardens and past the barracks was Norodom Boulevard, named after the nineteenth-century king of Cambodia who signed the treaty of protection with France in 1863.[37] Important military buildings flanked the boulevard. Beyond the cathedral, at the intersection with Pellerin Street, was a monument in honor of the French statesman Léon Gambetta, which had been inaugurated in 1889.[38] The monument comprised a large bronze sculpture of the famous statesman, absurdly attired in a heavy fur coat, his arm outstretched as if to enfold the city in a protective embrace. It stood atop a decorative pedestal skirted at its base by a sailor and a wounded naval infantryman.[39]

The palace of the governor general stood at the western end of Norodom Boulevard. The palace was a princely residence set among vast gardens and built at considerable expense. It had two pavilions at either end of a vast facade with a cupola at the center, accessible by a covered stairway or a sweeping ramp. There was a festival hall, a state dining room, the offices of the Governor General and the Privy Council as well as other administrative offices, and the private apartments of the governor.[40] The governor general seldom occupied the palace, however, after the capital of French Indochina officially moved to Hà Nội in 1902.

The towers of the municipal cathedral dominated Norodom Boulevard. The Apostolic Vicar of Cochinchina, Isidore Colombert, had blessed the foundation stone on October 7, 1877, and consecrated the cathedral on Easter Day, 1880. The Romanesque structure was built from red brick on stone foundations. It was ninety-three meters long and nearly thirty-six meters wide. Its two bell towers soared above the city to a height of fifty-seven meters. The bells in the two towers weighed almost twenty-nine tons and called the faithful to worship from across the city and the far reaches of the countryside. The cathedral had a traditional cruciform shape with a transept and a high vaulted nave that terminated in an apse. In canopies above the apse the faithful could view prominent figures of the Old and New Testaments coming to greet the Immaculate Virgin in the apse of the cathedral. They could also meditate on the suffering and resurrection of Christ by following the Way of the Cross, stopping at each of the fourteen stations in the side chapels that flanked the nave and the transept. The side chapels were dedicated to the veneration of the Blessed Virgin, the Sacred Heart, Saint Joseph, Saint Paul, Saint Francis Xavier, and other saints.[41]

In the square in front of the cathedral stood a bronze statue of Father Pigneau de Béhaine, the Bishop of Adran, leading the young Vietnamese crown prince, Nguyễn Phúc Cảnh, by the hand. Pigneau de Béhaine was born in Origny-en-Tirache, trained as a missionary in Paris, and arrived in Cochinchina in 1767. He became Bishop of Adran and Apostolic Vicar of Cochinchina in 1771. In 1777, Pigneau de Béhaine gave sanctuary to the Vietnamese leader Nguyễn Phúc Ánh, who was struggling against a massive uprising led by three brothers from Tây Sơn in Bình Định province. In 1787, the bishop took Nguyễn Phúc Cảnh, the young son of Nguyễn Phúc Ánh, to Paris on a mission to seek French assistance against the Tây Sơn rebels. After the bishop died in 1799, Nguyễn Phúc Ánh praised him lavishly in a funeral oration for his fidelity and assistance.[42] The governor general, Paul Doumer, presided over the inauguration of the statue erected in honor of Pigneau de Béhaine at a grand public ceremony on March 10, 1902.[43]

The Post Office occupied one side of the square in front of the cathedral. The municipal architect, Alfred Foulhoux, designed the building, which was erected between 1886 and 1891. The building had a neo-Baroque exterior and a wrought-iron interior. The names of famous philosophers and scientists, such as Samuel Morse, René Descartes, Pierre-Simon Laplace, Alessandro Volta, André-Marie Ampère, Michael Faraday, and Humphry Davy, commemorated Western scientific advancement on small rectangular plaques on the outside of the building. The first post office began working on January 13, 1862, and it opened to the public the following year. By 1864, letters from Saigon were being delivered in Biên Hòa, Cần Giuộc, Mỹ Tho, Chợ Lớn, Tân An, Tây Ninh, and Gò Công. The French had sent the first telegram in Cochinchina from Saigon to Biên Hòa on March 27, 1862. The line was later extended to Bà Rịa and Cape St. Jacques. A second telegraph line erected the same year linked Saigon with Chợ Lớn. In 1871, the French exchanged the first telegrams between France and Cochinchina. Submarine cables landing at Cape St. Jacques linked Saigon with cities overseas. A cable leading south linked the city with Singapore, Australia, New Zealand, India, Africa, and Europe. Another cable, extending north, joined Saigon with Hà Nội, Hong Kong, Shanghai, Nagasaki, and Vladivostok. By 1872, 6,600 kilometers of telegraph line had been strung across the colony, with 13,225 meters of cable running underwater. The

Catinat Street. Photograph: Ludovic Crespin.

first telephone network opened in Saigon on July 1, 1894. In 1906, the colonial government brought the postal, telegraph, and telephone services under a single agency, linking exporters in Marseille and Bordeaux and government departments in Hà Nội with offices and merchants on Catinat Street.[44]

Catinat Street began across the square from the cathedral and led down to the river. It was one of the oldest streets in the city. After the French conquest, it had been designated Street No. 16. In 1865, the governing admiral renamed the street for the French corvette *Catinat,* which had taken part in the bombardment of Đà Nẵng in 1856 and the attack on Saigon in 1859. The warship had been named in honor of Nicolas de Catinat, a Marshal of France during the reign of King Louis XIV.[45] The Treasury, the Mapping Office, and the headquarters of the Colonial Brigade stood on either side of the street followed by various administrative offices, shops, cafés, and hotels.[46]

The Municipal Theater dominated the middle of Catinat Street. It had opened in 1900 with an elaborate performance of Jules Massenet's *La Navarraise* attended by Prince Valdemar of Denmark, who had traveled to Siam and Indochina to support the Danish East Asiatic Company.[47] The performance was a great success, especially with the soldiers who had just returned from a campaign in China. The inaugural season included a number of new works, including Giacomo Puccini's *La Bohème* and Camille Saint-Saëns's *Samson et Dalila*. Saint-Saëns had visited Saigon for several weeks early in 1895. The theater usually hosted performances four times a week, from October to April, and regularly staged Gounod's grand opera *Faust* along with *Hamlet, Carmen, Lohengrin, Lakmé,* and *Werther*.[48] The French residents of the city eagerly awaited the arrival of renowned artists and performers from France and Europe at the beginning of each opera season.[49]

Beyond the theater, European trading houses, large grocery stores kept by Chinese merchants, basket weavers, tailors, shoemakers, and watchmakers flanked Catinat Street. The street became animated at dusk as people arrived to meet friends and acquaintances at the fashionable cafés and restaurants near the theater. Bonard Boulevard cut across Catinat Street and Charner Boulevard and was named for Admiral Louis Adolphe Bonard, who had served as the first governor of Cochinchina, from 1861 to 1863. It was filled with lawns and planted with trees. It was a popular place for leisurely promenades. Each Wednesday evening, musicians from the Navy and the Colonial Regiment performed at the electrically illuminated bandstand that stood at the intersection of Bonard and Charner boulevards.

A statue of the explorer Francis Garnier watched over the eastern end of Bonard Boulevard opposite the Municipal Theater. Garnier had been appointed inspector of indigenous affairs in 1862 and served as administrator of Chợ Lớn. Garnier instigated an expedition to explore the Mekong River, and in 1866 he set out with the Mekong Exploration Commission led by Ernest Doudart de Lagrée. In 1868, Garnier became the leader of the expedition after Doudart de Lagrée became too ill to continue leading the expedition and died. The commission eventually established that the river did not provide a navigable commercial route from Cochinchina to southern China. Late in 1873, Garnier went to Hà Nội to help settle a dispute between the Vietnamese authorities and the French adventurer and entrepreneur Jean Dupuis. After Garnier captured the city, the Vietnamese authorities sought the aid of the Chinese rebel leader Liu Yongfu and his Black Flag Army. Garnier died in a skirmish with Black Flag troops a few days before Christmas. To honor his heroism, the city erected a statue to his memory on Bastille Day, 1887.[50]

Northwest from the junction with Bonard Boulevard, Pellerin Street intersected with Lagrandière Street, named for a former governor. The Central Prison and the Palace of the Lieutenant Governor of Cochinchina both stood on Lagrandière Street. The palace was initially meant to be an exhibition hall for the display of goods and wares and was also designed by the municipal architect, Alfred Foulhoux.[51] Further northwest, Pellerin Street and Taberd Street, both named after prominent missionaries, crossed each other where the local Masonic lodge and the Philharmonic Society stood. Taberd Street also provided entry to the Municipal Park, with its spacious lawns, neat pathways, tall trees, and long shadows that provided respite from the heat of the day.[52]

To the west, the Vietnamese Rifle Regiment and a camp of the Colonial Infantry were located on the Camp des Mares, situated on the Plain of Tombs. The plain was a vast necropolis covered with bushes, leafy trees, and most prominently, a ruined stone funerary monument. The city had established a racing facility nearby with stylish and well-appointed spectator stands that gave it the appearance of a racecourse in Paris.[53]

Chasseloup-Laubat Street traversed the city from the southwest to the northeast and bordered the northern perimeter of the Municipal Garden, where the velodrome and the local sports society were located. The street had been named in 1865 for Marquis Chasseloup-Laubat, the minister of the Navy and the colonies as well as an enthusiastic proponent of French expansion in Indochina.[54] The street continued past the Palace of the Governor General, the water tower, and the barracks of the Colonial Infantry, alongside the Botanical Gardens and over the bridge across the Avalanche Arroyo into Thị Nghè.

The most important artery through Saigon was the Chinese Arroyo, which linked Saigon with Chợ Lớn. At the beginning of the twentieth century, modern means of transportation in Cochinchina were scant. The rail network was in its infancy.[55] The few sealed roads had to cross rivers and streams over frail bridges, poorly supported by the shifting soil of water-soaked rice fields, and were unable to carry heavy vehicles and merchandise. The rivers, streams, and canals of the colony provided the cheapest and easiest means of transportation for people and goods.[56]

The banks of the Chinese Arroyo bustled with activity. The north bank was home to the customs warehouse and served as the anchorage for doz-

ens of steamboats. The bank was covered with crates and barrels and merchandise of all kinds; countless thatched huts stood on stilts in the mud
and housed the growing population of the city's poor. The south bank was
on the islet of Khánh Hội, where riverine and seagoing vessels anchored,
their masts tightly arrayed side by side for almost a kilometer. The arroyo
extended westward into the countryside, past verdant palm and banana
trees, and lazily wound its way through rice fields laid out like a check-
erboard, into which tributaries and small canals discharged their waters.
The arroyo passed the villages of Cầu Ông Lãnh, Cầu Kho, and Chợ Quán,
with their diverse and various industries. Timber for construction and
wood for cooking and heating were stacked in carefully secured piles along
the bank. Nearby, sheds were filled day and night with the monotonous
sound of enormous handsaws cutting lumber. Coolies and day laborers unloaded lime, bricks, and tiles from junks to form enormous piles along the
bank. And local potters spread out seemingly endless rows of large, brown,
enamel vessels. Finally, after winding past the villages, the arroyo reached
Chợ Lớn.[57]

The banks of the arroyo were the most animated part of the city. Watercraft tethered to floating wharves constantly arrived and departed, filling the air with their whistles. They navigated the middle of the arroyo
cautiously—it was naturally narrow but was made narrower still by junks
that had been moored perpendicular to the channel. A junk was a vessel
larger than a sampan with a flat bottom, square prow, and lugsails capable
of crossing the ocean. The largest junks, heavily laden and slow moving,
could sail only with the current. At times, the congestion was extreme; the
sounds of collisions, cries, quarrels, and vociferations filled the air. The din
of the Chinese Arroyo contrasted with the quiet and calm of the Diversion
Canal, which traced an arc through Chợ Lớn. On the green and muddy
water of the canal, under the shade of enormous trees, empty and silent
junks were moored against the bank where they awaited the next harvest,
when they would be filled again with paddy from the provinces of the Mekong Delta.[58]

The main industries of Saigon and Chợ Lớn were perched beside the
Chinese Arroyo. Along the south bank stood the workshop of the engineer, plumber, and light fitter Charléty; the yards of Dupont et Bron,
builders and mechanics; and the ateliers of the importers Graf, Jacques

A rice mill in Chợ Lớn. Photograph: Ludovic Crespin.

and Company. Extending toward Chợ Lớn stood the warehouses of the Bonade trading company; the Mazet distillery; a sawmill, owned by Denis Frères; the Fontaine distillery; and finally, the great rice mills of Chợ Lớn. The mills comprised dozens of factories, warehouses, and other buildings along both banks of the arroyo. On the north bank of the arroyo stood the Ban Teck Guan, Ban Joo Guan, Ban Soon An, and Nam Long mills; the Yee Cheong, Orient, Union, and Kian Hong Seng mills stood on the south bank, along with other buildings belonging to the Ban Teck Guan mill. The mills were constantly filled with the noise of machinery and emitted a fine red dust that blanketed the quay where coolies unloaded paddy from junks and filled them again with milled rice. Tall chimneys of metal and stone, visible from Saigon, loomed above the mills and sullied the purple-gold tropical sunset with an endless trail of fluffy black clouds.[59]

French business interests built the earliest steam-powered rice mills along the Chinese Arroyo, but Chinese entrepreneurs soon began to compete with them. In 1869, Renard and Company and the American businessman Andrew Spooner built the first mill in Chợ Lớn; shortly thereafter, Alphonse Cahuzac built a second mill in Saigon. For seven years, they were the only such mills in the colony; the quantity of milled rice that Saigon

exported doubled and then tripled. In 1876, a group of Chinese entrepre-
neurs pooled their capital to establish the first Chinese-owned mill in Chợ
Lớn. Five years later, Denis Frères, who owned a large trading house in
Saigon, established another new mill in the city.[60] Chinese from the Straits
Settlements on the Malay Peninsula had established themselves in Chợ
Lớn shortly before, or soon after, the French conquest. By 1888, there were
twenty or thirty Straits Chinese families living on Fujian Street. In that
year, Tan Kim Ching, the eldest son of the businessman and philanthropist
Tan Tock Seng, opened a mill in Chợ Lớn.[61] Another Straits Chinese businessman, Khoo Cheng Tiong, established the Kian Hong Seng Mill, which
became one of the most prosperous enterprises in the city. Khoo Cheng
Tiong came from a poor family in Fujian. He migrated to Singapore and
started trading in the middle of the nineteenth century. He established a
rice importing company on Boat Quay in Singapore and a mill in Chợ Lớn.
When Khoo Cheng Tiong died in 1896, his second son, Khoo Teck Siong,
became the managing director of the company.[62] The Chinese entrepreneur Quách Đàm arrived in Vietnam in 1880 at the age of seventeen from
Chaozhou in the southern Chinese province of Guangdong. He worked
hard, selling buffalo skins and assorted bric-a-brac. Quách Đàm eventually amassed enough capital to become the proprietor of the Yee Cheong
rice mill on the south bank of the Chinese Arroyo.[63] Even the Union and
Orient mills, which were owned by German business interests, were leased
to a Chinese firm, the Ban Soon An Company.[64] By the beginning of the
twentieth century, Chinese firms dominated the milling of rice in Chợ Lớn
almost completely.

Paddy, or unhusked rice, traveled to Chợ Lớn along a network of canals
and waterways that linked the city to the more remote parts of Cochinchina. The French administration had developed and extended an existing
network of canals, which had first been excavated under the rule of the
Vietnamese Nguyễn dynasty. The new canals improved communication
with the interior and opened empty lands to settlement and cultivation.
Beginning in 1866, conscripted laborers carried out most of the excavation work, often shifting more than fifty thousand cubic meters of brackish water and alluvial sands each year. After 1893, French companies used
mechanical dredges and diggers to drain and excavate the land. Between
1890 and 1900, the machines excavated an average 824,000 cubic meters of

sand and water annually. In the years after 1900, they excavated an average of 2,750,000 cubic meters annually, opening new waterways to transportation and communication.[65]

These waterways allowed Vietnamese settlers to open the newly accessible lands of Cochinchina to rice cultivation. Between 1880 and 1893, settlers planted approximately four hundred thousand additional hectares in rice. After mechanical dredging began, the area of land devoted to rice increased sharply, from 926,000 hectares in 1893 to 1,134,000 hectares the following year. By 1900, rice covered 1,174,000 hectares of the colony; in 1904, on the eve of the typhoon, 1,392,000 hectares of Cochinchina had been planted in rice, as far south as the Hậu Giang River.[66] The crop traveled along the canals and waterways of Cochinchina to Chợ Lớn, where it joined rice shipped from the rich fields around Battambang and Mongkol Borey in Cambodia.[67]

Almost all the merchants shipping rice from the provinces to Chợ Lớn were Chinese. Chinese merchants in the provinces, often small store owners, advanced loans to Vietnamese cultivators against the harvest and purchased paddy from landowners. They then sold the paddy to larger Chinese merchants in the port and market towns of Cochinchina from whom they had often obtained credit themselves. The merchants in the market towns, many of them debtors of Chinese mills in Chợ Lớn, supplied the mills with paddy.[68]

Paddy from every province and every kind of rice plant poured into the mills together after each harvest. In the Orient mill, on the south bank of the Chinese Arroyo, a two-cylinder, 800-horsepower steam engine drove its machinery. The steam engines burned rice husks produced by the milling process to power the engines. A clutter of mechanical apparatus—sieves, grindstones, buckets on wheels, leather straps, and conveyor belts—worked at full speed on the three floors of the mill; the noise of the machines was ceaseless, and the machinery was constantly blanketed in a fine white dust. Workers brought paddy into the mill from the docks where it had been unloaded and emptied it into an enormous stone vat. Buckets on belts hoisted the paddy up to the third floor of the building, where the milling process began. The paddy first went through a sieve that removed stones and pebbles and other foreign bodies. It then passed between rollers that broke open the hulls and then, with the aid of a fan, through another sieve. The broken grains were removed, although not always very effectively. Another journey through the rollers and sieves improved the purity of the rice, but because so many kinds of rice passed through the mill together it always contained a high proportion of broken grains. Finally, the rice was polished as it passed between an emery cylinder and a metal sheet, which also produced rice flour. The rice moved from one part of the milling apparatus to the next, falling under its own weight from one floor of the mill to the next. Mechanical buckets on wheels elevated the rice again to repeat different parts of the process. By interrupting it before the rice was polished, the mill could obtain brown or cargo rice. The high proportion of broken grains that remained in the rice at the end of the process kept the price of rice from Saigon low.[69] The cargo rice, white rice, broken grains, flour, and paddy were all sorted into gunny sacks. Workers loaded the sacks onto barges, which took them to ships waiting in the port of Saigon.

Throughout the second half of the nineteenth century, the port shifted an ever-growing quantity of Vietnamese milled rice and paddy overseas. The Saigon Chamber of Commerce recorded that in 1860, the port of Saigon exported 58,000 tons of paddy; a decade later, the port shipped 130,000 tons of paddy and derivatives overseas; by 1880, that figure had reached 295,000 tons; in 1890, 548,000 tons left the port of Saigon; and in 1900 the port of Saigon shipped 748,000 tons of paddy and derivatives overseas. Before the typhoon in 1904, rice exports peaked in 1902 when the port shipped 992,000 tons of rice to ports overseas.[70]

The colonial government earned revenue by taxing the export of paddy and rice. When it opened to commerce after the French conquest in 1860, Saigon was a free port. But in 1879, the government began to tax the export of paddy and milled rice. It regularly increased the export duties as the value of the piaster, the local currency, declined.[71] In 1887, the government established the Customs and Excise Service, and after 1897 taxes on the export of rice contributed to the new general budget of French Indochina. The export of rice yielded several million piasters of tax revenue for the government each year, still a small fraction of the total value of rice exported.[72]

For the first three decades of the twentieth century, the main destinations for the rice exported from Saigon were the ports of East and Southeast Asia. Hong Kong and the ports of southern China were the largest importers of rice from Saigon. In the decade spanning 1870 to 1879, Saigon shipped 65 percent of its rice exports to those ports; in the following ten-year period, it shipped 68 percent of its rice there; and between 1890 and 1899, it shipped 50 percent of all its rice to the ports of Hong Kong and southern China. The Netherlands East Indies ranked second among Asian importers of rice from Saigon, and the Philippines ranked third. Although the Straits Settlements were important early consumers of rice from Saigon, they eventually received most of their rice from Burma or Siam.[73] In the last three decades of the nineteenth century, the demand for rice in Hong Kong and southern China busied Vietnamese farmers in the provinces of Cochinchina, kept the mills in Chợ Lớn working, and filled the port of Saigon with junks and steamships bound for Chinese ports.

Saigon had long been engaged in regional trade. In the early nineteenth century, small vessels carried goods down the Mekong River to the city from Cambodia and the Lao kingdoms. Junks from Saigon traded with Xiamen and Guangzhou, or Amoy and Canton as they were known, on the coast of southern China, as well as Bangkok, Batavia, Penang, Melaka, and Singapore in Southeast Asia.[74] Junks regularly sailed from Saigon to the new British settlement of Singapore. They carried rice and sugar and brought back cotton and woolen piece goods, opium, pepper, cloves, nutmeg, tin, sandalwood, saltpeter, and firearms. In the beginning the trade was very limited—Vietnamese already purchased Singapore's main export, British cloth, from Guangzhou. Chinese merchants carried out most of the early trade, but in 1825, the Vietnamese government declared it a royal monopoly. The government discouraged private trade by forbidding junks from carrying arms, leaving traders defenseless against pirates in the Gulf of Siam and along the east coast of the Malay Peninsula. But the private trade continued to grow. In 1844, Vietnamese royal vessels carried rice, sugar, local and Chinese silks, green tea, nankeens, cinnamon, rhinoceros horns, salt, ivory, buffalo skins, precious wood, and treasure to Singapore; they returned with camlets, linens, tin, opium, firearms, and goods from India.[75] After 1845, the Vietnamese government tightened trade regulations, and around 1850 the royal vessels stopped sailing to Singapore. But after the French conquest of Saigon and the reopening of the port, trade flourished.[76]

Chinese rice merchants organized this trade using networks spanning the South China Sea. After a Chinese exporter in Saigon received a tele-

gram with an order for rice, he contacted a mill in Chợ Lớn. The mill promised to supply the exporter with a quantity of rice at a fixed time for a fixed
price. After arranging with a shipping broker for space and with a bank
for exchange, the exporter in Saigon telegraphed an offer to the prospec-
tive customer. If the customer accepted, the exporter deposited half of the
purchase price in advance with the Chinese miller. When the exporter received notification that the shipping vessel had arrived at the mouth of
the Saigon River, the exporter paid the balance owed to the miller, who
then began to mill paddy.[77]

Chinese shipping companies owned most of the rice-carrying steamers
in the port. The records of the Chamber of Commerce show that most of
the cargo ships leaving Saigon sailed under French or British flags.[78] But
this is deceptive. Chinese shipping companies often manipulated their
capital statements and the nationality of their administrative personnel
so that they could sail their ships under a European flag. This allowed the
ships to avoid paying various tariffs and fees and to claim the protection of
the European powers in disputes or times of distress. Many of the vessels
carrying rice from Saigon to Hong Kong for Butterfield and Swire and for
Jardine and Matheson had been contracted to Chinese companies and had
Chinese livery on their bows.[79]

Hong Kong itself consumed only a fraction of the rice it imported
from Saigon. Hong Kong rice importers sold most of the rice imported
from Saigon and elsewhere to wholesale firms in Guangzhou. Retailers
in Guangzhou and districts of the Zhujiang, or Pearl River, delta finally
sold the rice to consumers there.[80] From the late eighteenth century, the
residents of the delta had started to use their land to raise mulberry trees
for silk production and export. Most of the silk came from five counties:
Shunde, which produced more than half of the silk from the delta, Nanhai,
Zhongshan, Xinhui, and Panyu. The residents of the delta bought more
and more rice from overseas: The new silk industry meant that mulberry
trees displaced rice fields in some places; the silk industry had made many
residents of the delta more prosperous, which allowed them to consume
fewer sweet potatoes and other root vegetables in favor of rice; and rice
from abroad was often less expensive than rice produced in Guangdong
or neighboring provinces.[81] By the early twentieth century, the amount
of rice imported from other countries exceeded the amount coming from
neighboring Chinese provinces.[82] Much of the rice imported from overseas

came from Saigon. Merchants in Hong Kong also sold some of the rice they imported to more distant buyers—for instance, German steamers carried rice from Hong Kong to Hamburg and Bremen and then on to Colombia in South America.[83]

Saigon was part of a region defined by the rice trade. The region extended from India in the east to southern China in the west. It encompassed the Philippines, British Malaya, the Netherlands East Indies, the kingdom of Siam, French Indochina, and British Burma.[84] In the second half of the eighteenth century, cultivators on Luzon in the Philippines and Java in the Netherlands East Indies started to plant crops such as coffee, tobacco, hemp, and sugar for export, which encouraged other cultivators to plant rice commercially rather than for their own consumption. When the Spanish liberalized trade in the Philippines, cultivators in Pampanga began to plant sugar for export. As farmers grew more and more sugar, they grew less and less rice for their own consumption.[85] Farmers from Ilocos, in the northwest of Luzon, moved into Nueva Ecija, Pangasinan, and Tarlac to plant rice, which fed Pampanga and the capital, Manila.[86] On Java, the Dutch East India Company promoted the planting of commercial crops, such as sugar, coffee, and indigo, in the second half of the eighteenth century, which led others to produce rice for the domestic market.[87]

From the middle of the nineteenth century, the ports of mainland Southeast Asia began to export growing quantities of rice to other parts of the region: Rangoon started to export rice from the Irrawaddy Delta after the end of the Second Anglo-Burmese War in 1852; Bangkok began to export rice in increasing quantities after King Mongkut signed the Bowring Treaty in 1855; and Saigon joined its neighbors as a rice exporter in 1860, after the French conquest. The availability of inexpensive rice in the second half of the nineteenth century made it possible to feed migrants from southern India to grow coffee and tea on the plantations of Ceylon; for Javanese to plant tobacco on the east coast of Sumatra; for Malays and others to plant gambir, pepper, tapioca, and coffee on the Malay peninsula; and for planters and smallholders to raise cash crops across the region.[88] The rice exported from Saigon helped feed the people of Hong Kong and the Pearl River Delta and supported the silk industry in southern China.

The rice trade profoundly shaped the lives of those who lived in colonial Saigon.[89] When exports grew, so did employment opportunities in commerce, shipping and transportation, warehousing, and stevedoring, among many others. The money earned from exports funded the purchase of imported goods and helped to underwrite the colonial government. A growth in imports typically accompanied or followed a growth in exports, creating employment opportunities in importing companies such as Denis Frères, Biedermann and Company, and Schroeder and at retailers such as Ogliastro and Ducrouzet, Speidel and Company, and Engler and Company. The sale of the largest imports, cotton and other textiles, created opportunities at cloth merchants, such as Mouriengager, Maugamadousin, and Zeinebon, and fashionable clothing stores, such as those of Madame Bonnefoy, Mademoiselle Eugénie Bourdin, and Madame Migieu. Retail merchants, such as Germain Lacaze, Poirrier and Company, and Hadjy Sahibe, sold household goods, from bedding and table linens to lamps and furniture. Many such goods eventually found their way into the junk shops and secondhand dealers of the city.[90] Government revenue rose and fell with the collection of taxes, wharf fees, and trade duties, which paid the wages and salaries of personnel at the Customs and Excise Service, the Department of Public Works, and the Department of Hygiene and Public Health. The growth of the export economy created many new opportunities for work in Saigon.

Vietnamese from the countryside migrated to the city and to the villages at its edge in search of such opportunities. The population of Saigon grew as migrants arrived in the city and as its boundaries expanded. In 1870, Saigon had only twelve thousand residents.[91] In the following year, it extended its limits and annexed the neighboring villages of Cầu Ông Lãnh, Phước Hòa, and An Hòa.[92] It also adopted a coat of arms and a Latin motto, *Paulatim Crescam,* which meant "Gradually I will grow."[93] By 1880, Saigon had gradually grown to a population of fourteen thousand, but many had come to live in villages just outside of the city.[94] In 1885, the population surged when several thousand Vietnamese sought refuge in Saigon from violence and unrest in southern Annam, caused by ongoing French pacification efforts. The government repatriated the refugees in 1887, leaving a population of 16,200 in 1888.[95] In 1894, Saigon annexed the villages of Hòa Mỹ, Phú Hòa, Nam Chơn, Tân Định, and part of the village of Xuân Hòa, adding 344 hectares to its area. The following year, it acquired a further eighty-two hectares when it absorbed part of Khánh Hội and Tam Hội. The municipality wished to tax the many Vietnamese who had come to live in

Soup merchants. Photograph: Ludovic Crespin.

the villages and to control them better—it gradually extended roads, police patrols, and public health inspections into its new territories.[96] With these additions, not only the area of the city but its population as well more than doubled, from 19,900 in 1893 to 44,800 in 1896.[97] By the end of the nineteenth century, Saigon had 51,000 residents.[98] After annexing the villages of Phú Thạnh and Tân Hòa it reached 55,800 in 1904.[99] The city expanded its boundary once more in 1907, when it absorbed the remaining part of Khánh Hội and the village of Chánh Hưng. The population, after the typhoons and natural disasters of the preceding years, was 53,000.[100] As the rice export economy grew, migrants moved from the countryside to Saigon seeking work.[101]

They settled in the archipelago of villages that comprised the neighborhoods of the city. The neighborhood of Cầu Ông Lãnh had been a village named for a bridge across the Chinese Arroyo that had been built by a Vietnamese military commander. Cầu Kho named both a bridge and a market beside a former imperial granary. Phú Thạnh and Xuân Hoà had once been communes in the canton of Bình Chánh Thượng, which abutted the city, while Tân Định had once been a hamlet in the canton of Bình Trị Trung. Dakao, the neighborhood adjacent to Tân Định, took its name not from a village but from the French corruption of "Đất Hộ," which referred to land belonging to a commune. It was home to the European cemetery where Ernest Doudart de Lagrée, Francis Garnier, and many others were buried.[102]

Many of the migrants who came to Saigon did not remain in the city permanently. Such migrants typically came from its hinterland in the neighboring provinces of Cochinchina—Gia Định, Chợ Lớn, Mỹ Tho, Bà Rịa, Tây Ninh, and Biên Hòa—or from the nearby provinces of southern Annam—Bình Thuận, Khánh Hòa, Phú Yên, and Bình Định.[103] Many returned to the countryside each June and July to help prepare the fields and transplant rice seedlings. Others left in January to help bring in the harvest or to celebrate Tết in their natal villages.[104] Sometimes they migrated to Saigon directly; sometimes they followed invisible paths, stopping first in one place and then in another but leaving no record, before arriving in the city.[105] The paths to Saigon were often circular, leading from the countryside to the city and back again.

But these paths did not always lead to stable or well-paying work. While some found such work, many did not: There were always many more migrants than there were jobs to be had. Instead of finding work in shipping companies, import firms, and stores, many migrants took up makeshift positions as servants and cooks, itinerant merchants, day laborers, rickshaw pullers, prostitutes, and beggars, among other transient occupations. They might have left the countryside for any number of reasons—debt and landlessness, a flood or drought or some other natural disaster, or merely a desire to escape the isolation of rural life. But most migrants came to the city because of the opportunities for work that the growing rice-export industry had created there. And even if they had little immediate chance of earning a good wage, the expectation of a better life over the distant horizon might make the decision to migrate seem reasonable.[106] At the beginning of the twentieth century, such an expectation seems to have guided many poor migrants who made their way to Saigon in the years that followed the typhoons.

CHAPTER TWO

A WOMAN WHO RAN AWAY

Did those twelve fairies curse the gal at birth?
They stole her love-thing, stuck it who knows where!
The devil take this mouse who squeaks and woos!
Let him go hang, that wasp which drones and courts!
Guess what she's got—a blossom or a fruit?
How does one tell the calyx from the stem?
No matter, really—all is for the best:
she will be spared a husband's mother's blows.
—*Hồ Xuân Hương, "The Girl Without a Sex"*[1]

On August 16, 1907, the colonial authorities summoned Lương Văn Sang to the Central Police Station in Saigon. He had to come to the city from the nearby countryside. It was the wet season, and the rains of the summer monsoon could make travel difficult, especially on foot.[2] The Central Police Station stood on Lagrandière Street, opposite the palace of the lieutenant-governor of Cochinchina. Only a block away was the Maison Centrale, the city's infamous prison, known to Vietnamese criminals as the *khám lớn* or "big jail."[3]

But Lương Văn Sang was not a criminal. The police wanted to question him about his daughter, Lương Thị Lắm, whom they had arrested for prostitution in 1906. She had lived a vagabond life, and the police were trying to determine her movements before the time of her arrest. At three o'clock in the afternoon, on August 22, Lương Văn Sang appeared before a Monsieur Léonardi. The inspector began with a number of standard questions.

"What is your name?" he asked first, for the record.

"My name is Lương Văn Sang," the man replied.

"What was the place and date of your birth?" the inspector asked next.

"I was born in 1856, in the village of Tân Ba," answered Lương Văn Sang.

"What is your profession?" was the third question asked.

"Day laborer," went the third response.

"And where do you live now?" asked the inspector.

"I live in the village of Tân Ba," Lương Văn Sang replied. "In the canton of Chánh Mỹ Trung, in the province of Biên Hòa."[4]

Biên Hòa was the largest province in Cochinchina. It was bordered to the north by the kingdom of Cambodia; to the south, by the province of Bà Rịa; to the west, by the provinces of Gia Định and Thủ Dầu Một; and to the east by the protectorate of Annam. The Đồng Nai River reached across the southwest of the province, flowing down from the Central Highlands toward the coast, where it spilled into the South China Sea. To the east of the river lay Bình Trước, the capital of Biên Hòa; to the west, Saigon, the capital of Cochinchina.

Biên Hòa was poor at the beginning of the twentieth century. In 1901, the population was a little over a hundred thousand people. Most of these were Vietnamese villagers. Chinese, Cambodians, highlanders in the upland areas, and a few French planters made up the rest of the population.[5] The province covered more than a million hectares, but only thirty-five thousand hectares had been planted.[6] Much of Biên Hòa was unfit for agriculture, as mountains, steep valleys, swamps, and barren plateaux covered much of the land.[7] The soil of the plains, sandy and rich in clay and iron, had the color of rust.[8] Rice did not grow well in Biên Hòa. What rice the villagers could grow was not very tasty or nutritious, and they could never grow enough of it. They imported most of the rice they ate from the provinces of the Mekong Delta and the western provinces. Tribal peoples in the highland areas gathered wild rice, which villagers in the lowlands prized.[9]

Maize was the other staple crop in Biên Hòa. Villagers grew both the white and yellow varieties, which they cooked simply, boiled in water without any seasoning.[10] They supplemented their austere diets with beans, potatoes, yams, and manioc. At the market, they could sometimes find oranges, mangosteens, mangoes, bananas, pineapples, tamarinds, and spices. And if they did not grow them themselves, they also bought betel and areca nut there. Betel and areca were an important part of Vietnamese hospitality and were often offered to guests.[11] But at the Central Police Station that day, Lương Văn Sang was not considered a guest.

Once Inspector Léonardi had established Lương Văn Sang's identity, the inspector turned his questions to the man's family circumstances.

"Are you married, a widower, or single?" the inspector asked.

"I am married to the Vietnamese woman Trí Mão," answered Lương Văn Sang.

"How many children do you have?" the inspector continued.

"We have five, two sons and three daughters," replied Lương Văn Sang.

Lương Văn Sang's family must have been very poor. A day laborer, he appears to have had no land of his own to farm and therefore no means of subsistence to fall back on when work was short.[12] He could, perhaps, rely on the help of neighbors and extended family during such times, but neither provided the same level of security as a farm. Tân Ba, Lương Văn Sang's village, was in the west of Biên Hòa, in a canton between Thủ Dầu Một and the Đồng Nai River.[13] At the beginning of the twentieth century, the village was known for the rivercraft built there; perhaps Lương Văn Sang took part in their construction. The village also had a market where goods from up and down the river were traded; Lương Văn Sang might have hauled these goods ashore or carried them from the wharf to the marketplace. Tân Ba also provided kaolin to potters in three villages to the south and another village to the west; Lương Văn Sang might have dug the kaolin from the ground or hauled it to the wharf.[14]

Whatever he did, Lương Văn Sang would have needed to work hard to feed his wife and five children and to provide a home for them. The homes of the poor were crudely fashioned: The roofs and walls were made from bamboo and covered with dried fronds from the Nipa palm; the few wooden supports were little more than mangrove branches that had been driven into the ground or, possibly, into stone pedestals; the door, instead of opening and closing, was a mere piece of cloth that could be raised or lowered. The Vietnamese called such houses *nhà lá,* houses of leaves. Warmth, when it was needed, came from the cooking fire kindled on the floor of beaten earth. The family would have slept on a cot, raised on two easels, where it also took its meals and received guests.[15] It was probably from such a house that, in 1905, Lương Văn Sang's daughter, Lương Thị Lắm, ran away.

Lương Thị Lắm was the object of Inspector Léonardi's inquiry, and now he turned his focus on her.

"Lương Thị Lắm is the oldest of all?" the inspector suggested.

"No," her father replied. "She is the youngest."

"How old is she currently?" probed the inspector.

"Twenty-one years old," her father responded.

"At what time and for what reason did she leave?" the inspector asked next.

"She left furtively," her father answered, "at the age of nineteen, toward the end of the month of February 1905."

Lương Văn Sang offered no explanation for why Lương Thị Lắm ran away, but there were several possible reasons. She was young and may have wanted to see something of the world. And life in Tân Ba was probably confining. But in the first months of 1905, it must have also seemed increasingly desperate. The typhoons of May and November 1904, and the flood, the drought, and the locusts that followed had all wreaked havoc in Cochinchina. In the market towns, gossip among Chinese with connections to Shanghai and Hong Kong had led to widespread panic over a possible Japanese invasion of Cochinchina. The Japanese had attacked the Russian fleet anchored at Port Arthur and imposing Russian men-of-war had put in at nearby Cam Ranh Bay on their way to battle. The Vietnamese feared that the Japanese would soon have designs further south.[16]

Villages in the provinces struggled to help the poor and the needy. Vietnamese villages typically had a number of associations that provided mutual protection and support: Such associations helped defray the costs of weddings, funerals, and burials, and they provided for the needs of the sick and the elderly.[17] But at the beginning of the twentieth century, communal solidarity had begun to unravel. The colonial government struggled to recruit Vietnamese notables to administrative roles in the villages.

The governor general recognized that with the imposition of French rule in Cochinchina, Vietnamese notables had lost all prestige and authority among the villagers and had no means of compelling obedience. At the same time, their administrative duties had multiplied and become more difficult. Those few notables who took up the task were often venal and dishonest.[18] As a consequence, theft and armed banditry increased sharply in the countryside, especially in the provinces of Biên Hòa, Vĩnh Long, Trà Vinh, and Cần Thơ. In one province, the notables had been so terrorized and the villagers were so afraid of reprisal that thieves and armed robbers could act with almost complete impunity.[19] Faced with ruin and unable to rely on their villages for safety and support, many Vietnamese abandoned their homes.

The disasters, the destruction of the harvest, and the collapse of the rice trade must have left the villagers of Cochinchina feeling very vulnerable. In May, a rebellion broke out in Biên Hòa. One day, two young buffalo keepers stopped at a house on the edge of a village to ask for water. The house belonged to a reclusive man, known in the village for his esoteric knowledge of Chinese characters and pharmacopoeia. At the house, the buffalo keepers came upon a group of people readying and sharpening swords and lances. The buffalo keepers quickly alerted the authorities. One of their number claimed that the Buddha had appeared to him in a dream. The Buddha told him that he was to proclaim himself *Minh Hoàng,* or the Luminous Emperor, and that he would become the king of Cochinchina. His divine mission was to protect the Vietnamese against all evils, enemies, illnesses, and ferocious beasts—all the troubles of the previous two years. Their waists and weapons girded in red sashes, the buffalo keepers declared a rebellion. It did not end before French soldiers fired on the group and razed the house at the edge of the village to the ground.[20] To the villagers of Biên Hòa, the hardship in the first months of 1905 must have seemed unrelenting.

When they encountered great hardship, Vietnamese of little means often turned to flight. This is just what Lương Thị Lắm had done.

"After she left did Thị Lắm give you the address of her new residence?" the inspector asked.

"No," Lương Văn Sang answered. "I later learned from someone in my village that my daughter, Lương Thị Lắm, was a tenant in a brothel in Chợ Lớn." Lương Thị Lắm had become a prostitute.[21]

Inspector Léonardi stopped the interview here. There was now a paper trail to follow. Prostitution in Saigon was legal, but it was regulated. The French had first developed a system for regulating prostitution in Paris and later exported it to their colony in Southeast Asia.[22] The Police des Mœurs, the Morals Police, registered prostitutes in the city and ensured that they complied with municipal rules and ordinances. Inspector Léonardi worked for the Police des Mœurs.

Inspector Léonardi and his colleagues employed a recondite language of bureaucratic control to document and regulate the lives of prostitutes in Saigon. A *maison de tolérance* was an illegal but officially tolerated house of prostitution or brothel, established with the permission of the police; the *tolérance* referred to police permission to run the brothel. A *fille en carte* was a prostitute who was inscribed or registered with the police. A *fille de maison* worked in a brothel, while the *fille isolée* worked on her own; both were *en carte.* Women who eluded police surveillance practiced *prostitution clandestine,* for which the police could arrest them. The police referred to such prostitutes as *insoumise*—the unsubdued. Prostitutes in Saigon had to regularly undergo a *visite sanitaire* during which doctors examined them for venereal disease in the *dispensaire,* the municipal dispensary or clinic.[23] The registration, examination, and regulation of prostitution in Saigon generated an extensive body of paperwork.

If Lương Thị Lắm had been a prostitute in a brothel in Chợ Lớn, she should have been registered with the police there. It is impossible to say with any certainty how many women worked as prostitutes in the city. Neither the municipal authorities nor the colonial government systematically compiled statistics on prostitution. And those numbers that the administration gathered are probably underestimates, since brothel owners and prostitutes both wanted to avoid being counted and regulated. The earliest figures appear in letters from one colonial administrator to another. A letter from the central commissioner of Police to the secretary general of Cochinchina in 1888 states that there were ninety-five prostitutes registered that year.[24] By 1893, that number had grown to 114, according to a letter from the governor general of Indochina to the lieutenant governor of Cochinchina.[25] Another letter, from the mayor of Chợ Lớn to the lieutenant governor of Cochinchina, indicates that in 1904, the year before Lương Thị Lắm ran away, the authorities were aware of a total of 310 prostitutes in Saigon and 240 in Chợ Lớn in 1904.[26]

Inspector Léonardi sent his colleague, Inspector Bernard David, to the police station in Chợ Lớn in search of further information about Lương Thị Lắm. Chợ Lớn was a larger city than Saigon, and it had a sizable Chinese population. In 1907, it numbered 172,520: There were 92,031 Vietnamese, 80,300 Chinese, and 289 French.[27] In the same year, the total population of Saigon was only 54,000.[28] Biên Hòa was close to Chợ Lớn; in some ways it had become closer under French rule. The French built roads that connected distant parts of the colony, laid railway lines, and established shipping routes. Lương Thị Lắm may have traveled on a river vessel owned by the Messageries Fluviales, which worked a route between Saigon and Biên Hòa and then went on to Chợ Lớn. She may have traveled downriver on a sampan or a junk. If she first headed to Bình Trước, the provincial capital, she could have taken a carriage to Saigon and from there then gone on to Chợ Lớn.[29] What seems most likely, however, is that without a *sou* to her name, Lương Thị Lắm made her way to Chợ Lớn on foot, a walk of some forty kilometers that would have taken the best part of a day.[30]

After some delay, Inspector Bernard reappeared with a dossier in hand. According to their records, the Chợ Lớn police had arrested Lương Thị Lắm for illegal prostitution on March 7, 1905. She had been working unregistered in Brothel No. 14. After her arrest, she registered herself in that brothel as Huỳnh Thị Kim. Neither Lương Văn Sang nor Inspector Léonardi commented on this fact. Why had she registered under a different name? It was common, at the time, for Vietnamese to go by many names. Most children did not receive personal names until they were one or two years old. At home, their parents deliberately called them by some other, uglier name to make them unappealing to malevolent spirits. They began to go by their personal names only when they reached adolescence. At home, with their parents and siblings, they often went by a name that indicated their order of birth. Intimates and friends called them yet other pet names.[31] Criminals and fugitives often used aliases to evade the authorities. Perhaps Lương Thị Lắm did not want to associate her own name with her new profession. In Chợ Lớn, in Brothel No. 14, she would be Huỳnh Thị Kim.

There were few jobs open to Vietnamese women in Saigon and Chợ Lớn in the early twentieth century. They were rarer still when Lương Thị Lắm came to Chợ Lớn in 1905 and 1906, after the rice exports collapsed.

Most poor women took up some kind of temporary work. Some worked as itinerant merchants who walked the streets, a bamboo pole across their shoulders, selling fruits and vegetables. Others hawked bowls of noodles or plates of rice for a few *sous* on the pavement. In the marketplace, women sold spun goods and small handicrafts that they had made at home, but Lương Thị Lắm had run away from home. A few women became midwives or fortune tellers.[32] The homes of the French and the rich Vietnamese also provided jobs as cooks, cleaners, and nannies. For such work, they might have received their room and keep and a small sum each week.[33] But Lương Thị Lắm came without references, and nobody in the city knew her. Vietnamese nuns worked in the hospitals and orphanages of the colony, but the Catholic Church had often raised them since they were orphans themselves.[34] This left the cafés, opium dens, and brothels as the few places open to Lương Thị Lắm, and of these, a brothel provided not only a wage but also a place to sleep. Many other women seem to have followed the same path as Lương Thị Lắm during the difficult years of 1905 and 1906: The Police des Mœurs in Saigon recorded a sharp increase in arrests for illegal prostitution in those years.[35]

In 1905, an ordinance issued in 1878 still governed brothels and prostitutes in Chợ Lớn. Its main purpose was to limit the spread of venereal disease. It required all prostitutes in the city to register themselves with the Commissioner of Police. It was thus Article Two of the ordinance that Lương Thị Lắm had broken, though she may not have known it. The police issued registered prostitutes with an identity card that they were required to produce to the authorities upon request. Every week prostitutes were required to undergo a medical examination during which a doctor inspected them for venereal diseases. If the doctor discovered an infection, he ordered the affected prostitutes to be warded in Chợ Quán Hospital until they were well again. When the police caught clandestine prostitutes, they jailed them until they too had undergone an examination. The police would then enter them in the register of prostitutes and require the same obligations of them as other prostitutes. The regulations forbade them to solicit in public, dress indecently, and do anything that might give cause for complaint to their neighbors or to passersby. They all had to belong to a brothel where they might be better monitored and surveiled. The police had to authorize each brothel, which could admit only prostitutes who had submitted to a medical examination. Every brothel had to close by midnight.

The penalties for breaching these regulations were severe. In 1884, the authorities sentenced Trần Thị Thanh, the owner of Brothel No. 11 in Chợ Lớn, to fifteen days in prison for employing an unregistered prostitute in her brothel.[36] In 1886, they sentenced Trần Ngọ, the owner of Brothel No. 4, to fifteen days in prison for keeping four unregistered prostitutes in her establishment.[37] In June 1891, eighteen year-old Nguyễn Thị Cúc twice provided false information to the police who had been hunting for her after she deserted the brothel at which she was registered. Nguyễn Thị Của, who was twenty-four years old, had deserted her own brothel six times. The authorities sentenced both to thirty days in prison.[38] In September of the same year, Nguyễn Thị Cơ was a prostitute registered in a brothel in Chợ Lớn that she left without authorization to work in a brothel in Saigon. She too went to prison for thirty days.[39] The ordinance of 1878 did not prescribe any specific penalty for clandestine prostitution itself. By 1893, however, the police regularly meted out penalties of thirty days or more in prison. The arresting officer usually recommended the punishment a prostitute received, which made the system open to abuse. A prostitute would do almost anything to avoid having to go to prison.[40] The governor general came to believe that the regulation requiring prostitutes to register with brothels was the main reason that there were so many clandestine prostitutes. In 1893, Saigon introduced a new ordinance to better regulate the prostitutes and the police who oversaw them. It formally recognized two categories of prostitute: One category included those who worked in brothels, while the other included prostitutes who worked in an apartment or from their own homes.[41] This policy stretched the resources of the police, who now had several places that they had to monitor. The ordinance also required both kinds of prostitute to register with the municipal police and to undergo a regular medical examination. But in 1905, when the police first arrested Lương Thị Lắm in Chợ Lớn, the ordinance of 1878 was still in force there.

The brothels of Chợ Lớn attracted not only Vietnamese women but Japanese and Chinese women too. Women of each ethnic group worked in separate brothels. Lương Thị Lắm would have worked alongside other Vietnamese prostitutes in Brothel No. 14. In 1904, some months before the police arrested Lương Thị Lắm, an inquiry by the mayor of Chợ Lớn

found that there were ninety-five Vietnamese working in the city's brothels; a further six walked the streets alone. The Chợ Quán hospital confined
eighty-seven Vietnamese prostitutes infected with a venereal disease.
Fifty-six of them had already failed their regular medical inspection; the
police had arrested the remaining thirty-one women for clandestine prostitution who had then failed the obligatory medical examination. A further twenty-eight Vietnamese prostitutes were registered, but they had
deserted their brothels and were not attending their regular examination.
The mayor also found that there were twenty-one Japanese prostitutes
in the city divided among three brothels; one more was confined to the
municipal dispensary. Most of the Japanese prostitutes who had come to
Southeast Asia were from poor families on the Shimabara Peninsula and
Amakusa islands.[42] French naval men seem to have been their exclusive
patrons. The remaining brothels in the city were Chinese, and there were
nine of them. They allowed entry only to Chinese patrons. There were
thirty-one registered prostitutes between them. Four of these were in the
municipal dispensary, and one was at large.[43]

Women from southern China had been working in brothels in Chợ Lớn
since the late nineteenth century. Most were Cantonese, some Hakka. The
brothels had purchased many women as young girls, often no more than
five years old, from traffickers in Shanghai or Hong Kong, for between 100
and 200 piasters each. Their parents had usually sold them to the traffickers because of poverty, but some of the young girls had been abducted.
Although the girls grew up in the city's brothels, child prostitution was
not common. Some of the girls became servants, while others became entertainers known as *pei pa jai* (琵琶仔) who played a four-stringed musical
instrument called a *pei pa* in Cantonese. They studied the art of conver-
sation, how to perform, and how to sing. When they reached the age of
fifteen or sixteen, they began to perform at banquets for wealthy Chinese
merchants. These merchants would sometimes purchase the most attractive or talented of these entertainers to become their second or third
wives. Those who did not marry out of the brothels became prostitutes. In
1880, there were forty-five Chinese women and sixty-six girls between the
ages of five and fourteen in eleven brothels in the city.[44]

The Chinese brothels were difficult for the city to regulate. Chinese entertainers occupied an ambiguous legal position. They were not usually

subject to the same regulations governing other prostitutes. In 1903, the municipal authorities decided to subject establishments housing Chinese entertainers to the same regulations as other brothels in the city. But the Chinese Chamber of Commerce intervened. It argued that requiring Chinese entertainers to undergo a weekly medical examination was degrading, so the authorities rescinded the new regulation. A police inquiry in 1908 discovered that the nineteen brothels in the city housed only twenty-four registered prostitutes. No brothel had more than two prostitutes recorded in the police registers, and most had only one. As it happens, the police often discovered that this lone registered "prostitute" was a servant in the brothel who easily passed the medical inspection. They were, in the words of the police commissioner, "the cloth that covers the merchandise."[45] At the same time, the brothels housed 216 entertainers. Many were very young. The police found 54 between the ages of ten and fourteen, 133 were fifteen to nineteen, 25 were between the ages of twenty and twenty-four, and only 4 were twenty-five or older.[46]

The entertainers and brothel owners used a language of fictive kinship inside the brothel. They referred to the brothel owners as their "mothers."[47] Many of the entertainers had come to Chợ Lớn when they were very young and had had little opportunity to know their own mothers or to experience any other kind of family life. This language could create a sense of intimacy and familiarity among unrelated women and girls leading difficult lives far from their native villages. It could also encode hierarchies of subordination and control within the brothel. A "daughter" was required to be dutiful and respectful to her "mother," to obey her, and to be grateful to her for providing food and a home.

The brothels themselves were also difficult for the police to survey and control. Their proprietors had built them to provide privacy and secrecy for their patrons. The chief of police noted, "I visited three of these brothels and I realized that their interiors, established to thwart police surveillance and avoid extra surprises, are perfectly designed: there are many corridors, dark, and branching off freely; concealed staircases, disguised doors only granting passage to the familiar. . . . These are labyrinths, where the disoriented policeman, lost, can never find Ariadne's thread to recognize his location and make his way out."[48] The interior of the brothels also mirrored the city of Chợ Lớn, with its crooked streets, narrow alleys, and paths that seemed to lead nowhere. Lương Thị Lắm worked in a brothel on one of those streets from March to September 1905.

The regulations of 1878 specified that the only way a woman could be struck off the register of prostitutes was if she ceased to work as a prostitute and if she could show that she had some other means of providing for her needs. Inspector Léonardi wanted to know how Lương Thị Lắm had come to leave the brothel she had worked in. From the way he put the question, he must have already known the answer.

"By what means," he asked Lương Văn Sang, "did you proceed to obtain Lương Thị Lắm's removal [from the register of prostitutes]?"

"On September 3, 1905," replied her father, "I composed and sent a petition to the public prosecutor's office in Biên Hòa, which was successful."[49]

"On what date," continued the inspector, "was your daughter Lương Thị Lắm, then called Huỳnh Thị Kim, struck off the register of prostitutes?"

"September 6 of the same year," Lương Văn Sang answered.

"And it was to you that she was entrusted when she was struck off the register?" continued the inspector.

"Yes," went the brief reply.

"When did you return to the village of Tân Ba?" the inspector asked next.

"The day after she was discharged," responded Lương Văn Sang.

"Did your daughter, Lương Thị Lắm, remain with your family for a long period?" asked Inspector Léonardi, again apparently already knowing the answer.

"Two months later," her father began, "that is to say in November 1905, she left in secret, as before, and departed for the village of Tân Linh, located along the railway line. Once there, she took up residence until the end of the month of June 1906. She returned to Tân Ba for ten days," during which time she must have recounted her movements to her father, "and then she left again for the third time, for an unknown destination," he reported. Like so many poor Vietnamese at the turn of the century, Lương Thị Lắm lived a nomadic existence, moving from place to place in search of better opportunities.

In July 1906, when Lương Thị Lắm left Tân Ba again, she went to Saigon. She arrived without work or a place to live, so she did what she had done before: She became a prostitute. But she did not remain one for long. The police arrested her on July 22, 1906, for clandestine prostitution. A doctor examined Lương Thị Lắm and discovered that she had contracted blennorrhea, causing an excessive discharge of watery mucus from her vagina, and her cervix was ulcerated. The doctor immediately admitted her to the municipal dispensary. Inspector Léonardi must have known all of these things when he asked Lương Văn Sang his next question:

"On October 1, 1906, you formulated a request to obtain the freedom of your daughter, Lương Thị Lắm?"

"Yes," her father replied. "But this time, my efforts were fruitless, because she was being treated in the municipal dispensary in Chợ Đũi."

The municipal dispensary stood in an area that was once a market, or *chợ*, that had specialized in selling *đũi*, a kind of coarse silk fabric. The market had become part of Saigon, but in 1905 it was still on its outer edge. Streets bordered the dispensary on all four sides: Jauréguiberry Street to the northwest; Pierre Flandin Street to the northeast; Esparges Street to the southwest; and Colombier Street to the southeast, where the entrance was located. Monsieur Colombier, a former soldier turned market gardener and florist in the city, had offered land to the Municipal Council in 1886 to build the dispensary.[50] A four-meter-high wall surrounded the dispensary's six buildings and its large garden. Two policemen stood in constant watch over the gates. They stopped prostitutes from leaving, but they also protected the dispensary from outsiders.[51] A French doctor, three European nuns, two Vietnamese nuns, and three attendants cared for the patients who occupied its eighty beds. Ten of them were reserved for sick or indigent Europeans, "exhausted by the climate and by privation," who paid two piasters each day for their treatment. Seven or eight of these beds were always occupied. The other seventy beds in the dispensary, of which there were often too few, were reserved for prostitutes who had failed a medical examination. The examinations took place every Saturday morning when a crowd of noisy, sometimes grubby, and often sick women gathered in Colombier Street.[52] Because of a peppermint tree that once stood on the grounds of the dispensary, its distinctive fragrance led the prostitutes and other townsfolk to refer to the dispensary colloquially as *nhà thương bạc hà*, the "peppermint hospital."[53]

The dispensary in Hà Nội, the capital of French Indochina in Tonkin, had an equally fanciful name: the *lục xì*. According to local lore, a jovial French doctor who examined the city's prostitutes during the nineteenth century would ask the women if he could have a "look-see," and the English expression slipped into common use. The French had built the first dispensary in Hà Nội in early 1889, shortly after they took control of the city. It was a makeshift structure, constructed from thatch and bamboo, near the women's prison on Pagoda of the Great Buddha Road. A typhoon destroyed the building in the middle of the same year. The city used another building on Hàng Cân Street until 1902, when it moved to a new facility on Huế Road. None of the buildings were ever adequate: there were rarely enough beds to accommodate the number of women admitted, the amenities were primitive with poor hygiene and security, and the institution itself inspired horror and revulsion in the people of Hà Nội. One doctor who worked at the dispensary remarked that "this sanitary establishment is more like a prison; the unfortunates are interned behind solid iron gates as if they were wild animals. The duration of their detention is not compensated for by the treatment they receive, as the treatment of the sick, due to a lack of materials and personnel, is notoriously insufficient." Vietnamese in Hà Nội considered the medical examination an affront; the possibility of long confinement in the dispensary terrified many prostitutes.[54]

It was important for prostitutes in Saigon to pass their weekly medical examination. Their livelihoods depended on it. Prostitutes in Chợ Lớn who knew they had a venereal disease would sometimes try to conceal it from the doctor or fake their recovery if they had already been interned. They developed several strategies. Shortly before the examination began, those who had urinary tract infections or blennorrhea would often urinate to flush their urinary tracts. They would then roll a cigarette paper to the thickness of a match and insert it into themselves to absorb any telltale discharge. They would remove the paper only moments before they mounted the examination table. Appearing healthy, they would pass the medical inspection. Others would sprinkle their genitals with an astringent powder, such as talc, disguised by being mixed with another reddish powder, which absorbed any discharge, disguising their symptoms. Instead of dissimulating, some prostitutes tried to evade the medical examination altogether. Many claimed that they were menstruating; an examination at that time would therefore be unrevealing. In order to convince the doctor that they were, indeed, menstruating, they would smear their genitals with the blood of a bird, duck, or chicken. Lương Thị Lắm may have tried to conceal her disease from the doctor during her examination too. The documents do not say. She had been in Saigon for only three weeks when the police arrested her. She may not even have known that she had a disease.[55]

Venereal disease was rampant in Saigon and its environs. In 1889, the number of cases of syphilis in Saigon had attracted the attention of the authorities. The police commissioner suspected that clandestine prostitutes who lived in villages on the edges of Saigon and Chợ Lớn were spreading the disease.[56] These villages were part of the province of Gia Định to the north or the province of Chợ Lớn to the south. Incriminating innuendo and rumors were rife in the villages to the north. Associating prostitutes with criminals and lawlessness, the notables there claimed that they wanted to eradicate prostitution from the canton completely. The police commissioner received word that there were four illegal prostitutes in one of the canton's villages, living in the house of one Kiệt. It turned out, on further investigation, that there were only three prostitutes, and they were living near Kiệt, not in his house. When the police pressed the villagers for information, they protested their ignorance, and the three women immediately disappeared. Some said that they had left for Mỹ Tho.[57] When questioned, notables from villages in the south told the police that the prostitutes in the villages of Cần Hòa and Khánh Hội in fact lived in Saigon and that they were registered with the police there. According to the notables, the prostitutes were seen in Khánh Hội only when new ships came into port.[58] These villages, both to the north and to the south, were just outside the reach of the Saigon police, which made them natural homes for petty criminals and clandestine prostitutes. To domesticate this wild area, the colonial administration decided to place the villages under the authority of the Saigon police. After 1889, prostitutes there also had to register themselves and undergo a medical examination.[59]

The new municipal clinic that opened in Saigon in 1904 saw poor patients for free. Many of the patients that visited the clinic suffered from syphilis. The disease was most widespread among the Chinese, for the most part unmarried men who moved from port to port on the littoral of the South China Sea. In 1904, the municipal clinic recorded 177 cases of syphilis in Saigon, 152 in 1905, 303 in 1906, and 267 in 1907. The sharp increase in 1906 followed the economic slump in 1905 and coincided with the increase in arrests for clandestine prostitution, which women had probably taken up out of hardship. Patients seldom came to the clinic in the early stages of the disease, when small, painless ulcers called chancres first became noticeable. Secondary syphilis, marked by a characteristic rash and sometimes genital warts, fever, and weight loss, had usually developed by the time doctors made a diagnosis. Tertiary syphilis, in which the disease had spread to the brain, the nerves, and the heart, was rare. Soft chancre and blennorrhea were much more common, both in their advanced stages. One French doctor complained that many Vietnamese, ignorant of how venereal diseases spread, tried to purge themselves of "peccant humors" by having sex more frequently. Up to 90 percent of the women who came to the clinic with a venereal disease had been infected with gonorrhea by their husbands. Many other women suffered from an inflamed uterus and consequently weakness, emaciation, a changed character, and sterility.[60] The municipal authorities hoped that subjecting prostitutes to regular medical examinations and confining the infected would help stem the spread of venereal disease among the residents of Saigon.

But the prostitutes in Saigon had many wiles. From 1907, a change in the regulations governing prostitution made it possible for them to engage in a new subterfuge, though the change occurred too late to be of use to Lương Thị Lắm. For a fee of four piasters, a doctor was allowed to visit prostitutes in their brothels or at home and conduct the medical examination there. Brothel owners and prostitutes exploited the darkness and weak lighting characteristic of their establishments to make it difficult for the doctor to find the signs of disease. One doctor wrote to the authorities in frustration:

> The prostitute lies stretched across an ordinary bed, which is more or less soft, the doors of the house availing onto the street, so that they need to be almost shut. It is under these very poor conditions, and in half-darkness that the doctor must search to discover, with great difficulty, disease, when it exists. Among the Vietnamese, Japanese, and Chinese, an ordinary chair serves for the sanitary visit, and in general, the keeper of the brothels has the visit take place in a more or less dark location, seeking in this way to conceal, as far as possible, the venereal diseases of their tenants.

In 1911, the authorities put a stop to medical examinations outside of the dispensary. Instead, they made it possible, for the same fee, for prostitutes to choose a day other than Saturday for the doctor to inspect them. This way they could avoid marking themselves as a prostitute by waiting in an often noisy and disorderly crowd in front of the dispensary.[61]

The inspector had one final question for Lương Văn Sang.

"How did you know," he asked, "that she had been arrested in Saigon by the police?"

Lương Văn Sang answered the inspector for the last time: "Nguyễn Văn Đại, agent fourth class of the municipal police . . . wrote a letter to me toward the end of the month of September 1906. In it he told me that Lương Thị Lắm, my daughter, his cousin, was being treated at the municipal dispensary."

On February 7, 1907, the dispensary finally discharged Lương Thị Lắm after exactly two hundred days there—an extremely long stay. In 1906, the year she entered the facility, the 826 prostitutes admitted to the dispensary spent an average of forty-five days there. Three days later, on February 10, father and daughter reunited.

Lương Thị Lắm continued to be a problem for the municipal authorities after she was discharged from the dispensary. It was not that she had engaged in clandestine prostitution again or contracted another venereal disease. She did not break another law, or if she did, the documents do not record that fact. Now she was an administrative and financial problem. Lương Thị Lắm had spent a very long time in the municipal dispensary. The cost of her treatment during that period was $80, a considerable sum. A rickshaw man in Saigon would have had to pull a thousand rides to make $80 in 1907.[62] Nobody wanted to pay it. Lương Thị Lắm could not pay it, and neither could her father. An inquiry had found him "absolutely insolvent." There was relevant legislation for dealing with circumstances such as this, but implementing it proved contentious. An ordinance passed in 1904 specified that when patients could not afford to meet the costs of their treatment in one of the colony's hospitals, it had to be met by their home village or, barring that, their home province. The city tried, therefore, to recover the cost of Lương Thị Lắm's treatment from the province of Biên Hòa. The administrator of Biên Hòa, however, demurred. The woman had spent too much time living outside of the province, he argued. Biên Hòa could no longer be considered her home province. The city must meet the cost of her treatment itself or try to reclaim it from somewhere else. He suggested Tân Linh, a village he thought was in the protectorate of Annam, which was the last place that Lương Thị Lắm was resident before her arrest in Saigon. Correspondence went back and forth between the president of the Municipal Commission of Saigon, the administrator of Biên Hòa, the lieutenant governor of Cochinchina, and even the governor general of Indochina. The wrangling lasted for more than eight months, well into 1908. In the end, the officials determined that Lương Thị Lắm had returned to Biên Hòa sufficiently often for it still to be considered her home province. Had she not returned for more than a year, she would have lost any right to claim it as such. With some reluctance, the administrator of Biên Hòa added the cost of her treatment to the provincial budget. He did request, however, that in the future all prostitutes from Biên Hòa arrested in Saigon and Chợ Lớn who required hospitalization be returned to the province, as the cost of medical treatment was less expensive there.[63]

By 1907, the cost of medical treatment for prostitutes interned in Saigon for lengthy periods had become a heavy burden for the provincial authorities. These prostitutes were usually migrants to Saigon from rural areas in nearby provinces of Cochinchina, such as Gia Định, Chợ Lớn, Thủ Dầu Một, Mỹ Tho, and Biên Hòa. Lương Thị Lắm was only one of many prostitutes whose arrest and hospitalization plagued provincial officials.

One case from the same period initiated a frantic correspondence between the French administrator of Chợ Lớn, the mayor of Saigon, and the lieutenant governor of Cochinchina. Đỗ Thị Tư was born in the village of Tân Giao, in the province of Chợ Lớn.[64] Her mother had died, and her father, a poor farmer, had entrusted her to the care of her uncle, Nguyễn Văn Học. He lived in the nearby village of Long Hậu Tây. Since June 1905, Đỗ Thị Tư had lived with a Chinese man named Tam. At the beginning of November, he abandoned her. Finding herself penniless and with nowhere to live, she turned to prostitution. She was twenty-one years old. Inspector Léonard Pacot arrested her on November 9, 1905, because she was unregistered. The inspector arrested and detained her just as she boarded a steamer anchored between Nhà Bè and Khánh Hội, just south of the center of Saigon. When questioned, Đỗ Thị Tư confessed that she had been living as a prostitute and that she had a venereal disease. The inspector had her admitted to the municipal dispensary immediately. Her uncle, Nguyễn Văn Học, twice wrote to the authorities to have her released, and on May 19, 1906, his request was granted.[65] She had spent a total of 190 days in the dispensary, at a cost of 76 piasters. An inquiry by the police found that her father was penniless and unable to meet the costs of her treatment. Her home province, Chợ Lớn, became responsible for the cost. As in the case of Lương Thị Lắm, the provincial administrator requested that such prostitutes be sent back to Chợ Lớn for treatment in the future.[66]

The administrator of Gia Định also found the cost his province was incurring unacceptable. Five minutes after midnight, on April 6, 1905, Inspector D'Leno of the Saigon police observed a transaction take place between a young Vietnamese woman, Nguyễn Thị Khê, and a Vietnamese man whose home she was about to enter on Garnier Quay.[67] Inspector D'Leno placed the woman under arrest. After spending the night in jail, she was questioned at nine o'clock the following morning. Nguyễn Thị Khê, who usually went by the name of Nguyễn Thị Cơ, was seventeen years old. She was born in Thủ Đức, in the province of Gia Định, the daughter of Nguyễn Văn Đông, a coolie, and Nguyễn Thị Kiều. She now lived with her brother in Gò Vấp and did not have a job. She told the police that she had never been a prostitute, although she did ask, now that she had been arrested, to be registered as one. Nguyễn Thị Khê said that she had intended to spend the night with the man she was caught with, but "there had been no question of price." After her interview a doctor examined her and admitted her to the municipal dispensary because she had a venereal disease. On September 17, 1905, her father, Nguyễn Văn Đông, wrote a letter to the French authorities asking that she be discharged. He claimed that she was mad and that the police must have found her wandering while going to visit her sister who worked in Chợ Lớn.[68] He appears not to have known the circumstances of her arrest, or perhaps he did not want to mention them. Nguyễn Thị Khê spent over a year in the municipal dispensary, 450 days in all. Her treatment cost 177 piasters and 60 centimes, a fantastic sum. Her parents were too poor to pay it, and so was her village. As with Đỗ Thị Tư and Lương Thị Lắm, the burden fell to the province of Gia Định, much to the administrator's consternation.[69]

These cases all illustrate the growing demographic mobility between Saigon and its rural hinterland, as migrants from the countryside came to Saigon looking for work. Lương Thị Lắm, Nguyễn Thị Khê, and Đỗ Thị Tư all spent long periods of time in the municipal dispensary. None of them were from Saigon. Of the forty prostitutes undergoing treatment in the dispensary in March 1907, just a month after Lương Thị Lắm left it, only one was from the city.[70] Many of the women would never recover and would require ongoing treatment. An inquiry in August 1907 found that ten prostitutes in the dispensary had incurable diseases. One woman, Nguyễn Thị Nên, from Tây Ninh province, had been in the dispensary since March 1905; another, 25-year-old Nguyễn Thị Huệ, from Gia Định, had been there since July 1905. They must have both known Lương Thị Lắm while she was in the dispensary. But the dispensary was not staffed or equipped to provide prostitutes with long-term treatment. It was also proving too expensive for their home provinces to do so. Yet these women could not go back to living in the city because they posed a serious risk to public health. The authorities could not send them back to their home villages because they would not be able to receive palliative care there. The inquiry recommended that the dispensary transfer the women to the Chợ Quán Hospital, in Chợ Lớn, which was better staffed and equipped.[71] The inquiry also recommended that the police send prostitutes from neighboring provinces arrested in the city to hospitals in their home provinces if they were diseased, instead of being treated in the municipal dispensary. One official seems to have dissented, however, when he scribbled on a letter relaying this decision that "it is also not enough that a prostitute comes from a province, or says so, in deciding that her hospital expenses will be borne by the budget of that province. In my opinion, girls that usually exercise their profession in Saigon should always be hospitalized at the expense of the municipality."[72]

Colonial troops stationed at the garrison in Saigon and sailors from the naval yard there provided many of the customers for prostitutes such as Lương Thị Lắm. One of those soldiers or sailors may have given her the venereal diseases that led to her confinement, diseases she may have then passed on to their comrades. The French military had established a presence in Saigon from the beginning of the conquest in 1859.[73] There were very few European women in the colony before the turn of the century, so French soldiers and sailors turned instead to Vietnamese prostitutes. Sometimes they entered long-term relationships with these prostitutes, even living with them.[74] In the early years of French colonial rule, Vietnamese visited prostitutes with much less frequency because, able to freely enter relationships with Vietnamese women, they did not need to. And in the twentieth century, the large number of soldiers visiting brothels discouraged Vietnamese men from going there.[75]

The municipal authorities struggled to deal with clandestine prostitution. The sources all agree that unregistered or clandestine prostitutes significantly outnumbered registered prostitutes. Some clandestine prostitutes were women who worked as prostitutes full-time, like those who were registered, but who wished to evade regulation. Others practiced prostitution in addition to or under the guise of some other trade or profession. Chinese singers who worked in the brothels of Chợ Lớn made up most of those in this group. Itinerant merchants and waitresses in cafés and restaurants may have added to their precarious incomes through occasional work as prostitutes.[76] Lương Thị Lắm, Đỗ Thị Tư, and Nguyễn Thị Khê had all been arrested for failing to register themselves and failing to attend a regular medical examination. The earliest authorities had required both obligations when they issued the first ordinance regulating prostitution in 1867.[77] All subsequent ordinances, issued in 1876, 1878, and 1893, had made the same demands. In an attempt to improve surveillance over prostitutes, the ordinance of 1878 required all of them to work in brothels. But this measure proved ineffective, as clandestine prostitution continued to be a problem.

In 1908, the municipal authorities took bold new measures to regulate prostitution in Saigon. A new ordinance established a reserved quarter in the city, and the city permitted brothel owners to establish their brothels only within that quarter. All other brothels in the city had to close by the beginning of the following year. The quarter was on the southwestern edge of the city and was bounded by four streets: Léfèbvre Street, Bourdais Street, Hamelin Street, and Boresse Street.[78] There were already several brothels there. Declaring it a reserved area consolidated the police presence there and was meant to make it easier to control. But it was a sordid part of the city, infamous for crime and disorder. Two Europeans had been killed there in the previous year.[79]

The new ordinance also regulated cafés and drinking places run by European women. The ordinance confined the cafés to certain streets in the reserved quarter. The proprietors of these establishments had once been known in the colony as "Valaques," because the first of them had come from Wallachia, in Eastern Europe. But by 1908, many of them were French, and most of them were prostitutes.[80] These women did not register themselves, and the authorities did not oblige them to attend a weekly medical examination. To do so would have been "an assault on European dignity." The colonial authorities were only too aware of the real nature of their business—they were the source of endless scandals.[81] A greater scandal may well have been the double standard applied to European and Vietnamese prostitutes, one that left Lương Thị Lắm confined in a hospital for two hundred expensive days, while French prostitutes plied their trade with impunity.

At this point, Lương Thị Lắm recedes beyond the horizon. She appears in no archival documents after 1908. Many forces shaped her life: natural disaster, the failure of the harvest and the collapse of the rice trade, urban migration, homelessness, colonial legislation, the municipal police, venereal disease, and the municipal dispensary, among others. Such forces no doubt shaped the lives of other prostitutes in the first years of the twentieth century as well. The love a father might have felt for his daughter is another force that should not be forgotten. Lương Văn Sang tried to have his daughter freed from confinement twice: the first time from Brothel No. 14 in Chợ Lớn, the second time from the municipal dispensary in Saigon. Lương Thị Lắm may have saddened her father or made him ashamed. But he loved her enough to seek her release when he could have turned his back on her. Or perhaps she was supporting her family with her work, so he deemed her release essential.

At the end of this story, however, one question seems to stand out: Why, on August 16, 1907, did Inspector Léonardi summon Lương Văn Sang to testify to his daughter's movements? Why did she not appear to give testimony herself? And what does this suggest? Patriarchy? Chauvinism? Condescension? Perhaps. But it also might suggest that, yet again, Lương Thị Lắm had run away.

CHAPTER THREE

BETWEEN HEAVEN AND EARTH

Clouds float through dreams, are nowhere to be seen:
you've borne and shed the load of rank and wealth.
Stars shift, things change within the realm of kings;
streams flow, flowers drop outside the gate of lords.
Life is a game of chess played here and there:
men's hearts are seas with shallow waves and deep.
Speak out or not—what difference does it make?
Keep brooding and your head will soon turn white.
—*Nguyễn Bỉnh Khiêm, "Clouds Float Through Dreams"*[1]

Few migrants to Cochinchina became as wealthy and well known as the Chinese rice merchant Quách Đàm. He was originally from Chaozhou prefecture, near Phoenix Mountain, in the southern Chinese province of Guangdong. Quách Đàm arrived in Cochinchina in 1880 and began his rise to prominence selling old bottles and buffalo skins. He soon amassed enough capital to venture into the rice trade. He established the Thông Hiệp Company, which had its offices on Gaudot Quay in Chợ Lớn; by 1916 he owned one of the largest and most profitable rice mills in Cochinchina. He became fabulously rich, and his name was heralded throughout the colony.[2]

In contrast with Quách Đàm, many Chinese migrants to Saigon and its hinterland toiled in obscurity and suffered from penury and want. Huỳnh Khánh Lương arrived in Saigon in 1890. He too was from Chaozhou. Huỳnh Khánh Lương took up residence in Chợ Lớn, but he also sojourned for several years in Cambodia. He paid his taxes when he could, which does not seem to have been very often. His daughter, Huỳnh Thị Phụng, sold vegetables for a living. She described her father to the colonial authorities, after he had spent twenty-six years in the colony, as "old, poor, miserable, and sick." Vương Vĩnh Thành came from Chaozhou like Huỳnh Khánh Lương. He had arrived in Cochinchina in 1896 and lived in the province of Long Xuyên in the Mekong Delta. In 1916, the police arrested him for running an illegal gambling den, and he spent two months in prison awaiting expulsion from the colony. His wife and six children lived in apprehension as they anticipated the outcome of his appeal. The vagrant Quách Quan was also uneasy. He had landed in Saigon in 1897 but never found the fortune he sought. He spent a month in prison for vagrancy in 1910 before the colonial government sent him back to China. Quách Quan returned to Saigon only to find himself destitute once again by 1916. Quan Thanh arrived in Cochinchina from Guangdong in 1902. He became a resident of Chợ Lớn and assumed the Vietnamese name Trần Văn Lợi. Quan Thanh spoke Vietnamese well and was easily identifiable to other pork traders by the smallpox scars that pockmarked his face. In 1916, he attracted the attention of the colonial authorities after he threatened his fellow Cantonese merchants in a provincial market and demanded that they each pay him ten piasters. The authorities ordered him expelled from Cochinchina.[3]

Cochinchina was an attractive destination for poor immigrants from China at the end of the nineteenth century and at the beginning of the twentieth. Saigon was flourishing: For the previous ten years, it had shipped growing quantities of rice to the ports of East and Southeast Asia. In the decade from 1892 to 1901, it shipped 45 percent of its rice to Hong Kong and the ports of southern China, 9 percent to the Straits Settlements, and 21 percent to India, Ceylon, the Netherlands East Indies, the Philippines, and Japan.[4] Accompanying the rapid growth of the rice trade, the Chinese population of Cochinchina had increased significantly in the same years: In 1892, there were nearly sixty thousand Chinese residents in Co-chinchina; by 1902, their number had grown to more than a hundred thousand.[5] They settled mainly in Saigon, Chợ Lớn, and their hinterlands in the neighboring provinces. They too would come to be buffeted by the winds that blew through the regional rice economy.

If the potential for wealth attracted Chinese to Cochinchina, tumult and turmoil in southern China often led them to emigrate. The establishment of Western dominance on the coast of southern China after the first Opium War caused profound disruption to the local economy and society. With the Treaty of Nanjing in 1842, the Qing government acquiesced to a number of British demands, including the cession of Hong Kong island and the opening of five treaty ports where Westerners could reside and trade exempt from Qing law. France and the United States soon demanded and received the same privileges. The new treaty ports of Shanghai and Ningbo abruptly opened Guangzhou to competition when it had once been the only place where Westerners could trade. A hundred thousand porters and boatmen around Guangzhou lost their jobs and turned to outlaw brotherhoods and banditry to survive. Many of the disaffected joined the Red Turban Rebellion that ravaged the region from 1853 to 1855. Fear of violent official reprisals led many rebels to flee overseas.

The Opium War also deepened an economic downturn on the southeastern and southern coast, leading to feuding among villages, chaos in the countryside, and rampant homelessness.[6] In 1851, Hong Xiuquan, a former village schoolteacher and failed provincial examination candidate who believed he was the younger brother of Jesus Christ, was proclaimed Heavenly King of the Heavenly Kingdom of Great Peace. The ensuing civil war between the Heavenly Kingdom and the Qing state from 1851 to 1868 devastated the empire. It killed as many as thirty million people and displaced many more.[7] Migrants crowded ships bound for the distant ports of Bangkok, Batavia, Saigon, and the Straits Settlements seeking refuge from violence and hardship. But it did not take a violent catastrophe or cataclysm to produce a sense of insecurity among the residents of Guangdong. In 1902, the harvest was particularly dismal: The first rice crop on the Han River delta failed, and then the second crop on the Pearl River delta failed as well.[8] The number of emigrants from Shantou, or Swatow, and Hong Kong destined for Southeast Asia increased sharply that year and in 1903.[9]

Among them was a man from Guangdong named Trần Dưỡng, who abandoned his native place for Saigon.[10]

Most Chinese migrants, like Trần Dưỡng, came from the provinces of southeastern and southern China. Wenzhou speakers came from the area around Wenzhou prefecture in Zhejiang province, near the mouth of the Ou River. Those who spoke Hokchiu originated in the coastal reaches of the Min river basin around Fuzhou prefecture and the port of Fuzhou. Hokkien speakers hailed from the littoral prefectures of Quanzhou and Zhangzhou, south of the Min River, and usually departed for Southeast Asia from the port of Xiamen. Teochiu or Chaozhou speakers came from Chaozhou prefecture in Guangdong province and were served by the port of Shantou. Hainanese speakers came from the southern island of Hainan, which had its largest port at Haikou. And Cantonese speakers from the Pearl River delta came from Guangzhou and Zhaoqing prefectures and left from the port at Guangzhou and, after the Treaty of Nanjing, from Hong Kong.[11] Many thousands of Chinese migrants arrived in Saigon from southeastern and southern China each year: 13,201 migrants in 1912, 13,624 in 1913, 10,143 in 1914, 10,118 in 1915, and 9,998 in 1916.[12]

Trần Dưỡng was Hakka. The Hakkas came from the border highlands of Guangdong, Fujian, and Jiangxi provinces in southern China. They traditionally worked in upland occupations such as mining, quarrying, masonry, and metalworking, as well as swidden farming and forestry. They spoke a language that was a descendant of Old Southern Chinese that had been spoken by Chinese migrants to the south of the empire before and during the Han dynasty and that broke away from the languages of the north long before the seventh century. The name *Hakka,* which means "guest people," seems to have been the Hakka way of saying 客戶, *kehu,* the category under which they appeared in the local population registers of the Ming and Qing dynasties. Unlike other Chinese women, Hakka women did not bind their feet to make them small, which allowed them to work on the hillsides alongside their men or on their own while the men sojourned somewhere else.[13]

Trần Dưỡng was one of between 1,500 and 2,000 Hakkas who had settled in Cochinchina by World War I.[14] Hakkas such as he had sojourned and settled in Southeast Asia since the middle of the eighteenth century. They began mining at Pontianak in western Borneo in 1776, then at Bau in Sarawak, and in Bangka and Belitung in the Netherlands East Indies.[15] Their tin mining settlements prospered in the sultanates of Selangor, Negri Sembilan, and Perak on the western coast of the Malay peninsula.[16] In Cochinchina, some Hakka owned small shops, some sold tea and cakes and fresh vegetables, some operated river craft; others worked as cobblers, wheelwrights, carpenters, blacksmiths, and masons, just as they had done in China.[17]

The Chinese in Cochinchina, as elsewhere, tended to work in occupations specific to the language they spoke or the area of China they came from. The largest group, the Cantonese, milled rice and monopolized the silk looms, sawmills, lime and ceramic kilns in Chợ Lớn as well as the construction of junks and sampans. They also managed workshops, large and small, for repairing water vessels, and they owned and operated most of the Chinese watercraft that went back and forth on the inland waterways of the colony. Petty entrepreneurs sold furniture, made shoes, sewed clothes, hewed stone, turned and fashioned wood, butchered meat, and ran restaurants. The Cantonese furnished most of the workers in the industrial enterprises in Saigon and Chợ Lớn, such as the Arsenal, the workshops of the Messageries Fluviales, and the company Dupont and Brun. They also specialized in the export of animal skins and horns, cardamom, and gamboge, a resin used in yellow pigments and as a purgative in traditional Chinese medicine. Most of the river boatmen and stevedores who loaded and unloaded ships at the port of Saigon were Teochiu speakers. Unique among the Chinese in Cochinchina, the Teochiu engaged in agriculture in large numbers and grew rice in the provinces of the Mekong Delta. Hokkien or Minnan speakers, from Fujian province, dominated the milling of that rice in Chợ Lớn and the regional trade in rice more broadly. They worked as clerks and compradores for European and Chinese trading houses in Saigon and in the prestigious stores on Catinat Street. They also engaged in more modest enterprises as bottle, barrel, and scrap merchants. The Hainanese had a few small shops in Saigon and Chợ Lớn, but they mostly worked as cooks and domestic servants for European families or on the pepper farms in Hà Tiên province and on the distant southern island of Phú Quốc.[18]

After he arrived in Saigon, Trần Dưỡng registered to pay his taxes in the city and then decamped for neighboring Biên Hòa, just when Lương

Thị Lắm might have begun to contemplate leaving the province. He made his home in Tân Lai, one of eight villages in the canton of Phước Vĩnh Thượng, roughly eleven kilometers from the provincial capital. Biên Hòa was part of the great hinterland that sustained the economic life of Saigon. The province supplied Saigon with firewood for its hearths, stone for its buildings and roads, and labor for its arsenal, rice mills, brothels, and commercial enterprises. Biên Hòa had long been a destination for enterprising Chinese settlers like Trần Dưỡng. After the fall of the Ming dynasty, Chinese loyalists, led by the Cantonese Chen Shangchuan, began to settle in the province. The island of Cù Lao Phố, located on a bend in the Đồng Nai River, became an important commercial port: Chinese junks and sailing boats and other foreign vessels often moored there. The boats came once a year, in November and December following the northeastern monsoon, and departed again in March and April with the winds of the southwest monsoon. The traders brought silks and fabrics, which they exchanged for sugar, salt, and forest products. Many Chinese settled on Cù Lao Phố and took Vietnamese wives.[19] Trần Dưỡng married a woman named Khưu Thị Tâm, whose family name suggests a Chinese father, and together they had three children.

Trần Dưỡng worked as a mason to support his wife and young family. Chinese dominated the quarries in Biên Hòa. There were nearly a hundred scattered across the province. The work was difficult and dangerous: Trần Dưỡng would have used explosives to blast granite loose from the open quarry where he worked in Tân Lai, which he would have then shaped with hammers and chisels. The masons in Biên Hòa fashioned gravestones, plinths, columns, and building blocks for construction in Saigon as well as grindstones for husking paddy in Chợ Lớn. They sold broken granite to cover the surfaces of provincial roads and municipal streets.[20] The city of Saigon had recently drained the marshland near the Chinese Arroyo and sealed nearly twenty kilometers of streets, avenues, and boulevards with gravel, as more and more Chinese and Vietnamese made Saigon their home.[21] The growth of Saigon made work for men like Trần Dưỡng in its hinterland while their labor made the expansion of the city possible.

For as long as he resided in Biên Hòa, Trần Dưỡng was the responsibility of its Hakka congregation. The colonial administration required all Chinese immigrants to belong to a congregation based on their place of origin and the language they spoke. There had once been seven congregations in Cochinchina, but by the first years of the twentieth century there were five, designated Guangdong, Fujian, Chaozhou, Hainan, and Hakka. Each congregation was collectively responsible for the conduct and well-being of its members: It maintained discipline and levied fines when its members misbehaved, and it built schools, hospitals, and cemeteries to provide for its members' welfare. The Chinese character for "congregation" or bang—幫—is the same as that for "help" or "assistance." The elected headman acted as an intermediary, relaying laws, orders, and regulations from the colonial administration to the congregation while conveying the concerns, requests, and complaints of its members to the administration.[22] In 1916, the headman of the Hakka congregation in Biên Hòa was a quarry owner and local notable named Trương Thất.

Trương Thất was a wily and devious figure. He and three other Hakka notables owned a company that sold commercial granite and had once engaged Trần Dưỡng and several other Hakka masons. But the notables were poor employers: They failed to pay the wages they owed, while they demanded that the masons work longer and longer hours. When the masons finally complained and sought their unpaid wages, the notables chased them away. The masons formed their own stone-cutting enterprise and went into business for themselves. They must have been fairly successful, because when their former employers tried to entice them to return, the masons adamantly refused.[23] Possibly bitter at the success of the masons or resentful of the competition they provided, Trương Thất decided to punish them and eliminate the nuisance they had become. In the middle of April, he penned an urgent letter to the French administrator of Biên Hòa province: Trần Dưỡng and the other Hakka masons had formed a clandestine branch of the Heaven and Earth Society, he wrote. The colonial administration had long anguished over the Heaven and Earth Society, a secretive organization that was notorious in Cochinchina for smuggling, counterfeiting, robbery, and racketeering. It had been especially active in Biên Hòa.[24] Trần Dưỡng and the other masons were a serious threat to order and public safety and should be expelled from the colony immediately, Trương Thất concluded. Trương Thất connived with Khưu Phước Trường, a Chinese merchant and business associate from Chợ Lớn, who made the same complaint to the Justice of the Peace in Biên Hòa.[25]

The Justice of the Peace played an important role maintaining order and dispensing justice in the province. There had once been a magistrate's court in Biên Hòa, but the province was thinly populated and there was not enough work for the court to do, so the administration replaced it with a Justice of the Peace. The Justice of the Peace had all the duties that a magistrate might have: He regulated administrative orders and payments, he conducted inquiries in civil affairs, such as disputes over tenancy, and he pursued investigations into crimes, such as robbery and fraud.[26] Trương Thất had made a serious accusation, so the Justice of the Peace ordered Trần Dưỡng and the other masons detained and questioned. He could not be sanguine about allegations concerning the Heaven and Earth Society. But after making further inquiries, the Justice of the Peace found no evidence that the masons had formed a branch of the society. He ordered them released and closed the case. The administrator of Biên Hòa reached the same conclusions and similarly considered the matter settled.[27]

Trần Dưỡng refused to be bullied and intimidated by his former employer. Together with the other masons, he made a complaint of libel against Khưu Phước Trường in the Magistrate's Court in Saigon. The Magistrate's Court had had two chambers: The first ruled on cases concerning Europeans, while the second decided cases concerning Vietnamese and other Asians.[28] Khưu Phước Trường appeared in the second chamber before the vice president of the court. After hearing the evidence, the judge found him guilty of slander. The judge ordered the merchant to pay a fine of one hundred francs, and to pay damages of one hundred piasters each to Trần Dưỡng and the other masons he had maligned.

The judgment came as a blow to Khưu Phước Trường. He was, after all, a merchant with a reputation to protect. He resolved to contest the decision in the Court of Appeal in Saigon, one of the most powerful judicial bodies in French Indochina. The court had jurisdiction over a vast territory that comprised Cochinchina, the penal island of Poulo Condore, the protectorate of Cambodia, and the provinces of southern Annam and Laos. The court heard appeals against judgments in civil, commercial, and criminal cases as well as findings against French citizens, subjects, and protégés who had been tried in consular tribunals in Siam and China.[29] Khưu Phước Trường hoped that the court would strike down the judgment against him and vacate his sentence.

When nothing emerged from his first complaint to the administrator of Biên Hòa, Trương Thất sent him a second anxious letter in the middle of July. Three former heads of the Hakka congregation in Biên Hòa and fifteen of its members joined him in signing the complaint. Trương Thất maintained that Trần Dưỡng and five of his fellow masons were men of questionable morality and poor conduct. They did not work, they gambled, and they kept the company of suspicious individuals, the letter falsely claimed. Although he offered no proof, Trương Thất alleged that the men were responsible for encouraging mischief in the province, even if they did not take part in it directly. Once again, Trương Thất urged the administrator to expel Trần Dưỡng and the other masons from Cochinchina immediately.[30]

After receiving the second letter, the administrator felt that he had to act. He sent a Vietnamese official, a prefect in the administration, to make inquiries in the village of Tân Lai, where Trần Dưỡng lived. The official arrived in the village in the last week of July and established himself in the communal house. He enlisted the aid of the canton chief in his investigation. The official began his inquiry by interviewing Trương Thất and the former heads of the Hakka congregation. Predictably, they vehemently denounced Trần Dưỡng and the other masons. They had intimidated other villagers into joining the Heaven and Earth Society, they had blackmailed those who were reluctant to join, and they had committed a number of other petty crimes, the accusers claimed. The reputation of the Hakka congregation depended on the expulsion of such delinquents from the colony. To verify the accusations, the official interviewed fourteen of the additional signatories to the second letter. He also questioned forty-four members of the Hakka congregation in Tân Lai and the neighboring village of Bửu Long. All of the witnesses gave the same damning testimony as Trương Thất. The official felt compelled to agree with the head of the congregation: The masons should be expelled from the colony and sent back to China.[31]

Trương Thất and the other Hakka notables had a further reason for wanting to be rid of their former employees. The Hakka had erected a pagoda in the village of Bửu Long at the end of the eighteenth or the beginning of the nineteenth century to honor the patron saints of masonry, carpentry, and smithing. They renovated the pagoda in 1894 using the bold, blue stone characteristic of Bửu Long. The Hakka invited two deities, Guan Yu and the Empress of Heaven, Mazu, to reside in the pagoda along with the patron saints. The pagoda soon became known as *Chùa Bà,* or the Pagoda of the Lady, because of the miracles that Mazu was said to perform there.[32] Trương Thất and the Hakka notables had borrowed $1,900 from the pagoda, a truly fabulous sum at a time when a coolie might earn only $1 for a day's labor. A mason the notables had once employed but had dismissed along with Trần Dưỡng kept the books for the pagoda. When he informed the notables that the loan had become due, they refused to repay it. They would return the money, they said, only if the masons returned to work for them. Such disputes were usually mediated by the head of the congregation. But since he was a protagonist in the affair, the colonial courts provided the only avenue of redress. No ledger shows that the Pagoda of the Lady was ever repaid.[33]

The Lady, Mazu, was a well-known deity in southeastern and southern China. The people of Meizhou, off the coast of Putian county in Fujian province, had first recognized Mazu as a deity in the late tenth century. According to local accounts, her given name was Lin Moniang. She was born into a seafaring family in 960 and died at a young age in 987. She was an unusual person—as a child she did not cry or show emotion, and as an adult she did not marry. Toward the end of her life, local people became convinced that she had supernatural abilities that allowed her spirit to guide seafarers safely through storms. The first sign of this came when she had a dream in which she saved her brothers from peril at sea, only to learn upon their return that they had indeed been in danger and that they had been rescued by a mysterious female spirit. Soon after her death, seafarers along the coast of Fujian began to report similar miracles, and she soon became their patron saint. She became prominent further afield after the imperial court began to confer a succession of titles upon her: "Divine Kindly Lady," "Imperial Concubine," "Heavenly Holy Mother," and the most exalted, "Empress of Heaven."[34]

Mazu was honored and revered among the Chinese in Cochinchina and especially in Saigon and Chợ Lớn. She had protected their journey across the South China Sea, and she watched over the seamen who plied the shipping routes between Saigon and the Chinese littoral. As an object of piety, she protected their profit. The Chinese community came together to honor her at the Pagoda of the Seven Congregations on Cây Mai Street, which was the common property of all of the congregations. Each congregation also had its own shrine or pagoda where they venerated her. The Hainanese offered her sacrifices at a chapel on Marins Street. The Hokkien honored her at Tam Sơn Pagoda, or the Pagoda of the Three Mountains, on Canton Street. The Hokkien had originally dedicated the pagoda to a prince consort from Fuzhou, but when prayers and sacrifices to him proved ineffective, they invited Mazu to take his place. Those from Zhangzhou prefecture in Fujian offered their own sacrifices at a separate pagoda on Cây Mai Street. The Guangdong congregation worshipped Mazu at a small temple in the quarter of Cầu Ông Lãnh, a small chapel in the Chợ Quán quarter, and at the grandest and wealthiest pagoda in Chợ Lớn on the corner of Cây Mai and Canton streets.[35] The large brass bell that the temple used to mark time and summon the monks to prayer bore an inscription dating to the tenth year of the reign of the Qing Daoguang emperor (1830 in the Western calendar), although the pagoda itself was considerably older. Chinese supplicants lit joss sticks and bowed before a gilded statue of Mazu when they sought guidance and favor in uncertain times, such as when they sought to marry or had to compete for paid employment or when they were about to embark on a new commercial venture or had become ill for some unknown reason.[36] The veneration of Mazu helped bind communities of settlers and sojourners in foreign lands. Chinese seafarers and oceangoing passengers usually made their way to the pagoda to give ritual thanks to Mazu for their safe arrival; those about to depart made offerings for a safe onward journey. They could do so along the Chinese coast from Zhejiang to Guangdong and across the South China Sea, from Taiwan to Singapore, Pontianak to Batavia.[37] Shared rituals linked Chinese in distant parts, Bangkok or Biên Hòa, to kith and kin across the region; and it helped cement trust among traders who might otherwise never meet each other.

When the Vietnamese official returned from Tân Lai, he submitted his report to the administrator of Biên Hòa. The administrator felt compelled to agree with its recommendation: Trần Dưỡng and the other masons should be expelled from Cochinchina. It was very likely, he thought, that they had been involved in the violent disturbances that had troubled Saigon and the provinces at the beginning of the year.[38] The head of the Immigration and Identity Service in Saigon agreed.[39] A metropolitan law passed in 1849 declared that "the Minister of the Interior may, through the police, order any foreigner traveling or residing in France, to leave French territory immediately and have him taken to the border."[40] The metropolitan government had begun to apply the law to foreign visitors to France's colonies in 1874.[41] Édouard Rivet, the acting governor of Cochinchina, cited the law when he ordered Trần Dưỡng expelled from the colony at the end of August.[42] The acting governor had a reputation for maintaining peace and order: He had joined the colonial administration in 1893 and had previously served as the administrator of four southern provinces and as the acting head of the colonial administration in Tonkin.[43] He ordered Trần Dưỡng and the other masons detained while they waited to board the steamer *Kimchow,* scheduled to leave Saigon for China on September 14.[44]

The order of expulsion was a crushing blow. Trần Dưỡng had lived in Cochinchina for thirteen years, married, and established a family. One mason had lived in the colony for twenty years, another for thirty-eight. They would leave behind their homes and their wives and children. They would abandon the land and life to which they had become accustomed for an uncertain and frightening future in a place they had once left behind. Trần Dưỡng, transforming what must have been agony into action, immediately appealed the decision. The lawyers, Messrs. Vabois and de Mérona, wrote to the acting governor on the masons' behalf. The advocates explained that the men had been falsely accused of participating in the Heaven and Earth Society and that they had sued Khưu Phước Trường for calumny. Rather than pay the fine and damages to which he had been sentenced, Khưu Phước Trường and Trương Thất had conspired with other Hakka leaders to have the masons sent back to China. The advocates asked that the acting governor suspend the expulsion order and conduct a new inquiry into the dispute among the Hakkas.[45] But the acting governor summarily dismissed the request: According to the administrator of Biên Hòa, the masons had incited unrest in Saigon and the provinces at the beginning of the year; at least now they had been discovered and would soon be appropriately punished.[46] But what so troubled the colonial administration at the beginning of 1916? Why did it take Trương Thất's accusations against the masons so seriously? And why did the Heaven and Earth Society provoke so much anxiety among colonial officials?

Despite the outbreak of war in Europe in 1914, the economy of Cochinchina had grown steadily in 1916. Farmers in the provinces of the Mekong Delta continued to bring more and more land under the plow: By 1916, they had planted 180,000 hectares in rice. The port of Saigon shifted 1,245,000 tons of paddy, milled rice, and flour that year.[47] And the Government of Cochinchina collected more land revenue than ever before, to the tune of $2,080,000 in 1916.[48] The growing affluence of Saigon continued to attract people to the city, which had grown to 67,000 residents by 1916, although it was dwarfed by Chợ Lớn, which numbered 183,000.[49] The municipality, finding itself with a significant budget surplus that year, embarked upon several major public works: It built a new police building near the Marais Boresse, new municipal stores and warehouses on Bangkok Street, and two new buildings at the Municipal Free Clinic, and added new guttering to the European cemetery.[50] Two years earlier, in 1914, the grand new Central Market had opened near the Marais Boresse. The market enclosed eleven thousand square meters and comprised four pavilions separated by two passageways at right angles to each other, while a square cupola topped the center of the market. One pavilion sold meat, another fish, the third tropical fruit, and the last eggs and poultry; fruit and vegetable stalls lined the passageways.[51] In 1916, the new market and the other markets in the city were bustling with commerce: Fish had been in short supply since the beginning of the year, which had made it more expensive; heavy rains in the last two months of the year damaged many crops and created a shortage of vegetables, but pork and poultry were in great demand, especially in Singapore. For these reasons the markets sold $155,430 worth of goods in 1916—an increase of 9 percent over the previous year.[52] The residents of Saigon and the provinces were able to share their prosperity with others less fortunate in the north: At the end of 1915 and the beginning of 1916, they raised significant sums to assist Vietnamese in Tonkin, who were affected by recent flooding of the Red River.[53] When it flooded, as it did all too often, the river cascaded over the dikes and embankments meant to contain it, it ruined the harvest in the low-lying coastal provinces, and it did enormous damage in the villages, the deluge completely sweeping away all but the most robust structures.[54] But for many residents of Saigon, and for Chinese merchants and craftsmen in its hinterland, the early years of World War I were years of relative plenty.

Recent events, however, had made the administration increasingly apprehensive about the role of the Chinese in the colony. After the Xinhai revolution in 1911, the administration had banned the importation of Chinese-language newspapers and periodicals to prevent radical ideas from the young Chinese republic from infiltrating the colony. Early in the new year of 1915, Prime Minister Ōkuma Shigenobu of Japan had presented Yuan Shikai, the new president of the Republic of China, with what would become known as the Twenty-One Demands. These demands included special economic privileges in Manchuria, Shandong province, and the Yangzi River Valley; the right to lease farm land in Manchuria and reside there with extraterritorial legal status; and permission to post Japanese troops in China. The demands roused strong opposition from Chinese newspapers, students, and municipal chambers of commerce. Boycotts of Japanese goods spread from Guangzhou and the southern coast across China.[55] In March, the Chinese congregations in Chợ Lớn decided to join their brethren and boycott the importation and sale of Japanese goods in Cochinchina. The war in Europe had made it impossible to import products from France, and Cochinchina had come to rely upon Japan to supply manufactured goods. The colonial administration feared that the boycott would cause a shortage of important goods and a sharp rise in prices. Chinese merchants also took advantage of the war to spread rumors and panic in the provinces at harvest time to force down the price of paddy.[56] The war had disrupted transportation between Cochinchina and the other ports of East and Southeast Asia. This disruption, in turn, helped push the local price of paddy lower still, while the scarcity of imported goods forced up the prices of other commodities in the cities and the countryside. The rice trade and therefore the economic welfare of the colony depended almost entirely on the prudence and good will of the Chinese merchants who dominated it. The administration introduced a range of measures to restrict the movement of Chinese in and out of the colony while war was going on in Europe. To enter the colony, a Chinese migrant had to pay a deposit and provide a guarantee from a local sponsor approved by the administration in addition to paying the customary taxes.[57] When applying for a passport to leave the colony, the Chinese had to declare the name of the ship on which they intended to depart.[58] Trần Dưỡng and the other Hakka masons did not have to commit any crimes or misdeeds to become the objects of anxiety and suspicion—it was enough that they were Chinese.

While France was at war in Europe, the potential for sedition or rebellion was a problem of paramount importance. Unrest in the kingdom of Cambodia at the end of 1915 and at the beginning of 1916 had shaken the highest levels of the colonial administration. In November 1915, some two hundred cultivators from the district of Khsach Kandal descended on the capital, Phnom Penh, to petition King Sisowath for relief from their labor obligations. The king assured the petitioners that their grievances would be investigated and urged them to return home, which they did. But they returned to the capital on January 5 and 6, 1916, and this time they numbered several hundred. As in November, the king assured them that he would attend to their complaints and they left peacefully. But on January 7, two thousand cultivators from the environs of Phnom Penh descended on the royal palace. Once again, the king peacefully dispatched the crowd after promising to take up their concerns. In the following weeks, wave upon wave of cultivators from the surrounding countryside marched on the capital to bring their troubles before the king. By January 24, a crowd of some five thousand farmers had formed in the village of Lovea Em, across the Mekong River from the capital. The following day, they crossed the river and assembled before King Sisowath. They presented their complaints respectfully and departed after listening to the king's admonitions. The colonial authorities estimated that thirty thousand cultivators had brought their complaints to the capital in the first weeks of the new year. On January 30, King Sisowath addressed a crowd of ten thousand cultivators gathered on the eastern bank of the Mekong River in the village of Tonle Bet. The following day, the king confronted a gathering of between three and four thousand cultivators. On February 1, the monarch traveled to Khsach Kandal, where the unrest had begun, and addressed a crowd of cultivators who were preparing to attack the provincial administration.

On each occasion, the words of the king reassured and quieted the crowds, but after his departure the unrest returned. Itinerant cultivators sacked a copra and sugar palm plantation, they harassed Vietnamese fishermen on the Mekong River, and they threatened the residence of the Cambodian governor at the settlement of Beng Chuoi, west of Kompong Cham. The colonial administration sent thirty troops to restore order to Beng Chuoi, and the Cambodian authorities also made a number of arrests. On the afternoon of February 6, cultivators attacked the administration at Beng Chuoi to free those taken prisoner. Five of the rebels were killed and a number wounded. To restore order, King Sisowath returned to the region for several days. Unrest was widespread: Cultivators traveled from throughout the kingdom to lay their complaints before the king in Phnom Penh, they attacked local and village officials, and they attacked other Asians and their property. They sacked the buildings of the Vietnamese fishing monopoly in Takeo province, they looted the Chinese markets near the former royal capital of Oudong, north of Phnom Penh, they burned Chinese shops in Kampong Chhnang, and they attacked a Vietnamese Catholic village in Takeo province, forcing the residents to retreat across the border into Cochinchina. Only at the end of February did quiet finally return to the kingdom.[59]

The administration in Saigon watched vigilantly for signs of unrest in the city and in the southern countryside. It soon became evident that a major rebellion was stirring in the provinces of Cochinchina too. On January 20, in the province of Trà Vinh, the recruitment of volunteers for military service in Europe caused considerable unrest. In Biên Hòa, in the canton of Chánh Mỹ Trung, a band of Vietnamese tried to hamper the recruitment of volunteers and attacked local notables; several militiamen were wounded. At five o'clock in the evening, on January 25, a riot broke out in the Biên Hòa prison. The prisoners seized weapons from the guard post and opened fire on the provincial administrator, who returned fire with a hunting rifle. Seventeen prisoners escaped. On the same evening, at close to eleven o'clock, a mob of almost fifty individuals rioted in the village of Tân Uyên, looting the market, wounding a forest warden, and killing a Vietnamese worker before fleeing into the night. In the province of Bến Tre, a group of nearly two hundred rebels assembled in the village of Mỏ Cày on the night of February 2. The rebels, armed with picks, machetes, and clubs, marched to a drum and carried a red flag bearing the characters 義和, or "Nghĩa Hòa," a sign of the Heaven and Earth Society, while they looted as many as twenty homes. Troops dispersed the mob and made a number of arrests. In Thủ Dầu Một province, rebels in groups of five or six looted houses bordering Biên Hòa and Gia Định provinces. The tattooed rebels were deserters from the military forces, voluntary military recruits, and criminals who had been released on appeal. In Bà Rịa, the authorities reported that the men had deserted the villages and that secret meetings were taking place in clandestine locations. On the night of February 12, a group of almost a hundred rebels assembled in Cửa Lấp, about eight kilometers from Cape St. Jacques, and planned to descend upon the cape. The group dispersed, but not before the police arrested thirteen individuals. In Gia Định, the authorities learned at the end of January that a group of rebels planned to disrupt the celebrations during Tết. The rebels spread the rumor that the government was defenseless since it was obliged to send not only money and materials but also soldiers and workers to France to fight in the war. On February 7, the provincial administrator arrested several individuals, including a man who claimed that he would soon be crowned king and that he had gathered thousands of followers, just as Phan Xích Long had done in 1913. In early February, the administrator of Tân An province signaled that unrest was about to break out in his bailiwick. Open exhortations to rebellion circulated among villagers in the province, auguring an uprising that would chase the French from Cochinchina. And on February 12, the wife of a canton chief sought refuge in Chợ Lớn after learning that the residents of Đa Phước village intended to attack Saigon to rescue the Vietnamese from colonial rule and massacre the French in the city.

The attack took place on February 15. At three o'clock in the morning, the moon was beginning to descend in the sky. Three hundred rebels, who had been concealed beneath banana leaves, climbed out of junks and sampans that had been moored at the mouth of the Chinese Arroyo, between the signal mast and Cầu Ông Lãnh Bridge. Members of the Heaven and Earth Secret Society filled the ranks of the rebels. They all wore white pants and short black tunics and white kerchiefs tied around their necks. The kerchiefs were made of cotton or silk, according to rank, and carried symbols of martial prowess and Chinese characters in red. Stitched into the sleeves of the tunics were protective amulets that the rebels thought provided immunity from bullets as well as various exhortations to bravery and courage in combat. The rebels were armed with lances, machetes, and old swords. At the head of the group was a flag bearer who carried a banner with the emblem of the self-proclaimed emperor Phan Xích Long, who had been imprisoned since the failed uprising he led in 1913. The rebels meant to free Phan Xích Long from the prison in Saigon where he was confined. The rebels divided into three groups along the Belgian Quay: one group went down Mac Mahon Street; another group headed for Nemésis Street; and the last group set out for Marchaise Street. Silently the rebels began to make their way toward the center of the city.

The rebels soon confronted resistance. Those marching down Mac Mahon Street encountered an automobile returning from a hunting trip, which was carrying two French passengers and a Vietnamese driver. The rebels surrounded the automobile and hacked at one of its tires. The Frenchmen had hunting rifles in the vehicle but they were not loaded. Slashes from a sword wounded one passenger on the back and cut his arm through to the bone. The other passenger used his empty rifle to parry repeated machete blows from a rebel who had taken up a position on the running board of the automobile. The driver eventually managed to break the vehicle free of the rebels. "Death to the French!" and "Great Leader!" cried the rebels as the vehicle sped toward the Central Police Station to warn the authorities. At the corner of Canton Boulevard the rebels met two policemen on patrol, one French and the other Vietnamese, mounted on bicycles. The policemen immediately engaged the rebels, firing shots from a service revolver into the crowd. The bullets killed two rebels and wounded several others. The rebels fought back ferociously: a machete blow injured the hand of the French policeman while several blows felled his Vietnamese colleague, who lay on the ground wounded while the rebels retreated toward their sampans. The rebels rejoined the two other bands and made their way down Filippini Street toward the Central Prison. At the corner of Espagne Street, a group of fifty rebels broke away and attempted to force open the back gate to the palace of the governor of Cochinchina. The sturdy iron gate held, however, defeating the rebels, who rejoined the group marching upon the prison.

The cries of "Death to the French!" and "Great Leader!" redoubled. The corporal of the prison guard, having no warning of the impending attack, dispatched a sentry to investigate the commotion. He believed that the noise might have been made by new recruits returning late from the brothels in the Boresse quarter of Saigon. The sentry encountered the rebels on Filippini Street, where they attacked him. He fell, mortally wounded, but not before injuring one of the rebel leaders. The corporal sounded the alarm and closed the gate to the prison as the rebel band arrived and attacked two soldiers. The sergeant in charge of the guard post opened a box of cartridges to distribute them to the guards just as a lance thrust through the bars of the gate slashed his chin. The cartridges having been distributed, the guards opened fire. The rebels' protective amulets proved ineffective. Two fell dead, and a third died in front of the Central Market while retreating. The others withdrew down Mac Mahon Street and Marchaise Street toward the Belgian Quay. Some scrambled into sampans and used oars to escape; others hurriedly followed the Chinese Arroyo toward Chợ Lớn, with individuals peeling off into boats anchored along the waterway.

The gendarmerie in Chợ Lớn had been alerted to the approaching rebels and confronted them in front of the "Rizerie" station along the tramway that ran between the city and Saigon. Four rebels fell during the struggle; some threw themselves into the arroyo to escape, while others fled into the nearby undergrowth. With the aid of the Chợ Lớn police, the gendarmes took twelve of the rebels prisoner and apprehended several others in nearby huts.[60]

The attack on the prison had been part of a much larger plot carried out by members of the Heaven and Earth Society. A small army had been raised in Saigon and its environs. The rebels that landed on the Belgian Quay were to be joined by another group from the Boresse Quarter. The idea was that together they would attack the Central Prison. The freed prisoners would join their liberators and together they would arm themselves with weapons cached in sampans along the Chinese Arroyo and attack the main munitions store. If the attack on the prison failed, they would torch a building. The explosion of the munitions store or the flames of the burning building were meant to serve as a signal to another group of rebels, which would be lying in wait on the Avalanche Arroyo behind the Botanical Gardens, that the moment had come to loot the city and massacre its French residents. Phan Xích Long, the mystical pretender to the Vietnamese throne freed at last from prison, would install himself in the palace of the governor and take over the reins of government. But the rebellion had been foiled.

The colonial administration responded swiftly and severely. A council of war convened five days later quickly sentenced thirty-eight of the rebels to death. According to Ernest Roume, the governor general of French Indochina, such harsh sanctions conformed with the Vietnamese understanding of justice, commenting that they "reassured honest people and gave pause to brigands." But the number of capital sentences troubled him: They implied that the colonial administration was afraid of the Vietnamese, even though it was never in peril; and they made it seem bloodthirsty and merciless. The governor general suggested that several of the sentences be commuted, but the civilian and military authorities in Cochinchina demurred.[61] The executions quickly became a public spectacle and attracted a large crowd. Frenchmen with their wives and children traveled from the distant countryside to witness the event. A platoon of Vietnamese infantrymen methodically shot the rebels, who knelt on the ground in groups of four, blindfolded and lashed to stakes. A battalion of French soldiers waited at the ready with machine guns in case the Vietnamese infantrymen lost their nerve. On the following day, peddlers hawked picture postcards of the event on the streets of Saigon.[62] They were macabre souvenirs of the failed attempt by members of the Heaven and Earth Society to free Phan Xích Long and overthrow French rule in Cochinchina.

Chinese migrants had first brought Heaven and Earth Society rituals and lore to Cochinchina at the end of the eighteenth century. The first meetings of the society had taken place in China in the 1760s when restive and disaffected men—teachers of Chinese boxing, wandering monks, itinerant healers, and gamblers—from the southeastern Chinese provinces of Fujian and Guangdong assembled together. The group "united their hearts" by drinking a mixture of wine and ash from burned incense. They resolved to recruit new members to the gathering and to plunder the storehouses, county treasury, and homes of local notables.[63]

The Heaven and Earth Society quickly spread throughout southern and southeastern China. Members of the society provided each other with protection and support during difficult and uncertain times. An early member of the society explained to the Qing authorities:

> The name Heaven and Earth Society comes from the fact that Heaven and Earth are the source of being for mankind. The only meaning is respect for Heaven and Earth. Originally, the reason for people's willingness to enter the society was that if you had a wedding or funeral, you could get financial help from the other society members; if you came to blows with someone, there were people who would help you. If you encountered robbers, as soon as they heard the secret code of their own society they would bother you no further; if you were to transmit the sect to other people, you would also receive their payments of "gratitude." Therefore, those who want to enter the society are many in number.[64]

Chinese migrants soon established the Heaven and Earth Society on the water frontier of the Mekong delta. One of its earliest adherents was the Chinese pirate He Xiwen, known in Vietnamese as Hà Hỷ Văn, who was originally from Sichuan province in southwestern China. He had become a member of the Heaven and Earth Society and joined a band of pirates that raided along the coast of the South China Sea. In 1786, he offered his assistance to the southern Vietnamese leader Nguyễn Phúc Ánh, who was fighting to suppress the Tây Sơn Uprising. In 1771, three brothers from Tây Sơn district in Bình Định province—Nguyễn Lữ, Nguyễn Nhạc, and Nguyễn Huệ—had started a rebellion that sent armies marching north and south causing widespread bloodshed.[65] He Xiwen died among his troops and received many posthumous honors after Nguyễn Phúc Ánh eventually defeated the rebellion and ascended the throne as Gia Long, the first emperor of the Nguyễn dynasty.[66] Later Chinese migrants established the Heaven and Earth Society wherever they settled. By 1880, it was active throughout the coastal provinces of the Mekong Delta. In that year, riots broke out among rival society members in the province of Sóc Trăng. Gangs brawled and plundered with impunity, with the colonial administration seemingly impotent in its attempts to intervene. The intermittent violence lasted for more than two years before finally abating.[67] By the time of the attack on the Saigon prison, the Heaven and Earth Society was most active in the provinces of Châu Đốc, Bến Tre, and Biên Hòa.[68]

The society had developed a body of fantastic and elaborate lore about its origins. According to that lore, early in the reign of the Kangxi emperor (r. 1661–1722), the Xi Lu barbarians were alleged to have threatened northwestern China. The Kangxi emperor sent out an urgent plea for assistance. The monks of the Shaolin monastery in Gansu province answered the plea and defeated the barbarians. The grateful Kangxi rewarded the monks but, respecting their vows, bestowed no titles upon them. Later, a traitorous official persecuted the Shaolin monks with great cruelty. Eighteen monks survived and wandered the empire for more than four years. When they were on the verge of being captured, a white stone incense burner miraculously appeared in a river. Inscribed on the bottom of the incense burner was an exhortation to "Restore the Ming and Extirpate the Qing." Inspired, the monks founded the Heaven and Earth Society and vowed to carry out the instruction, which they consecrated with a solemn blood covenant. The monks became the first brothers of the Hong family. A young descendant of the Zhu imperial family, which had founded the Ming dynasty, later joined them in their quest. In a final battle, the Qing forces defeated the Shaolin monks once again. The five surviving monks scattered and established the Heaven and Earth Society throughout the empire.[69]

New members of the society endured a lengthy and elaborate initiation ceremony. The ceremony enacted a journey through the mythical landscape of life and death. At its conclusion, the initiate was reborn a member of the society and a brother of the Hong family. In Saigon and the provinces of Cochinchina, the ceremony was a pale imitation of those performed in China. It was described in poems, manuals, and magical texts, which the colonial authorities found obscure and unintelligible whenever they discovered them. The initiates were usually taken to a field far from other houses and buildings so as not to arouse the suspicion of the authorities. Members of the society marked out a square using palm branches to fashion a makeshift lodge, leaving an opening on each of the four sides to represent passages or gates. The members placed one or two small tables in the center of the square, which served as an altar to the five founders of the origin story, on which they placed a roasted pig, fruit, and various other ritual objects. The master of the ceremony, who was usually Chinese, wore a white turban with his hair loose, the left leg of his trousers hitched up, and the left sleeve of his shirt rolled up. A vanguard member who spoke for the initiates led them through each of the gates. Two members stood on either side of each gate armed with swords. As the initiates passed through the gates, they were asked a number of questions. To "Where do you come from?" they answered, "The East"; to "Where are you going?" they responded, "In search of brothers"; and to the question "Are you faithful?" they replied, "Faithful and devoted." A band of white cloth placed over the second gate represented a golden bridge. The passage through a gate of swords or under a bridge reinforced the imprecations of the blood covenant that concluded the ceremony: Members would be killed by those same swords if they broke their promises. The characters for "City of Willows," 木楊城, *Mộc Dương Thành,* were inscribed above the third gate of the lodge. The City of Willows represented a safe haven, where members of the society would be free from persecution. Triangular pendants suspended above the fourth gate proclaimed that it was a "hotel of obedience to the Hong," the family that the new members were to join. And on the altar to the five founders a flag carried the exhortation: "Overthrow the Qing, restore the Ming."

After passing through the gates, the vanguard and the initiates arrived in front of the table where the master of the ceremony was waiting for them. The master proceeded to read the thirty-six oaths of the covenant before the initiates. After each oath, each initiate took a stick of incense. Following the reading of the oaths, the officiant instructed the initiates to place their hands behind their backs. He pierced the tips of their middle fingers with a silver needle and collected a few drops of their blood in a bowl of water or wine. The officiant then had each of the initiates drink from the mixture. The blood covenant sealed the membership of the initiates in the new society. The new members then crossed over the Mountain of Fire, which was represented by three rocks surrounded by embers. The Mountain of Fire was part of the landscape of the underworld and also appeared in the Ming dynasty–era novel *Journey to the West* (西遊記). Passing over the mountain was an act of purification before rejoining the world of the mundane. When this formality was complete, each new member performed six greetings, three standing and three kneeling. The ceremony ended with a proclamation of the names of the brothers and the officers of the gathering, followed by a festive banquet.[70]

Members of the society identified each other by way of a number of discrete signs. The three surnames Lý, Châu, and Hồng often appeared in that order on society documents. The character for Hồng, 洪, the common family name of members of the society, could be decomposed into the numbers 3 三, 8 八, and 21 二十一, and the use of these numbers in sequence or in combination was a sure sign of affiliation with the society.[71] Some members of the society had Chinese characters tattooed on their arms in blue ink, which signaled their membership to those who recognized their significance. One tattoo, "君子殺身以成仁" / "Quân tử sát thân dĩ thành nhân," was a Confucian saying that meant "The superior man will take his own life to keep his benevolence intact." Another tattoo, "丈夫縱橫宇宙" / "Trượng phu tung hoành vũ trụ," proclaimed that "a man of prowess roams the whole world freely."[72] Signs and counter-signs helped distinguish the initiated from the uninitiated, brother from layman, friend from foe.

Many men joined the society of their own volition, but it also used violence and coercion to fill its ranks. The court records of Long Xuyên province from 1911 were filled with such incidents. Phan Văn Chánh, a society member in the village of Mỹ Phước, planned to conduct an initiation ceremony and urged his fellow villager, Phan Văn Nhi, to join. When Phan Văn Nhi begged off, Phan Văn Chánh beat him savagely about the head. When Đoàn Văn Bạch refused to join the society or to pay the hundred piasters it demanded from him, members of the society destroyed his home in the canton of Định Hòa. In the village of Mỹ Hội Đông, a notable asked a villager to join the society. When the villager refused, members of the society felled his areca and coconut trees, smashed the water wheel he used to irrigate his fields, and threw excrement into his barrel of salted fish.[73] Members of the society menaced, maimed, and murdered throughout the provinces of Cochinchina, cowing the population as they evaded the authorities.

The colonial administration struggled to understand the workings of the Heaven and Earth Society, with its recondite lore, clandestine ceremonies, secret signs, furtive meetings, and criminal undertakings. But the French understood its potential for sedition. They knew that the society had figured in the uprising led by the mystic Hong Xiuquan that had devastated the Qing empire during the nineteenth century. And they were aware that it had become an important vehicle for Sun Yat-Sen and Chinese nationalists early in the twentieth century. Its declared goal was to overthrow the Qing dynasty. In Cochinchina, this goal became the overthrow of French rule.[74] A society manual, titled "Advice to Farmers and Scholars," captured during a police raid made vivid its goal of insurrection:

> According to the *Spring and Autumn Annals*, Cochinchina is a political unit. The French are verily one of the three categories of barbarians. They intend to make war on us. We are going through a time of trouble—it is fate that makes us unhappy and so many of our countrymen suffer. The means of regaining independence are still etched in these books. In the past, one distinguished good from evil and made examples. Every man must discern the one from the other: you are warned. So much the worse for the imbeciles who will be deceived!
>
> . . .
>
> As for the French, they are separated from us by thousands of leagues of water and mountains. They built iron boats with chimneys. Though they had many bronze cannons and leaden cannon-balls, they had to wage war against us for several years, and many officers and generals died. They have conquered the three provinces. . . . Have they not been seen opening the graves, demolishing the pagodas and temples, committing acts of inhumanity, tearing down houses, raping young girls and children, and engaging in acts of sacrilege? . . . Heaven will not leave us in this chaos and will not allow them to enjoy happiness. No one is stronger than Heaven; on every part of the globe, everything has a master.[75]

Members of the Heaven and Earth Society had attacked the Saigon prison early in 1916 to free Phan Xích Long and overthrow the French, bring order to chaos, and enact the will of Heaven. When Trương Thất wrote to the administrator of Biên Hòa only two months later and reported that Trần Dưỡng and the other masons had formed a branch of the society, he all but expelled them from Cochinchina himself.

The administration had denied requests from Trần Dưỡng and Messrs. Vabois and de Mérona to halt the expulsion. By the middle of September, the masons had been ejected from the colony. It fell to their wives, who remained behind, to plead on their behalf. One wife wrote that her husband had lived in Cochinchina for thirty years. He had refused to join the company owned by Trương Thất and the Hakka notables who had made false claims against him in order to have him expelled from the colony.[76] Another wife asked the acting governor to take pity on her and her child, who had been "deprived of natural support" and was in the "deepest grief." She petitioned him to investigate the events in Biên Hòa once more. One woman, a peddler of sundries, insisted that her husband was innocent and that Trương Thất and the other Hakka notables had schemed against him. She gave the names of 190 witnesses, all of whom, she said, would offer the same testimony.[77] A village notable also testified to the administration that her husband was honest and kind.[78] When the acting governor failed to act or to reply, she petitioned him yet again.[79] Khưu Thị Tâm wrote a desperate letter on behalf of her husband Trần Dưỡng:

> I, the undersigned, Khưu Thị Tâm, residing in Tân Lai, in the canton of Phước Vĩnh Thượng (Biên Hòa), have the honor of informing you that the Chinese Liêu Thắng, Huỳnh Phụng, and Huỳnh Khánh, former heads of the congregation of Hakkas, and Trương Thất[,] the current head of the same congregation[,] have, with the aid of Khưu Phước Tường of Chợ Lớn, created a company called "Đông Thắng" and have forced my husband, Trần Dưỡng, to join it for a fee of five piasters.
>
> My husband who is only concerned with the trade and sale of granite refused to become a member of the company they had founded, despite their threats.
>
> So, Khưu Phước Tường, seeing his powerlessness, carried out his threat and denounced my husband as a member of a secret society before the Biên Hòa Tribunal during May of this year. My husband was arrested, imprisoned for several days, and was released after he was found not guilty.
>
> My husband then made a complaint against Khưu Phước Tường before the Tribunal of Saigon, which sentenced Khưu Phước Tường to a fine of 100 francs and 100 piasters in damages for slander on June 10.
>
> It was following this affair that Khưu Phước Tường, the current head of the congregation, Trương Thất, and their associates, viciously denounced my husband before the administrative authority as a member of a secret society and a danger to public safety. They provided their relatives or members of their company as witnesses to the enquiry made by the prefect of Biên Hòa in order to have my husband cruelly expelled from the country by the police.

My husband, struck by this administrative action, has already been unjustly expelled, because of the false and vicious denunciation made by his enemies, leaving me with three young children who cry night and day for their absent father. I am deeply unhappy here and lack the means to feed my children.

My children and I come before you respectfully and throw ourselves at your feet to plead for justice. We beg you to have a French official conduct an inquiry among the notables of the village of Tân Lai, where my husband has spent thirteen years with irreproachable conduct. The deputy head of the canton of Phước Vĩnh Trung, and the Justice of the Peace of Biên Hòa know this affair well, as well as the Chinese witnesses whose names I will indicate on the day of the enquiry to render justice to my husband, to my children, and to me.[80]

But Khưu Thị Tâm never received a reply. There was no further inquiry. And neither she nor her children nor their father received justice. Trần Dưỡng had been sent back to China.

CHAPTER FOUR

A HUMAN HORSE

The wheels of history stoop your back and pull;
try hard to climb the uphill road ahead.
. . .
The world goes through a play of change and flux—
this human horse may turn a dragon yet.
—*Phan Trọng Quản, "A Ricksha Man's Impromptu"*[1]

On December 3, 1914, a French gendarme stopped and questioned a young Vietnamese man in the village of Cái Sơn in the southern province of Vĩnh Long. The gendarme asked the man about his name, his age, his place of origin, and his livelihood, and requested proof that he had paid his taxes for the year. The answers he gave were translated, transcribed, redacted, and then included in a laconic official report. "My name is Trần Văn Lang," the man answered:

> I am 19 years old. I do not know my place of birth, I have no profession and no fixed abode. I do not know who my parents were, I am unmarried, and I have no previous conviction. I know how to read romanized Vietnamese.
> I do not have a tax payment card for the current year.

I have twenty cents to my name and I arrived in the province of Vĩnh Long, from Nha Trang (Annam) six days ago with the hope of finding work here.

I spent last night at the home of a notable in the village of Hòa Mỹ.[2]

The colonial authorities were particularly preoccupied with establishing the identity of those they governed. Only then could taxes be fairly collected, provincial budgets for public health and education accurately allocated, and criminals located and punished. Lương Thị Lắm had once pretended to be a woman named Huỳnh Thị Kim. The gendarme merely wanted to be certain that Trần Văn Lang was who he claimed to be. But after questioning him, the gendarme promptly arrested the young man for vagrancy and for not having a tax payment card.

The police learned that Trần Văn Lang was born in 1895. He grew up in the hamlet of Chánh Mẫn in Bình Định, a coastal province in the protectorate of Annam.[3] Bình Định shared a border with Quảng Ngãi to the north; Phú Yên to the south, which it later annexed; Kontum to the west; while the South China Sea lay to the east. Mountains covered much of the province and barricaded it against its neighbors. The Côn River flowed from highlands in the west to the coastal plains where it emptied into Quy Nhơn Bay close to the capital. Towers built of stone and brick studded the land, built by Cham peoples from the kingdom of Vijaya during the twelfth and thirteenth centuries.[4] Vietnamese troops annexed the province in the late fifteenth century, and it was the southernmost frontier of the Vietnamese kingdom until 1611, when Nguyễn Hoàng conquered the basin of the Đà Rằng River to the south as far as Cả Pass. By the middle of the seventeenth century, Bình Định had become the staging ground for expeditions further south into the Mekong Delta.[5] At the end of the eighteenth century its villages had kindled the Tây Sơn Uprising.

In the first year of Trần Văn Lang's life Bình Định was in turmoil yet again. The patriotic Cần Vương (Save the King) movement had just come to an end. It had begun in 1885 when the Hàm Nghi emperor fled the imperial capital and called on his subjects, both the scholar-gentry and the peasantry, to oppose the French. After a little more than a decade, the movement was all but defeated, and its most important leader among the scholar-gentry, Phan Đình Phùng, had died of dysentery.[6] But the rebels in southern Annam were unwilling to lay down their arms. They had begun to regroup near the town of Bồng Sơn, in the north of Bình Định, close to the border with Quảng Ngãi. The leader of the rebels, Trần Đức, was based in Quảng Ngãi. Trần Đức had a forged letter from Hàm Nghi that called on those still loyal to him to take up arms and rid the land of foreigners. His lieutenant in Bình Định was a local notable from Bồng Sơn named Huỳnh Phống Tương. Huỳnh Phống Tương enlisted villagers from the surrounding countryside to rebel. Some joined him because they did not think the cause yet lost; others had rebelled in earlier years and escaped capture or had been released for want of evidence. The senior rebels received grand titles such as general, colonel, and lieutenant colonel. Their plan was to attack the imperial citadel in Bình Định and the French residence in Quy Nhơn. Rumors of the plot spread and the Vietnamese prefect of Bồng Sơn, who had sided with the French, found out about it. The French arrested the rebels and tried fifty-four of them in May. Eight were sentenced to death, and the others received prison sentences of between five and twenty years.[7] On the last day of October, a violent typhoon slammed into Bình Định. It washed out roads and isolated the province further still. Many called it the worst storm in living memory.[8]

The first year of life is typically the most dangerous, but Trần Văn Lang survived the tumult. He told the gendarme that he did not know who his parents were—he may have been trying to conceal their identity, but he could also have been an orphan. Many other Vietnamese gave the same answer when questioned by the colonial police about the identity of their parents.[9]

Perhaps the most remarkable fact about his youth is that sometime before his nineteenth birthday, Trần Văn Lang learned to read romanized Vietnamese. Throughout his boyhood, the schools of Annam still provided a predominantly traditional education in which students studied the core of Chinese literature, known universally as "the Four Books and the Five Classics," as well as history in preparation for the imperial examinations. Such schools seldom taught romanized Vietnamese or did so only very poorly. It took until 1910 for the Vietnamese imperial government to oblige schools in the villages to teach Vietnamese in the Latin script.[10] But there were very few such schools in Bình Định. Instead of being organized village by village, the schools in the province were organized canton by canton, with each canton containing twenty villages on average. Very few students were ever able to attend. When they did, there were many challenges: The provincial authorities were largely indifferent to the functioning of the schools; the teachers were poorly compensated and soon abandoned their duties; it was almost impossible to obtain new teaching materials; there were almost no books of interest to assign; and the schools were equipped with only very crude paper, pens, and ink. It would have been very difficult to learn to read and write romanized Vietnamese in the villages of Bình Định. But Trần Văn Lang did it.[11]

Bình Định was a relatively prosperous province, but opportunities for young men like Trần Văn Lang were limited. Bình Định was sparsely populated: During the reign of Emperor Gia Long at the beginning of the nineteenth century, the province had roughly 38,400 residents; after the middle of the century, when Emperor Tự Đức sat on the throne in Huế, 41,800 people lived in the province; in 1898, the population had reached 53,300. By 1909, that number had grown to 66,900.[12] The hilly terrain meant that there was little scope for settled agriculture, other than on the coastal plains. Many people fished off the shore to feed themselves. Chinese merchants dominated commerce. There were almost fifteen hundred Chinese traders in Bình Định. They purchased goods produced in the hinterland or manufactured nearby, which they sent to emporia established in bays along the coast. They shipped the goods on to Hong Kong and Shanghai and the other ports of southern China. A French commercial house based in Nha Trang had branches in the province that purchased rice, manioc, silk cocoons, and products collected from the forest for sale in Quy Nhơn and Nha Trang. But the Vietnamese and French struggled to compete with the Chinese. The French had more success manufacturing in the province. One entrepreneur established a factory that spun and wove silk using the most modern machinery, employed more than 500 Vietnamese workers, and used almost all of the raw silk produced in the region, including from as far away as the province of Quảng Nam further north.[13] Vietnamese in nearby villages produced silk seersucker on looms in their homes for the manufacturer. Artisans fashioned ornate wood carvings, sometimes inlaid with metal, glass, or ceramic or patterned after statues found among the minority peoples of the highlands; potters made vases for flowers, water jugs, pipes for smoking, and decorative statues.[14] Such crafts required apprenticeship and long training or were learned in the home. It would not have been easy for Trần Văn Lang to find work in Bình Định beyond tilling its fields or fishing its waterways. The isolation of the province and the limited opportunities it afforded might have prompted Trần Văn Lang to strike out for more fertile fields.

Or perhaps Trần Văn Lang was troubled by the deep sense of anxiety that had come to pervade Bình Định in 1913, despite its tranquility and prosperity. The province was seemingly calm: Its inhabitants crisscrossed the countryside going from one market town to another; the roads were busy with travelers, especially along the Old Mandarin Road between Quy Nhơn, the seat of the French resident, and Bình Định, site of the citadel and the Vietnamese imperial administration; the markets themselves were overflowing with people and wares; and in the fertile river basins of the lowlands the farmers reaped an abundant harvest. Yet a pervasive malaise took hold of the population in 1913: Rumors of some arcane and impending peril began to spread from the larger towns into the villages and into individual homes. The provincial mandarins had started to question people, sometimes repeatedly, about vague plots and rebellions, and their surveillance was becoming increasingly intrusive. In the south of Bình Định, in what had once been the province of Phú Yên, the mandarins erected watchtowers every few hundred meters along the main road. At night nobody could travel without being stopped and questioned at each watchtower. The villagers and townsfolk became uneasy because the mandarins seemed frightened by some looming danger that was never specified. Observing the growing disquiet among the people, the mandarins increased their interrogations, which seemed only to multiply the dread among the people. Panic slowly took hold of Bình Định. The price of rice, which had brought affluence to the countryside, began to fall precipitously as rice merchants tried to move their stock as quickly as possible. Some people buried their money and valuables to preserve them from calamity. The population stood ready for some ineffable menace.[15]

Cochinchina and Tonkin had already been terrorized. In Cochinchina, Phan Phát Sanh, under the name Phan Xích Long, and his followers had mounted an abortive attack on Saigon in late March. In Tonkin, a mandarin from the province of Thái Bình and two French military officers in Hà Nội had been dramatically assassinated in separate public attacks. On

April 12, the chief of Thái Bình, Nguyễn Duy Hàn, had been traveling in a rickshaw down the main street of the provincial capital. At 11:30 in the morning, Phạm Văn Tráng shouted, "The Vietnamese revolution begins!" and threw a bomb that killed Nguyễn Duy Hàn as he passed by. Phạm Văn Tráng and his co-conspirators had singled out Nguyễn Duy Hàn for his devotion to the colonial administration and the ferocity with which he pursued its opponents. Two weeks later, on the evening of April 26, Nguyễn Khắc Cần and Nguyễn Văn Túy hurled a bomb onto the crowded terrace of the Hà Nội Hotel on Paul Bert Street in the colonial capital. The bomb killed two commandants in the French army and one Vietnamese and wounded twelve others. The unexpected attacks prompted French administrators and Vietnamese mandarins to conduct intensive local investigations and broader inquiries throughout the provinces. But there was no plot in Bình Định. It was the relentless questioning and conspicuous watchfulness of the mandarins themselves that caused so much fear and apprehension. Once the perpetrators of the attacks in Cochinchina and Tonkin had been arrested and tried and the surveillance and interrogations had ended, calm returned to the province.[16] Shortly after, the authorities discovered the presence of Heaven and Earth gatherings in Bình Định, which had been going on since 1907. The mandarins quietly conducted inquiries and discreetly arrested the leaders of the gatherings without causing further distress or any unrest.[17]

But such calm might not have assuaged Trần Văn Lang, for he decided to leave Bình Định and make his way south to Nha Trang. The journey would not have been easy. The train line from Saigon did not extend as far north as Quy Nhơn. The steamer that brought supplies and took away goods to Saigon stopped there only twice each month, and one of the two weekly mail vessels that plied the coast had stopped calling at Quy Nhơn. Trần Văn Lang probably could not have afforded a ticket on a passenger vessel. It is likely that he would have had to cross the Varella massif at the Cả Pass on foot, a traversal that took at least four hours, before he descended into Khánh Hòa province toward Nha Trang.[18] Khánh Hòa had been hit by a typhoon the previous November, which left a number of casualties. It damaged the robust administrative buildings of Nha Trang and destroyed many of the less sturdy homes. The fields of the province remained replete, however, and the people rallied to bring in the harvest. News of the attack on Saigon and the bombings in Tonkin reached even the smallest villages, through word of mouth and newspapers from Saigon, but the population remained placid. The people made their tax payments without any ire, and for the first time the admininstration issued payment cards in receipt.[19]

When he arrived in Nha Trang, Trần Văn Lang found work as a cook for a French priest.[20] He did not say how the priest treated him, but the conditions must have been tolerable—he remained in the service of the priest for more than a year. But working for the priest paid poorly, and "because of the low wages," Trần Văn Lang left the parochial house in November 1914. He made his way south to the Mekong Delta and stopped when he reached the province of Vĩnh Long.

Trần Văn Lang might have taken a number of routes to get to there. Road, river, and rail had increasingly knitted the distant parts of Cochinchina together.[21] Two main roads traversed the province: Highway No. 4 extended to Sa Đéc, Provincial Route No. 7 to Trà Vinh.[22] A number of smaller roads linked Vĩnh Long with market towns such as Vũng Liêm, Cần Thơ, Cái Môn, and Chợ Lách. But canals formed the main arteries of communication. By 1914, it was possible to travel by ferry from Saigon to Tân An, Mỹ Tho, Vĩnh Long, and Cần Thơ.[23] Steamboats could navigate the largest canal, the Mang Thít, carrying delta rice to Saigon and bringing people and goods to Vĩnh Long via a network of subsidiary waterways. Since 1885, a railway line had linked Saigon with the nearby port of Mỹ Tho, and from 1913, locomotives regularly steamed between Nha Trang and Saigon. But in 1914, no train line extended into the Mekong Delta as far as Vĩnh Long.[24] It is possible that Trần Văn Lang took the train from Nha Trang as far as Saigon and then took a ferry to Vĩnh Long. He told the gendarme that he spent the night of December 2, 1914, "at the home of a notable in the village of Hòa Mỹ," which was on the banks of the Cổ Chiên River, a short distance from the provincial capital.

Five provinces bordered Vĩnh Long: Mỹ Tho to the north; Trà Vinh and Cần Thơ to the south; Bến Tre to the east; and Sa Đéc in the west. To the northwest lay Đồng Tháp Mười—the Plain of Reeds—a vast wetland area that included the Cambodian provinces of Banam and Svay Rieng and extended south into Cochinchina as far as Mỹ Tho and Sa Đéc.[25] The Tiền Giang River, the northern fork of the Mekong, bounded Vĩnh Long in the north before dividing into the Hàm Luông and Cổ Chiên rivers and flowing into the South China Sea. Canals crisscrossed the province in all directions, bringing water to the paddy fields that covered the landscape. The province had neither forests nor mountains; only in the southwest, toward Trà Vinh, did the occasional sandy plot rise above the paddy fields to break up the monotony of the terrain.[26]

Trần Văn Lang did not say why he went to Vĩnh Long instead of Mỹ Tho, Sa Đéc, Trà Vinh, or one of the other provinces in the Mekong Delta. Perhaps its auspicious name drew him: In Vietnamese, Vĩnh Long (永隆) means "eternal prosperity," and it was one of the most fertile provinces in the Mekong Delta. It had an area of 122,000 hectares, more than three quarters of which had been planted in rice fields in 1912. In that year, it produced 115,000 tons of paddy; only Bến Tre among the other delta provinces produced more.[27] The province also gave its name to the best-known variety of rice in Cochinchina, which had a long grain but was brittle with an irregular shape.[28] According to the governor of Cochinchina, the harvest in the first months of 1914 was "even more abundant than the previous year," which had brought "the influential majority of the population material satisfaction."[29] Vĩnh Long was at the center of the rural rice economy linked to the port of Saigon. That year, the port moved 1,293,000 tons of paddy, rice, and flour—the most to that date.[30] When Trần Văn Lang arrived in the province at the end of 1914, just before it was time to bring in the next harvest, it must have seemed like a good place to find work.

And there was work in Vĩnh Long after the harvest too. In the off-season, laborers repaired the bunds in the rice fields and cleared the irrigation channels. Many villagers used the time to repair their houses, replacing thatching, often with the aid of kin and neighbors, or fixing roof tiles. They also repaired and replaced tools essential for the next year's growing season—water scoops, plows, harrows, knives, sickles, threshing sledges, and baskets. Some of the villages had small industries. There was a Chinese-owned brick works in Hòa Mỹ, where Trần Văn Lang might have earned a wage, just as there was in Sơn Đông, Tân Hội, and Tân Hóa. Chinese proprietors also operated a dozen sawmills in the province. There were a few jewelers as well as a number of blacksmiths in Vĩnh Long.[31] There were many opportunities in Vĩnh Long for somebody seeking work.

But Trần Văn Lang had no time to find any. He had been in Vĩnh Long for only six days when the gendarme arrested him. He lacked a tax payment card, and he was a vagrant. The tax payment card played an important role in Cochinchina: It was both proof that the bearer had paid his or her taxes and an identity card. The government required every Vietnamese male between the ages of eighteen and sixty to pay a head tax. Only ministers of religion, soldiers and sailors in reserve or active service, and heads of districts and prefectures were exempt.[32] The burden of the head tax fell particularly heavily upon the poor; taxes had once been paid collectively by villages, rather than individually by their inhabitants, so hardship had once been shared. In the earliest years of colonial rule in Cochinchina, the new government had no means of determining who had paid their taxes and who had not. In 1884, it started to issue tax payment cards, which soon took on the additional role of identity cards. Colonial officials began to request them from Vietnamese whenever they dealt with the administration. The cards followed a uniform template and recorded the name of the taxpayer, his or her personal particulars, and where he or she had paid the tax; it also carried the taxpayer's fingerprints. The base tax in Cochinchina was only $1, but additional surtaxes had brought the total levy to $5.85 by 1913. In that year Cochinchina collected $710,000 in head taxes from its residents.[33] Trần Văn Lang did not have a tax payment card, though he may have paid his taxes in Annam. Annam had started to issue tax payment cards only the year before, and it was not compulsory for Vietnamese in the protectorate to carry their cards with them.[34] When stopped by the gendarme in Vĩnh Long, Trần Văn Lang could not have paid the head tax even with all the money he had, which was just $0.20.

In addition to declaring himself insolvent, Trần Văn Lang told the gendarme that he had "no profession" and "no fixed abode." He was a vagrant, and vagrancy was a crime. Before the French conquest, hardship or calamity drove many Vietnamese from their villages to become wandering thieves, bandits, pirates, and sometimes leaders of rebellion.[35] But the colonial state was more effective than its predecessor at keeping Vietnamese in their villages, punishing those who strayed illegally, and collecting taxes. New canals, roads, and railways carried rice from the provinces to Saigon and also made it easier for people to move around Cochinchina.

At the same time, the colonial administration improved its surveillance of Vietnamese society, employing greater numbers of policemen, security officers, and gendarmes to inspect tax payment cards and arrest vagrants.

There is no way of determining the number of such Vietnamese who wandered the countryside and drifted into the cities of Cochinchina. But records from the Saigon Central Prison document the growing number of people punished for vagrancy under French rule. In 1879, the Saigon Central Prison recorded only seventeen such cases. A year later, twenty-four of the entries were for vagrancy. In 1881, after the introduction of the tax payment card, the Saigon Central Prison recorded forty-three entries for vagrancy. In 1882, the prison documented seventy-one entries for that crime. Three years later, in 1885, the prison began to record entries for petty theft and vagrancy together, noting 148 entries for both crimes. Over the next decade, these crimes of poverty increased dramatically in Saigon. The rate of imprisonment more than doubled, then tripled again. In 1895, the prison recorded 983 entries for theft and vagrancy. By 1900, there were 2,639 entrants to the Central Prison for these crimes. Hardship in the countryside might have driven Vietnamese from their villages in search of work or charity, but the new means of transportation made it easier for them to move around the colony and become vagrants. Many went to Saigon, and some, like Trần Văn Lang, went to work in the rice fields of the Mekong Delta. In 1914, when the gendarme arrested Trần Văn Lang in Vĩnh Long, the courts in Cochinchina convicted 1,528 people for vagrancy and begging.[36] Trần Văn Lang had no livelihood and no official documents, so the gendarme arrested him.

The administration viewed vagrants as a menace and as a potential source of disorder. In the late nineteenth century, they had terrorized residents in and around Saigon. In 1899, vagrants were allegedly responsible for several thefts and murders in the villages of Thủ Đức, Phú Mỹ, and Hòa Hưng and for acts of violence and brutality against residents of Saigon near the municipal cathedral.[37] Colonial officials attributed the rise of criminal gangs in and around Saigon to the growth of vagrancy. One report noted that "these gangs are not content to rob from passersby . . . they attack houses right in the village, and more often their misdeeds are unknown to the police and to the administration because of the terror they provoke in the inhabitants and in the notables; they do not dare complain for fear of reprisals." Sometimes conflict broke out between rival gangs of vagrants. One report mentions that an episode of such conflict "took place right in the city of Saigon during June 21, 1901 at the time when workers were leaving the arsenal; it was only thanks to efforts taken by the police that a serious brawl was avoided." But the police were not always successful at anticipating and preventing vagrants from causing violence. "Sometime later, a bloody brawl broke out in the middle of the night right in a village in Phú Nhuận: three individuals from Saigon were gravely wounded and were taken in by notables. As soon as their wounds were dressed, they left in a carriage without having identified their aggressors. The next day, all the people from Phú Nhuận who went to Saigon were abused by the friends of the injured three."[38]

In later years, some vagrants adopted a new strategy: Instead of menacing people or begging on boulevards they became, or pretended to become, Buddhist monks. They shaved their heads, donned yellow robes, and committed a few Chinese characters, prayers, and sacramental phrases to memory. Such monks attracted credulous followers, especially among Vietnamese women in the city, who presented them with money and gifts. On one occasion, the police seized a number of tracts that were meant to provoke alarm among the faithful and to separate them from their money and possessions. Some monks claimed miraculous powers, especially the power to heal. Others led the pious on pilgrimages to the sacred Seven Mountains in Châu Đốc, to Black Lady Mountain in Tây Ninh, and to the rebuilt Vĩnh Tràng Pagoda in Mỹ Tho. The police began to view all mendicant monks with suspicion and regarded them as little more than parasites, indolent charlatans who were unwilling to work.[39]

Trần Văn Lang never had the opportunity to deceive anyone or foment disorder in Vĩnh Long. After taking him into custody, the gendarme took Trần Văn Lang before the Prosecutor of the Republic in the provincial capital. But the prosecutor found insufficient evidence to charge him with vagrancy. The administrator of Vĩnh Long did not want an alleged vagrant loitering in his province, so he had Trần Văn Lang transported to the Central Police Station in Saigon, the hub of the rice-growing hinterland. While Trần Văn Lang was being held in the city, a member of the security police decided that he wished to employ the vagrant. Trần Văn Lang had, after all, recently worked as a cook. Even during his imprisonment, this unwilling migrant to Saigon was offered employment that so many of his fellows sought. "I beg the favor of remaining in Saigon to pay my taxes," Trần Văn Lang implored the commissioner of police, "since an employee of the security police wishes to take me into his service." But the commissioner demurred. He did not want a purported vagrant, a potential source of unrest, lingering in Saigon. So, on December 11, 1914, eight days after his arrest in Vĩnh Long, the government of Cochinchina sent Trần Văn Lang back to Annam.[40] He was not to number, like so many others, among the poor of the city.

In 1918, another migrant from Annam who called himself Nguyễn Văn Thủ made his way to Cochinchina in search of work. He too carried no official document that might have identified him to the authorities by this name. Nguyễn Văn Thủ first found a job with the Biên Hòa Industrial and Forestry Company, to the northeast of Saigon, where he worked as a coolie and wood cutter. Biên Hòa was densely forested: Groves of enormous century-old trees climbed dozens of meters into the air, their reddish brown or white trunks encircled with knotted vines; palms and rattans formed dense thickets tangled with vines and orchids, while ferns, cycads, lichens, and mosses clung to their trunks; timber trees grew in the sandstone soils near the Đồng Nai and Bé rivers; hopea and melia trees lined their shores, and mangroves and bamboos crowded their saline estuaries along with rotins, rushes, palms, and vines.

French entrepreneurs had started the Biên Hòa Industrial and Forestry Company in 1911 to exploit the forest wealth of the province. Several other logging companies soon followed in its path. The French milled timber in Biên Hòa for construction and manufacturing, but also to make charcoal and to use as firewood: The lucrative commerce in mangrove timber kept the hearth fires of Saigon and Chợ Lớn burning. Except for Cambodia, Cochinchina earned more from forestry than any other territory of French Indochina.[41] Nguyễn Văn Thủ stayed with the forestry company for only four months before he left it to work on a neighboring rubber plantation.

Rubber thrived in Cochinchina. A navy pharmacist had sent two thousand rubber plants from Malaya, where he was stationed, to the Botanical Gardens in Saigon in 1897.[42] A canny Saigon policeman established the first rubber plantation on the outskirts of the city in Gia Định province, where he planted fifteen thousand trees. It took six or seven years for the rubber trees to mature. In 1906, the second year of tapping, the policeman made a profit of 100,000 francs. His success quickly attracted others to rubber planting. In 1910, the planters founded the Association of Rubber Planters of Indochina in Saigon. By that time, they had planted 1,700,000 trees in 4,800 hectares. Three years later, 3,400,000 trees covered 12,500 hectares.

The fortunes of the rubber industry fluctuated greatly. During World War I, military requirements and the expansion of the automobile industry, particularly in the United States, had greatly increased the demand for rubber. But the rubber planters in Cochinchina struggled. Most of its French personnel had been mobilized, the war had made transporting the commodity from Cochinchina difficult, and the value of the piaster varied wildly. With the support of the colonial government, the Bank of Indochina began to underwrite French investment in rubber to help stabilize the industry during the war.[43] In 1918, Nguyễn Văn Thủ took advantage of the demand for labor on the plantations of Cochinchina, when he went to work at Dầu Giây for a plantation called Suzannah.

Suzannah was the first rubber plantation in the red soil region of Cochinchina. A railway engineer had established it in 1905 while laying the train line from Saigon through Biên Hòa to Nha Trang. The train line cut the full length of the plantation, more than six kilometers. By 1922, the plantation spread over 3,400 hectares of red soil. More than 170,000 rubber trees covered the plantation's 900 hectares. In 1921 the plantation produced 278,000 kilograms of rubber, and in 1922 it produced 320,000 kilograms. Although global overproduction had caused the price of rubber to collapse after World War I, the colonial government continued to underwrite the growth of the rubber industry. Each day, workers on the plantation extracted between 1,000 and 2,000 kilograms of liquid rubber from the trees. In 1922, Nguyễn Văn Thủ was one of 450 workers at Suzannah. His fellow laborers were mainly Vietnamese from Annam and Tonkin, but some were Cham and people from the nearby hills. Many from Annam and Tonkin were indentured, brought to the plantation by professional labor recruiters. Between 1919 and 1922, an average of 2,286 contracted laborers came to work on the rubber plantations of Cochinchina each year.[44] The workers at Suzannah shared a hospital, a birthing center, an orphanage, and a school with the neighboring plantation at An Lộc.[45] Yet the rubber plantations found it difficult to retain workers. The pay and rations were meager, the work demanding, the supervisors violent, and malaria was rife as well.[46] In each year, between 1919 and 1922, on average 125 workers died, and another 366 workers deserted the plantations.[47] In June 1922, Nguyễn Văn Thủ abandoned the plantation at Suzannah too and went to find work in Saigon.

Well-paying employment in Saigon's commercial economy would not have been easy to find. Although the economy continued to expand, it had been in tumult since the end of World War I. The peace coincided with warm El Niño winds, which brought a drought to mainland Southeast Asia.[48] At the close of 1918, the governor noted that the rice harvest showed signs of being unsatisfactory. At the beginning of 1919, it was clear that the crop in the center and west of Cochinchina had failed. Many farmers deserted their lands and migrated to provinces in the southwest of the colony, where the fields continued to yield rice. The residents of Bến Tre, Gò Công, Mỹ Tho, and Tân An sought relief in Bạc Liêu, Rạch Giá, and Sóc Trăng, where the harvest had been better. The administration provided relief to needy farmers, established camps for distributing food in the areas with the greatest need, and dispensed rice from government stocks. Such measures could not arrest an escalation in banditry, however. By the middle of the year, migration had become widespread in the populous central rice-growing provinces linked to Saigon, as farmers and their families moved to escape hunger and ruin. Prosecutions for vagrancy and begging in Cochinchina surged in 1919. The harvest in neighboring Cambodia had been particularly poor: Large numbers of Khmer migrants, mainly from Svay Rieng province, crossed into Cochinchina. They headed toward provincial centers seeking charity, claiming that famine had pushed them out of Cambodia. Many made their way to Saigon. Poor Khmer begged in the streets with children in groups of two or three. There was hardly enough rice to feed the people in the countryside, let alone Khmer refugees, or to send to Saigon for export.[49]

The volume of exported rice plummeted. In 1919, Saigon exported 754,000 tons of paddy, rice, and flour—48 percent less than it had exported in 1918, the largest year-on-year drop in rice exports that the port had experienced.[50] The demand for Vietnamese rice remained high, however. Harvests had been poor across Southeast Asia in 1919, and cultivators in Siam also struggled to get rice to market.[51] The ports of southern China and Hong Kong continued to purchase more than a third of all of the rice that Saigon exported.[52] With a reduced supply and high demand, the price of rice in Saigon almost doubled: The price of 100 kilograms of paddy jumped from $3.57 to $6.69, while the price of second-grade rice leaped from $5.98 to $11.01. Prices remained high in 1920 when the harvest failed to recover fully amid continuing disorder in the regional rice economy.[53] Prices of many goods in Saigon soared.

Vietnamese reacted angrily to the sharp increase in the price of goods in the city. Many blamed Chinese merchants for the malaise. An author in one Vietnamese newspaper wrote that "the Chinese have made outrageous fortunes on the ruin of the native populations whose general misery they exploit in playing the ups and downs of their products." Worse yet, "while Vietnamese are crushed under the weight of an expensive life and the slump of their harvests, Chinese firms multiply and Chinese trading companies branch out toward infinity."[54] A month later, another author explained that "to ensure the monopoly of the rice trade, the main if not the only product, of our land," the Chinese "have stretched across Cochinchina a vast net with a mesh to secure great profits for themselves, and only let go of the crumbs for small fry like us. The cultivation of rice excepted, all of the operations of buying on the spot, transportation, handling, and milling which result in this trade are in their hands."[55] Vietnamese resentment against the Chinese simmered for months until it finally boiled over in protest.

A newspaper campaign urged Vietnamese to boycott Chinese goods and merchants in Saigon. In August, two Chinese-owned coffee shops on Hamelin Street increased the price of a cup of coffee from two to three cents, angering their customers who were mainly Vietnamese. Vietnamese newspapers like *Tribune Indigène*, *Echo Annamite*, *Thời Báo* (*The Times*), *Lục Tỉnh Tân Văn* (*News of the Six Provinces*), and *Công Luận Báo* (*Opinion*) told their readers to avoid buying coffee from Chinese stalls and later to boycott Chinese shops and goods completely. Vietnamese and Chinese traded insults in the press, and occasionally brawls broke out between the two groups. Despite the acrimony, the boycott campaign in the Vietnamese press lasted only a few months.[56] The surge in prices in Saigon that led to the campaign did not persist beyond the end of 1920.

The poor were forced to hock what little they had of value in the pawnshops of the city in order to pay for essential goods. The firm Ogliastro, Hui Bon Hua, and Company ran three pawnshops in Saigon—in the center of the city, in Dakao, and in Cầu Kho—and it was also involved in importing and exporting as well as real estate.[57] In 1919, residents of Saigon who needed additional cash pawned 313,883 items, borrowing more than $2,223,000. However, the value of the piaster rose dramatically, from 6.56 francs in 1919 to 11.57 francs in 1920.[58] In 1920, the residents of Saigon pawned only 217,519 items and borrowed $1,324,000. Because of the increase in the value of the piaster, many borrowers abandoned the items they had pawned, leaving the pawnshops with countless objects that they could not sell, especially jewelry.[59] A ring or broach pawned for $10 might be redeemed for $11, but because the value of the piaster increased, $11 later bought more than it once had, which led many people to abandon the items they had pawned.

A deep slump followed the surge in prices, which was almost as disorienting for residents of this rice-exporting city. One hundred kilograms of paddy, which had fetched as much as $8.30 in January 1920, sold for as little as $3.70 in January 1921. A sudden contraction in the economy was everywhere evident. The governor of Cochinchina noted that "after a short period of great activity thanks to the unaccustomed increase in the price of paddy, there has been a great depression in the economic life of the country, as a result of the sudden drop in prices. . . . Unable to sell their grain at the expected prices, the Vietnamese find themselves short of money which has affected domestic trade deeply."[60] The Vietnamese hoarded what little cash they could. Coffee shops, restaurants, suppliers of provisions, and clothing shops in Saigon remained empty. In the last months of 1920, several of the larger Chinese trading houses declared bankruptcy. European-owned companies in the city struggled to remain afloat.[61] At the same time, enterprising Vietnamese of means were opening more and more shops, boutiques, and trading companies and assuming a greater role in the commercial life of the city.[62] But the number of new jobs in the commercial economy could not match the growing number of migrants to Saigon, who took up various kinds of temporary work. At the beginning of the 1920s, the population of the city grew by several thousand. By the time Nguyễn Văn Thủ arrived from the plantation at Suzannah in 1922, it had reached 95,000.[63] Like so many of his fellow migrants, Nguyễn Văn Thủ had few skills, no capital, and no patrons to support him. Like so many others, he pulled a rickshaw.

Invented in Japan in 1869, the rickshaw played an important role in the social and economic life of cities across Asia. The vehicle became a familiar sight in Yokohama, Beijing, Shanghai, Rangoon, Calcutta, and Singapore.[64] Although it eventually hastened the pace of life for many in Saigon, the contraption was slow to arrive in the city. The first rickshaws in French Indochina appeared on the streets of Hà Nội in 1884, two years after the city fell to the French.[65] Vietnamese in the city viewed the new vehicles, which had been imported from Hong Kong, with amazement. The residents of Hà Nội were not accustomed to seeing anything on the streets other than pedestrians. "The crowd does not know what to do when it sees one coming," a French observer noted.[66] Until 1886, there were only two horse-drawn carriages in Hà Nội: one belonged to the Apostolic Vicar of Tonkin, the other to the head of the Department of Public Works.[67] Vietnamese in Saigon were much more familiar with wheeled vehicles. Oxcarts and carriages, buses, and trams, all drawn by horses, had made their way through the city long before the rickshaw arrived.[68] In 1888, rickshaws belonging to a Chinese entrepreneur in Chợ Lớn started to circulate in Saigon. The appearance of this new contrivance soon prompted a French entrepreneur to apply for a monopoly to rent out the vehicles in Saigon. The Municipal Council set the initial tariff for a trip at $0.05, or $0.12 for each hour.[69] The number of rickshaws in Saigon grew slowly: By 1900, there were only 395 in the city.[70]

The vehicles all shared the same basic design. They were small, light, hooded carts with large-diameter wheels, drawn by a puller running between two shafts. The hood could be raised or lowered, and there were front and side curtains to shelter the passenger against the sun or the rain. The earliest rickshaws had hard wooden seats and iron-rimmed wheels that made traveling in the vehicle jarring and uncomfortable. By 1908, a superior class of rickshaw had begun to circulate in Saigon with wheels

Rickshaw pullers on Lagrandière Street. Photograph: Ludovic Crespin.

that ran on ball bearings and had solid rubber tires. A ride in one of the older, second-class rickshaws cost \$0.08, while a trip in one of the newer first-class vehicles cost \$0.10.[71] Despite being more expensive, the first-class rickshaws proved so popular that fewer and fewer second-class vehicles remained on the road. By 1913, they had become so rare that the Municipal Council stopped regulating their circulation.[72]

The gradual growth in the number of rickshaws in Saigon coincided with the improvement of its roads.[73] The replacement of beaten dirt or gravel with asphalt was essential for the growth of the rickshaw industry. Sealed roads ensured a smoother, more comfortable journey and prevented rickshaws from constantly getting stuck in the mud during the wet season. As the boundaries of Saigon expanded, so did the length of the streets that crisscrossed the city. In 1880, they doubled from twelve and a half kilometers to twenty-five kilometers. By 1908, when the boundaries of the city were fixed, the city had 93 kilometers of streets.[74] While rickshaw pullers had greater distances over which to run, the path became much smoother after 1905, when the city began to seal the streets with asphalt.[75] The Department of Public Works continually invested in improving the roads, sealing streets and filling potholes. In 1920, the department resealed 10,791 meters of road in Saigon and, in 1921, 8,000 meters more.[76] The regular improvement of the roads in the city made the task of pulling a rickshaw a little less burdensome for men like Nguyễn Văn Thủ.

The Municipal Council regulated many aspects of rickshaw pulling in Saigon. When Nguyễn Văn Thủ first pulled a rickshaw in 1922, municipal bylaws issued in 1913 continued to govern the profession in the city and lent order to the working lives of thousands of rickshaw pullers.[77] When compared with regulations issued earlier, the bylaws reveal many of the tensions and strains that rickshaw pullers and their passengers experienced. Rickshaws were an important source of revenue for the Municipal Council. It levied a variety of taxes and fees on rickshaws and rickshaw companies in Saigon. Every proprietor of a firm required a business license that could cost hundreds of piasters, depending on the size of the firm. Every quarter, these proprietors also had to pay for a permit for each rickshaw to circulate in the city. In 1896, the permit cost $3.75. After 1913, it cost $4.50. The Municipal Council also charged proprietors for the placard it required each rickshaw to carry, displaying the tariff. After 1913, the placard cost $0.20.[78]

With the tariff set by the municipal council, Nguyễn Văn Thủ and his passengers had very little leeway for negotiating the price of a trip. Within Saigon, for a trip by the most direct route that took ten minutes or covered up to two kilometers, Nguyễn Văn Thủ could charge $0.10. If the ride took longer, the passenger paid an additional $0.05 for each five minutes or part thereof. If Nguyễn Văn Thủ made a return trip, which included a fifteen-minute rest, he could charge only $0.15. A passenger could also rent a rickshaw by the hour. For the first hour Nguyễn Văn Thủ was allowed to charge $0.25 and then $0.20 for each subsequent hour. If passengers wanted Nguyễn Văn Thủ to take them beyond Saigon, the same tariff applied until the rickshaw crossed the city limits. Then Nguyễn Văn Thủ could charge an additional $0.30 for a trip from Saigon to Chợ Lớn, or $0.60 for a return trip that included a rest for one hour. A trip to Bình Hòa, northwest of the city near Gò Vấp, cost $0.15 extra, or $0.25 for a return trip that included a half-hour break. A trip to Chợ Quán cost an additional

$0.10, or $0.20 for a return trip after a half-hour rest. Nguyễn Văn Thủ was not obliged to take passengers to other destinations beyond the city but could do so if he and the passenger came to an agreement on the price for such a trip.[79] By regulating the price of a rickshaw ride, the Municipal Council sought to reduce the number of disagreements between pullers and their passengers. These disagreements were often acrimonious and sometimes violent. The detailed tariff protected both Nguyễn Văn Thủ and his passengers.

Nguyễn Văn Thủ was allowed to take his rickshaw through the streets in search of passengers, so long as he kept to the right of the road and did not move alongside another rickshaw, obstructing the way. He was forbidden to solicit passengers by stationing himself in front of groups of people outside the railway station or the theater and shouting at them. If he was waiting for a passenger, he had to park his rickshaw alongside the pavement or on the side of the street and parallel to the direction of the road.[80]

A passenger wanting to summon Nguyễn Văn Thủ had only to shout "Kéo!" ("Pull!") or to raise his or her arm in the direction of a passing or stationary rickshaw. Most pullers understood little or no French, so guides to the city advised tourists not to bother stating the desired address or location. The guides instructed tourists simply to tell the puller "left" or "right" while the rickshaw moved through the streets and to say "Thôi!" ("Enough!") once the destination had been reached.[81] But most passengers in Saigon were not tourists; they were Vietnamese who lived in the city.

Not all Vietnamese rode around Saigon in rickshaws. Many lived where they worked, in a shop, a crowded apartment building, or a thatched hut on the edge of the city. Food was a much greater expense than transportation for most residents of the city.[82] The majority of Nguyễn Văn Thủ's passengers came from the new middling sort—teachers, civil servants, shopkeepers, professionals, and other well-to-do folk.[83] Travel by rickshaw was a show of status and relative means: The vehicle was more expensive than taking a bus or a tram but less costly than a horse-drawn carriage, called a *malabar*, or an automobile.[84] Traveling in a rickshaw pulled by Nguyễn Văn Thủ and his fellows, the new middling sort displayed both their social status and their relative wealth compared to the many poor residents of Saigon.

If rickshaw passengers came mainly from the middling ranks of Saigon society, most rickshaw pullers, like Nguyễn Văn Thủ, came from its lower ranks. The Vietnamese referred to such men as *người ngựa*—as "horse men."[85] They stood above a day laborer or a coolie in the social hierarchy but beneath a skilled tradesman, such as a mechanic. It was easy for a man to become a puller. He needed only to scrounge together enough money for the first day's rental and find a proprietor ready to rent him a rickshaw. Since the puller rented the rickshaw from day to day, pulling was easily entered into and easily abandoned. During the planting season and at the harvest, pullers often returned to the countryside to help work in the fields. Proprietors noted the high seasonal turnover among those who pulled their rickshaws.[86] By the early 1930s, a rickshaw puller could earn as much as $1.50 each day, while a coolie earned between $0.60 and $1.50.[87] Most rickshaw men were poor but not utterly destitute. Hard work kept pullers like Nguyễn Văn Thủ from joining the vagrants and mendicants who wandered the streets of Saigon.

Pulling a rickshaw was no easy way to earn a living. The Municipal Council even regulated when and where pullers were allowed to rest. If Nguyễn Văn Thủ became tired, he was obliged to take his rickshaw to one of several designated points in the city where he was allowed to rest. These included the square in front of the municipal cathedral, between the entry to the Post Office and Taberd Street; the square in front of the theater; at the intersection of Charner and Bonnard boulevards; in front of City Hall; in front of the Office of the Justice of the Peace; in front of the pier on Commerce Quay, at the end of Catinat Street; around the Mỹ Tho train station (but not in front of it); in Rigault de Genouilly Square; and along other several designated streets. As the population of Saigon grew and the streets became increasingly congested, the Municipal Council insisted that the streets be kept free from obstruction so that traffic could circulate freely. If Nguyễn Văn Thủ tired while carrying a passenger and wished to rest, he was obliged to take the passenger to the nearest rest place or to pull the individual until he encountered another available rickshaw. He had to compensate the passenger for this inconvenience and forfeit the sum of $0.05, half the price of a standard fare.[88]

To ensure that pullers did not tire too often, the Municipal Council required them to be at least twenty years old and to have sufficient physical strength for the job. Nguyễn Văn Thủ was twenty-seven years old in 1922 and in good health. Pullers were not allowed to work if they had an infectious disease or an obvious injury. While this regulation was meant to protect the puller and his passengers, it was generally ineffective. Pullers became notorious for their poor health and, alas, their tendency to die young.[89]

Tuberculosis was the main cause of death among rickshaw pullers. In the hospitals of French Indochina, tuberculosis accounted for 20 percent of admittances and 70 percent of the deaths during the 1920s. Doctors believed that the disease was much more widespread among the general population, especially in the cities. The poor, including rickshaw pullers, lived in cramped and poorly ventilated conditions. They were often malnourished and had poor hygiene, which left them particularly susceptible to the disease.[90] The puller acquired his famous hunched back not only from the posture he adopted pulling his rickshaw but often from the tuberculosis that ravaged his body as well. If the disease invaded his spine, it destroyed the anterior parts of his vertebrae, causing them to collapse forward, leaving him with a sharp, angular hunch. Tuberculosis also caused a chronic cough, fever, night sweats, weight loss, and blood-tinged sputum.[91]

Several of these symptoms were indistinguishable from the effects of smoking opium. Many rickshaw pullers in Saigon smoked opium. They did it to relieve pain, to aid sleep, and probably to escape from the harsh reality of their daily labor.[92] The misery of Saigon's rickshaw pullers helped contribute to the revenue of the colonial government. The government imported raw opium principally from Benares in British India but also from Yunnan, Persia, and Turkey. The Customs and Excise Service prepared the opium for sale as *chandoo* at its refinery on Paul Blanchy Street, mere steps away from the shops and fashionable hotels on Catinat Street. Following the British process used at Canton, it took three days of boiling, roasting, and fermenting for the refinery to prepare the opium. Workers hand-packed it into metal tins in quantities of one hundred, forty, twenty, ten, and five grams. They sealed the tins and labeled them with the special revenue labels of the Customs and Excise Service. Licensed vendors sold the *chandoo* to opium smokers.[93]

Opium smoking was an expensive addiction for a poor rickshaw puller. A puller, who could earn as much as $1.50 a day, spent $0.30 or more daily on opium.[94] The poorest addicts could seldom afford to buy prepared opium from the monopoly. Instead, they smoked or ate dross, the blackish residue that formed inside a pipe after it had been smoked. Between 40 and 60 percent of the opium smoked in a single pipe was left as dross. It was more harmful than opium since it contained the same amount of morphine but also a number of toxic alkaloids. After removing the dross from the pipe with a scraper, smokers could consume it in a number of ways: They could smoke it with prepared opium or decoct it with tea or alcohol for smoking a second, third, or fourth time or roll the dross into pills to eat or to add to tea or coffee or other drinks or even to their water pipes. Poor addicts also ate what the refinery called *écorce d'opium,* made from the outer wrappings of the raw opium that the British shipped to Saigon. The refinery powdered the wrappings, packed them in tins, and sold them in Cochinchina and Cambodia.[95] While opium was a balm to rickshaw pullers, it helped to fill the coffers of the colonial treasury.[96]

Despite the misery and indignity pullers experienced, the Municipal Council never seriously contemplated putting an end to the profession. When it was discussed at one meeting, a member of the Colonial Council declared that "he had chatted with several pullers and that they did not seem to him more miserable, in fact quite the opposite, than the coolies of the cement-works in Tonkin whose lungs are consumed by cement, the ferrymen who row for hours in the sun and the rain, or the peasant who works in the mud of the paddy fields under the blazing sun." The problem was not simply one of indifference to suffering. Thousands of people depended on rickshaw pulling for their livelihood, and it continued to be the most convenient way to move around the city. As the council member explained, there was no adequate substitute.[97] For Nguyễn Văn Thử and many others who arrived in Saigon with no capital and few contacts, pulling a rickshaw allowed them to earn a living and to survive in the rapidly expanding city.

After living in Saigon for nearly three months, Nguyễn Văn Thử decided to make the city his home. On September 5, 1922, he applied for a certificate to serve as proof that he lived in the city and that he was not a mere vagrant. Nguyễn Văn Thử told the Security Police, who provided such certificates, that he had been born in Saigon and that he lived with his lover Nguyễn Thị Tâm in Chợ Đũi, the quarter of the city close to the municipal dispensary. The Security Police recorded Nguyễn Văn Thử's particulars and took his fingerprints. Procedure required them to check his details against their records. Two days later, the Security Police sent off a hurried note to the Immigration Service: The rickshaw puller Nguyễn Văn Thủ had not been born in Saigon.

He was really a man from Bình Định named Trần Văn Lang.[98]

As police forces became more organized, identifying recidivists was a perennial problem for police forces around the world. Until 1832, the courts in France had repeat offenders sent to the galleys or punished for a crime branded with a hot iron. After that practice ended, prisons were meant to keep detailed descriptions of inmates so that recidivists could be identified and punished more harshly. But the arbitrary and disorganized nature of the descriptions made it difficult to identify former criminals. The police began to photograph convicts, but the photographs were often taken carelessly and haphazardly. The need to sort through tens of thousands of photographs to identify a former criminal eventually led French authorities to abandon this method of identification.[99]

After he entered the Paris police force in 1877, a man named Alphonse Bertillon revolutionized criminal identification by developing a system of identification based on three principles: the almost absolute fixity of human bone structure after the age of twenty, the great diversity of dimensions of the human skeleton, and the ease and precision of measuring those dimensions. Bertillon selected a number of measurements of the human skeleton, the combination of which he considered unique, for identifying former criminals. His system of criminal identification was quickly hailed as a success, and its use soon became widespread in France. Bertillon later standardized criminal photography, and he clarified the procedure for describing a person's distinguishing features. His system spread beyond France to the United States, Belgium, Switzerland, Russia, British India, Germany, Austria, Portugal, Cochinchina, and eventually the other territories of French Indochina.[100]

The government of Cochinchina created the Identity Service in 1897. Its director had studied the principles of anthropometry in Paris with Bertillon, as had two of its other employees. The main tasks of the service were to measure and photograph convicts, defendants, and prisoners for future identification, with the exception of prostitutes and individuals detained for petty offenses.[101]

The service maintained detailed identification cards that allowed it to identify recidivists. The cards carried several pieces of information, including the individual's name and surname, date and place of birth, address, profession, names of the person's mother and father, dates of remand into custody, and the reasons for remand. The card also recorded a number of anthropometric measurements: height, length, and width of the skull; length of the left and middle fingers of the left hand; length of the left foot; length of the left cubit; length of the right ear; height of the bust; and length of the arms extended horizontally. The card had a "spoken portrait" that noted the main physical features of the individual using various conventional abbreviations. It also described and noted the location of any tattoos, warts, scars, moles, or birthmarks. The cards also bore the fingerprints of the subjects, taken from both hands. Finally, the card had two photographs affixed to it showing the face from the front and from the side. It also had a registration number and the date and place of issue. In the beginning, the service organized the cards according to the anthropometric information, but after 1902, it began to use fingerprints as the main form of classification.[102]

In 1914, the Identity Service recorded Trần Văn Lang's particulars on one of these cards before the government of Cochinchina sent him back to Annam. The two photographs show a young Vietnamese man dressed in a dark-colored shirt buttoned to the neck with bright buttons. His hair is closely cropped, and he has a small, round face with clear skin and a modest frame.[103] Nguyễn Văn Thủ would have looked different by 1922. But the length of his left cubit would have remained the same, as would the length of the left and middle fingers of his left hand. His fingerprints would not have changed. These pieces of information, among others, allowed the Security Police to discover that Nguyễn Văn Thủ and Trần Văn Lang were one and the same.

Nguyễn Văn Thủ had deserted the plantation at Suzannah. Hundreds of workers had abandoned the plantations of Cochinchina in the previous four years. The director of the plantation wanted Nguyễn Văn Thủ returned so that he could complete the rest of his contract. But now he was back to being Trần Văn Lang, and he categorically refused to take up his former alias's place on the plantation. And so, for the second time, the government of Cochinchina expelled Trần Văn Lang from the colony.[104]

For the second time, it kept him from occupying the vast ranks of the poor in Saigon. But Trần Văn Lang would not be missed, except perhaps by his lover, Nguyễn Thị Tâm. Somebody else would become a human horse and take up the shafts of his rickshaw, ready to pull it through the streets of Saigon.

CHAPTER FIVE

A HOLY CHILDHOOD

A baby bird, with drooping wings,
goes looking for its nest, forlorn,
around the silent, lonesome woods,
all wet and dripping with the rain.
—*Tố Hữu, "Orphans"*[1]

The commune of Vence is in the Alpes Maritimes department in south-eastern France. The medieval square in the center of the commune has had many names, but in 1923, it was called the Place Clemenceau after the French prime minister during the Great War. A curved row of shops and houses defined the plaza's southwestern side, the Cathedral of Our Lady of the Nativity overlooked the goings-on from the north, and on the plaza's eastern side, the town hall stood on the site of a thirteenth-century episcopal palace. Henri Giraud, the mayor of Vence, presided over the town hall.[2] One of the tasks of his deputy-assistant was to issue certificates of indigence to the poor of the commune. On October 25, he issued one to Miss Aimée Lahaye, aged thirty-five.

Certificates of indigence were official testimony to the poverty of the individuals who received them. They usually established the circumstances

107

of the bearer's indigence: sickness, old age, widowhood, unemployment, or some other misfortune. They also entitled the bearer to a number of concessions: lodging in poor houses, free treatment in hospitals, exemption from local taxes, and a burial paid for by the commune.[3] The certificate issued to Aimée Lahaye stated that she was born in Saigon in 1887. Aimée had arrived in Vence in 1921, shortly before her thirty-fourth birthday. In 1923, after living in the commune for two years, she had no savings and was without work. She was utterly destitute.[4]

The years after the Great War were difficult ones in Vence. The war had led to a steep decline in the population of the commune. In 1921, it had 3,090 residents, 408 fewer than the last count before the war. The conflagration had claimed the lives of 108 men, and many others had left because of the conflict. The commune was not prosperous. The villagers grew olives, fruit trees, a few grapevines, and vegetables and flowers used to make perfume. They used traditional farming techniques; the poor quality of the soil, the uneven terrain, and difficult access to credit all stifled agricultural innovation. The villagers raised poultry but not enough livestock to meet their needs. Before the war, workshops in the village had fashioned ceramics and textiles for sale along the Mediterranean coast, mills had produced olive oil, distilleries had made lavender oil, and bakeries had made pastries. Three quarries, three ironmongers, a brickwork, and several building firms had each employed as many as ten workers. After the war, most of these industries went into decline.[5] It would have been difficult for Aimée to find work in Vence in 1921.

Aimée was one of many foreign-born residents living in the commune. Although its most famous foreign residents, D. H. Lawrence, Marc Chagall, and Chaïm Soutine, had not yet arrived, the census in 1921 recorded 388 foreigners living in Vence, which made up almost 12.5 percent of the total population. There were 234 Italians, forty English, forty Swiss, twenty Americans, one resident from the Low Countries, four Germans, four Austro-Hungarians, and four Iberians living in the commune.[6] The census did not register whether there were any Indochinese—any Vietnamese, Cambodians, or Laotians—living there. Thirty-two foreigners were listed merely as "others," among whom Aimée Lahaye may have numbered. But what had brought Aimée to Vence in 1921? What was a woman born in

Saigon doing in the south of France? How had she become so destitute? And what became of her?

Modern histories of Vietnam record several important occurrences in 1887, the year that Aimée Lahaye entered the world. After crushing an insurrection in the province of Châu Đốc, the colonial government destroyed the village of An Định and dispersed its residents.[7] Later in the year, the French united the colony of Cochinchina and the protectorates of Annam-Tonkin and Cambodia under a single administration to form the Union of Indochina.[8] In Saigon, Nguyễn Trọng Quản published *The Story of Master Lazaro Phien,* the first novel in romanized Vietnamese to follow the conventions of Western storytelling.[9] And Aimée Lahaye was born in the province of Thủ Dầu Một on October 6, 1887, a Thursday. Her father, Henri Lahaye, was a colonial forest warden; her mother was Vietnamese.[10] He argued that part of the province needed to be replanted with trees to prevent landslides and preserve its waterways that agriculture might flourish there. He encouraged the colonial administration to divide Thủ Dầu Một into two areas, one where ethnic minorities could clear the forests freely to plant kitchen gardens and another where such clearing would be forbidden so that the slopes could be planted with useful trees.[11] When Aimée was less than three weeks old, a ball of fire, white and deep purple, streaked across the night sky—it was a meteorite crashing to earth in Tây Ninh.[12] Understandably, perhaps, some took it as an omen: Her father died early in the new year.

Life alone with a young infant to care for would have been difficult for her mother. Hardship sometimes led the most destitute mothers to rid themselves of their children—and there were many ways for a Vietnamese woman to deal with an unwanted child. Repeated blows to the abdomen, inserting a needle or sharpened object into the cervix, or introducing camphor, musk, or the ox knee plant could all end a pregnancy before term.[13] If she gave birth to the child she could abandon it by the roadside or in a doorway, kill it outright, or let it die through willful neglect.[14] She could also sell the child, if somebody could be found to buy it. A form of bond service was common in Cochinchina in the second half of the nineteenth century. Poor parents, or those in debt, could sell their children as servants into more prosperous families. They could later buy them back or leave them to be raised and cared for by their new families.[15] Many such children were named Nuôi, which means "fostered" or "adopted," and grew up in Vietnamese families, their sale or "adoption" unrecorded by the colonial authorities. But no family adopted Aimée Lahaye.

Soon her mother died too.

Aimée became a ward of the Holy Childhood Association.

The Holy Childhood Association supported a number of orphanages in Cochinchina. Moved by tales of infanticide in China, the bishop of Nancy, a man named Charles-Auguste-Marie-Joseph de Forbin Janson, had established the Holy Childhood Association in France in 1843. Most of its members were children from established families who pledged a small sum of money to the association each month. The association grew rapidly in its first three decades when French children joined it in hordes. Soon, children from all over the world, but especially from Belgium, Italy, Germany, and the United States, swelled its ranks to support the principle that orphans in China should be protected from the terrors of being parentless. The money raised was used to baptize abandoned children, to buy them and raise them in Christian families, and to build schools and orphanages. The association eventually established orphanages beyond China, in India, in Africa, and by the 1880s, across Southeast Asia.[16]

The Sisters of Saint Paul de Chartres founded the orphanage of the Holy Childhood in Saigon in 1860, during the first year of French rule. In 1859, the local bishop had asked the sisters to come to Cochinchina to care for Christian children who had been orphaned through religious persecution as well as other abandoned infants.[17] The orphanage was a new institution in Cochinchina, distinct from the communal relief houses and mutual aid societies that had cared for such children under Vietnamese rule.[18] Located in a marsh in the southern part of the city, the first orphanage was little more than "a grass hut on stilts, like a chicken coop, its feet soaked in a swamp, bathed by the rising tide."[19] By the first days of 1861, the orphanage had moved to a new building that was larger and sturdier. It had been built from materials taken from the homes of Vietnamese mandarins who had fled Saigon during the French conquest. Local merchants and French military officers also assisted with its assembly.[20]

The orphanage did not occupy this new building for long. In 1862, the colonial government drafted new plans for the city; a street was to cut through the orphanage. In compensation, the government gifted lands for the erection of a new building on Citadel Boulevard, recently named Luro Boulevard for a colonial administrator. The boulevard began on the banks of the Saigon River and ended at the crumbling fortifications of the eponymous citadel. The orphanage faced onto Street No. 15, later named Sainte Enfance or Holy Childhood Street, before it became Espagne Street in 1870.[21] Travelers who made their way up the winding Saigon River to the city could see from miles away the chapel spire that ascended above the orphanage.[22] It was this orphanage that the infant Aimée entered after the death of her parents.

There were two main buildings in the orphanage, situated at right angles to one another. A walkway, covered to protect the sisters and the children from the sun and the rain, linked them. A low L-shaped wall formed a rectangle with the buildings, and a bed of flowers decorated the center. One of the buildings contained classrooms, a sewing room, and an infirmary. A refectory and laundry occupied the first floor of the second building, and a dormitory took up the whole second floor. The children slept on small iron beds containing a mat, a blanket, and a pillow. Like hundreds of other children over many years, Aimée must have peered up each night at the darkened rafters before drifting off to sleep.[23] Perhaps her dreams were happy; perhaps they were colored by fear. She may even have dreamed of her mother and father.

Vietnamese in Saigon viewed the orphanage with anxiety when it was first established. Reflecting on its earliest days, the nun in charge, known as "the Superior," wrote in 1864 that "the pagans are familiar with the orphanage now and no longer fear that we eat their children."[24] During the conquest, Vietnamese officials had demonized the French and their institutions. But many Vietnamese continued to be wary of the orphanage—once a child entered it, the sisters were always reluctant to let him or her leave. In 1864, the water carrier Trần Văn Quảng fell ill. Unable to care for his six-year-old daughter, he took her to the orphanage, where the sisters accepted her. But when he recovered, the sisters refused to return his daughter to his care, offering him no explanation.[25] The Cantonese laborer Lao Gia worked at the arsenal, building naval vessels. He lived with his wife and his one-month-old daughter on Adran Street, which the French had named for Bishop Pigneau de Béhaine. After Lao Gia injured his foot with a tool, he could no longer work and the family became destitute. Lao Gia took his daughter to the orphanage of the Holy Childhood. The sisters admitted his daughter but refused to return her to her parents after their fortunes improved.[26] In 1860, Nguyễn Thị Kéo, the seven-year-old daughter of a widowed tea merchant, went missing while accompanying her mother in a village near Chợ Lớn. The girl could not be found. One day, while passing by the orphanage, her mother recognized Nguyễn Thị Kéo through the fence. The girl told her mother that she did not have enough to eat and that she was made to do too much work. She summoned her courage and escaped from the orphanage. But the sisters were undeterred. They employed a Vietnamese man to hunt for escaped children, and one day he recognized Nguyễn Thị Kéo at the market near her home. Despite her mother's shouts and cries, he seized the girl and took her back to the orphanage.[27] Trần Văn Phụng was a rope merchant. He lived with his wife, Nguyễn Thị Sang, and their five-year-old son, Trần Văn Lanh, on a boat moored near the Chinese Arroyo. When his son went missing one day, he assumed that he must have had an accident and perhaps fallen into the river, dragged under by the current or washed out to sea by the tide. But one day Trần Văn Phụng recognized his son in the street accompanied by the sisters. The boy had not drowned after all. The authorities had found him wandering alone and taken him to the orphanage. The sisters refused to return Trần Văn Lanh to his parents, despite their clamors and protests.[28] There is no record of any of these children being returned to their families. The Sisters of Saint Paul de Chartres seemed convinced that they would be better provided for in the orphanage where they would also receive a Christian education. In 1870, one administrator recorded that "an inexplicable and muted unrest excited the Vietnamese. The rumor spread among them that the Europeans were abducting their women and children to sell them overseas, and an extraordinary anxiety and childish fears drove the Vietnamese from our cities."[29]

The number of children at the Holy Childhood ebbed and flowed but never fell below 150. In 1862, the orphanage accepted more than 160 children. In the following year, the number diminished to 150. By 1864, it had risen again to 200, then fell in 1867 to 170. When Aimée arrived in 1888, she was only one of many children in the care of the orphanage. Most of the children were between six and ten years old. From church pulpits, through Vietnamese notables, and in the pages of the official newspaper *Gia Định Báo* (*News of Gia Định*), the colonial government spread word about the new charitable establishments in the city: the hospital at Chợ Quán and the new orphanage on the Boulevard de la Citadelle.[30]

Children entered the orphanage by various means. The colonial administration deposited many there, such as those found wandering alone in the streets. Vietnamese notables from nearby villages did the same. Priests brought children from their parish whose parents had died or were too sick to care for them. Poor parents, knowing that they could not care for a sick or hungry child, often left them at the orphanage too. Sometimes the orphanage paid for children, purchasing them from destitute parents for a small sum, usually two or three francs. Some children, all alone in the world, even made their own way to the orphanage.[31] And Aimée? Perhaps her desperate mother took her to the orphanage after the death of her father. In that way, she could have chosen to give her daughter a home and a future, rather than have a priest, a French official, or a Vietnamese notable make the decision for her.[32]

The orphanage usually recorded the admittance of each new child in a register. It noted an entrant's name, sex, actual or supposed age, and place of origin; the name of the person or persons who had brought the child was also recorded. If the child was a foundling, the register noted the circumstances in which he or she had been discovered.[33] But no such registers have survived to testify to Aimée's infancy at the Holy Childhood.

Abandoned infants were the most vulnerable of the children admitted. After recording their details, the sisters wrapped the infants in swaddling clothes and lay them to sleep in little cradles covered with mosquito netting. A nun, aided by young Vietnamese girls, watched over them. The sisters fed the youngest infants, who had not yet been weaned, on goat's milk or cow's milk. It was difficult for the nuns to find Vietnamese wet-nurses.[34]

Boys and girls at the orphanage grew up differently. Both took classes where they learned how to read, write, and speak French. The sisters permitted the boys to stay in the orphanage only until they turned fourteen years old. Those who displayed academic talent were sent to the city's Collège d'Adran or Institution Taberd, while the others were left to make their own way in the world. The sisters were often able to place these boys with Christian families, sometimes in the parish of a French priest who could offer them guidance and support. In addition to reading and writing, the girls at the orphanage also learned how to sew and to make clothes. When they came of age, many took religious vows and entered the novitiate attached to the orphanage; others became domestic servants for European families in the colony; some took up work as seamstresses or in the clothing stores of the young city; many took husbands, their marriages often arranged by the Superior of the orphanage and priests in the colony.[35] But Aimée did not grow up like many of the other girls at the Holy Childhood.

Aimée was Eurasian—the daughter of European and Asian parents. She was almost certainly illegitimate, but her father seems to have acknowledged his paternity. To the French in Saigon she would have been a "métisse"; to the Vietnamese, a "Tây lai." To both groups she would have been an outcast, born into twin prejudices.[36] Some Eurasian children had been orphaned by the death of their fathers; other fathers had abandoned their children. By the second decade of colonial rule, abandoned Eurasian children were already considered a social problem in Saigon. The "pitiful fruits of debauchery and concubinage," they "roamed the streets of the city" living a "blighted childhood," often after being "abandoned by their mothers, who, to save their miserable lives, almost always had to find another guardian."[37]

The Catholic Church soon became such a guardian. In 1874, using much of his own fortune, Father Henri de Kerlan founded the Institution Taberd so that Eurasian children in the colony could receive an education and go on to take up respectable positions in colonial society.[38] In the same year, the Sisters of Saint Paul de Chartres founded a boarding school at the Holy Childhood in Saigon for abandoned Eurasian girls.[39] The sisters rigorously separated the Eurasian girls from the Vietnamese children and provided them with a French education. The sisters also taught the girls essential skills so that they could find employment in the colony when they were of age. The year that Aimée Lahaye was born, there were no fewer than forty-eight Eurasian girls at the Holy Childhood.[40]

The colonial government encouraged the girls to marry French soldiers and civil servants in the colony. In the first decades of French rule, there were few French women in Cochinchina. Orphaned Eurasian girls raised in the Holy Childhood who spoke French and who had received a Western education were among the small number of women considered suitable spouses for French men in the colony. From the early 1880s, the government provided Eurasian girls at the Holy Childhood about to marry with a dowry or with a sum of money to purchase a trousseau, a collection of clothes and household linens and other belongings collected by a bride in preparation for married life.[41] In 1883, for instance, the government allocated $250 for the trousseau of one Eulalie Boyer. In 1887, Sister Candide, the head of the Holy Childhood, wrote to the governor of Cochinchina requesting a dowry for Josephine Larrieu so that she could marry a customs officer who worked in Hội An. The government allocated $250 to her as well. It allocated the same sum to Emélie Blanc when she married another customs officer in 1895. Likewise, the government designated $250 for Bathilde Silvestre, whose parents were from Pondicherry, India, when she married a policeman in Saigon in 1904.[42] These were fantastic sums. At the turn of the century, a rickshaw puller in Saigon usually charged $0.08 for a ride across the city.[43] For a poor Vietnamese laborer, $250 represented many months of back-breaking work. For a Eurasian girl growing up in the Holy Childhood, it was a fortune.

The Sisters of Saint Paul de Chartres founded several other orphanages for poor children in the provinces of Cochinchina. The first was in the province of Mỹ Tho in 1864. In the following decade, the sisters opened five more orphanages.[44] By 1887, the year that Aimée Lahaye was born, 989 children were living in orphanages throughout the colony.[45] This number continued to increase—just a year later it had risen to 1,089.[46] The Holy Childhood continued to open orphanages across the colony, in Gò Công in 1891, in Trà Vinh in 1893, in Tây Ninh during the following year, and in Thủ Dầu Một in 1904.[47]

It is a miracle that Aimée survived her infancy. The youngest children seldom lived for long in these orphanages. In 1863, the Superior of the Holy Childhood in Saigon reported that once they were baptized, "almost half went to rejoice in heaven."[48] Some died from sicknesses caught in the orphanage. In 1867, smallpox spread throughout the institution and claimed the lives of five children.[49] But most of the infants and children brought to the orphanage were already dying. Their parents had been reluctant to part with them until death was certain but knew that they would be properly cared for and buried at the orphanage.[50] In 1887, the Apostolic Vicar of Western Cochinchina lamented that "despite the annual number of baptisms, the catalogue of our Christians does not increase. . . . [A] great number pass into the other world." The Church baptized 6,070 people, mainly Vietnamese, in Cochinchina that year. Of these, 5,158 were children. But 1,770 adult and infant Christians died, along with as many as 2,528 "pagan" infants. "Dying, for the most part, shortly after baptism," the bishop wrote in a sanguine mode, "if they do not number in the Church militant, they have the advantage of entering into the Church triumphant."[51]

Abandoned infants seldom survived long in the other orphanages in Cochinchina. Even as late as 1907, of the 960 orphans admitted to the nursery of the Holy Childhood in Chợ Lớn, no fewer than 840, almost 88 percent, perished.[52] A report penned many years later painted an equally tragic picture. Referring to a nursery in Chợ Lớn, the report stated that "the Vietnamese only bring their infants [to the orphanage] at the point of death because the family wants to avoid the cost of burial. This results in considerable mortality." Describing infants in a nursery in Gò Vấp, the report lamented that "these unfortunate little abandoned children are already dying when they are taken to the orphanage. The number of survivors is, for this reason, very low." At the orphanage in Thủ Đức, "the number of infants received since its opening, on July 2, 1912, is 964. And of this total, four children alone have survived, two boys who were sent to an agricultural colony in Trà Vinh and two girls who work in the orphanage as wardens of the children and dressmakers." That is to say, less than half of one percent survived their infancy. At the so-called nursery in An Lợi Xã the conditions were appalling: "two cradles were placed in the corner of an old, decaying, Vietnamese home, dirty and cluttered with unused furniture." An elderly Vietnamese nun oversaw the nursery, aided by a younger sister. The register was poorly kept, listing only the dates of infants' baptisms but not their dates of birth and death. The infants were baptized *in articulo mortis*. The French priest who oversaw the nursery described it as only "the courtyard of Paradise," a place for a child to linger while waiting to die.[53]

During the first decade of the twentieth century, infants died in much greater numbers in the orphanages of Cochinchina than they did in the general population. In 1905, 24 percent of infants born in Cochinchina died during the first month after birth, and 38 percent died within the first year. By 1909, infant mortality in the general population had declined significantly, largely due to a French campaign to eliminate umbilical tetanus. Only 6 percent of infants born alive died in the first month of life, although 29 percent died within the first twelve months of birth.[54] Many births and early deaths may have gone unrecorded, so the figure was probably higher yet. At any rate it was still tragically high. In the colony's orphanages, it was higher still.

Despite the alarming number of infant deaths in its orphanages, the colonial government supported the Holy Childhood in the first decades after the conquest. The relationship began in 1862 when Admiral Bonard created a number of bursaries at the orphanage to help raise and instruct orphaned children. Every subsequent year, the colonial government allocated funds for the same purpose. In 1877, the first year for which records remain, the sisters received 61,000 francs for their charitable works. Ten years later, when Aimée Lahaye was born, the government allocated 31,600 francs to the sisters to support their schools and orphanages in addition to a number of scholarships for individual children.[55] Entering the Holy Childhood the following year, Aimée must have benefited from this state disbursement.

She was fortunate. This government funding did not continue much beyond her adolescence. Changes in the laws regulating religious institutions in France had a profound effect on the orphanages of the Holy Childhood.[56] One law made all public institutions completely secular from the beginning of 1903. The colonial government stopped giving subventions to the religious institutions in Cochinchina.[57] The Sisters of Saint Paul refused to accept any more abandoned children, and those already in their care were encouraged to find a guardian to claim them. The number of children in the orphanages of the Holy Childhood dropped sharply. In 1900, 2,129 children entered the nine orphanages in Cochinchina, adding to the 710 already there. By 1905, one orphanage had closed, and there were only 549 children in the remaining eight.[58] Since its founding, the Holy Childhood in Saigon alone had admitted 1,200 children.[59] In 1905, there was one less charge at the Holy Childhood: Aimée Lahaye left the orphanage at the age of eighteen to seek work in the city.

Although it was the first, the Holy Childhood was not the only orphanage that cared for Eurasian children. At the beginning of 1894, when Aimée was six years old, several residents had founded the Society for the Protection of Abandoned Métis Children. The society sought to identify the Eurasian children in the colony so that they could be admitted to a school or charitable institution. Members of the society feared that their mothers would have a corrupting influence on them. With the death or departure of their father, the mother they believed "inevitably lapses into the vice out of which she came. She is virtually always a model of debauchery, laziness, and immorality." Her daughters would become prostitutes and her sons would become outcasts.[60] The group intended to rescue Eurasian children from this ignoble fate.

Donations and annual subscriptions supported its work. Later in the same year, several other residents formed another society with similar objectives. These two societies soon merged to form the Society for the Protection and Education of Young French Métis of Cochinchina and Cambodia. "The hour of reparations will finally come to this class of *métis*, which has been so long rejected," the new group announced in the press. "All our efforts will be to give it the place, the rank, that it must take among us." The society hoped to place abandoned Eurasian children in schools and to pay for their fees and upkeep.[61]

But it soon ran into financial difficulties. By 1903, the society could not meet its expenses for the year. At the same time, the colonial government had stopped sending cash to the Catholic institutions of Cochinchina. Many Eurasian children were forced to leave the Holy Childhood and the colony's schools and entered the care of the Society. In 1904, it began to receive a subsidy from the colonial government to help cover its rising costs, but it continued to struggle. In the following year, it planned to build an orphanage of its own to house its charges but could not raise sufficient funds.[62]

The children the society cared for faced prejudice and discrimination. In 1904, some French residents in Saigon insisted that the city's schools separate the Eurasian from the French children. They feared that the Eurasian children, being part Vietnamese, would have a corrupting influence on the French students. To protect its wards from further humiliation, the body removed the word *métis* from its name in 1906, becoming the Society for the Protection of Childhood of Cochinchina. It also reconstituted its statutes. The new purpose of the society was to "assure in Cochinchina the protection, the education, and the instruction of children of both sexes without resources and support, without distinction by race or religion. . . . It maintains the abandoned children at its expense," the statutes stated, "in the buildings that it owns."[63]

These buildings comprised an orphanage in Chợ Lớn on Drouhet Boulevard. The orphanage opened in 1907 and was sensibly planned: The main building was symmetrical, with two single-story wings extending from a central two-story building.[64] Shutters with louvers let light and air into the dormitories, refectory, and classrooms. The orphanage later erected a new dormitory in a separate building to house the boys as well as several new classrooms, but the orphanage endured a lot of wear and tear.[65] Over time, it became shabby and run-down. The dormitories remained clean, spacious, and well aired, but many of the beds lacked blankets and the mosquito nets needed repair. The toilets and bathrooms seemed to remain sanitary. The girls' refectory, while large and perfectly tidy, lacked sufficient tables and benches to seat them all at once. The boys' refectory was a mere lean-to built against the side of the main building; it too needed more tables and benches as well. The kitchen and common areas were tidily kept, but several of the doors and windows needed fixing. The three newest classrooms received sunlight and a breeze only on one side and were poorly lit; in contrast, there were too few trees to shade the paths in the garden.[66]

The number of children playing in the gardens of the orphanage grew in the following decades. In 1907, when the orphanage first opened, it was home to only twenty orphans, all girls. By the following year that number had risen to 39 and in 1909 to 49. By then the orphanage had already begun to turn some children away. In 1910 it began to admit boys. While in principle the orphanage received children from any background, in practice most of its wards were Eurasian.[67] Not all of them were orphans. In the years after World War I, the number of children in the orphanage grew considerably. By 1921 it had reached 148.[68] The number of children residing in the orphanage grew with the number of Europeans in the colony.

But limits on space and resources restricted the number of children it could admit.

Upon admission, the orphanage gave each new child a trunk containing several items of clothing and linens. The regulations stated that the boys' trunk should include two white suits, four darker suits, two vests, four pairs of pants, six towels, five pairs of pajamas, eight handkerchiefs, four pairs of stockings or socks, six cloth napkins, and two loincloths. The girls received eight blouses, six nighties, six pinafores, six towels, two white dresses, four pairs of socks, four petticoats, one pair of sandals, one pair of white shoes, one pair of black shoes, six cloth napkins, eight handkerchiefs, and six pairs of pants. The children were handsomely outfitted. The older girls worked in the sewing room, making and repairing clothes for the other children.[69] The children regularly outgrew their clothes as they aged, of course.[70]

The orphanage fed the children well. The regulations stipulated the amount of food to be served to children of different ages each day. Those older than ten years of age were supposed to receive 400 grams of white rice, 250 grams of meat (beef, pork, veal, mutton, or poultry), 200 grams of fresh fish or 150 grams of dried fish, 26 grams of fish sauce, 200 grams of fresh vegetables, 10 grams of condiments (including pepper, spice, lemon, and vinegar), and two or more cakes or pieces of fruit or 100 grams of dried fruit. The younger children received 200 grams of rice, 180 grams of meat, 160 grams of fresh fish or 150 grams of dried fish, 250 grams of fresh vegetables, 10 grams of condiments, and the same quantity of cake and fruit as the older orphans. The orphanage served Vietnamese meals every day, except for Thursday and Sunday. On Sundays, the children received wine with meals. For breakfast, each child was given bread and coffee, and in the afternoon bread and fruit—a banana or an orange—for a snack.[71] The two main meals each day normally comprised a soup made with vegetables and a little meat, and some cooked vegetables and meat, all served with rice. Sometimes duck eggs replaced the meat. Although the orphanage eventually replaced some of the meat with more vegetables, the meals remained well prepared and well served and the food was sufficiently abundant. The children had no complaints.[72] They were doubtless better fed than the children raised in poor Vietnamese homes, whose bellies remained empty when the harvest failed.

The orphanage provided several forms of recreation for the children. It kept a small library stocked with donated (and occasionally purchased) books. It also kept several games for the children to play together. A member of staff also led the children in regular exercise—the regulations specified that competitive sports were preferable to rhythmic exercises or calisthenics.[73]

The children also had to attend daily lessons. They had to be able to provide for themselves as adults and to take part in the economic life of the colony. A teacher instructed the youngest children in elementary mathematics, as well as how to speak, read, and write in French. When they got older, the children attended schools in Chợ Lớn. In 1928, they started attending a new French school in the city. But the young teacher lacked authority, and the boys behaved so badly that many of the other children at the school left. The orphanage had to arrange for the girls to receive instruction in the orphanage and for the boys to attend the nearby Franco-Vietnamese school instead. The girls made good progress in the orphanage, but the boys had difficulty learning French with a Vietnamese teacher and following the Franco-Vietnamese curriculum. Later, the orphanage arranged for the boys to receive lessons at the orphanage too.[74] At the age of fifteen or sixteen, many of the girls began working in the sewing room, where they learned a craft and produced clothes for the other orphans. When the boys reached the same age, the orphanage sent them to study at a school for mechanics or at an agricultural school, but they seemed to achieve only limited success. The most academically able children attended the Collège Chasseloup-Laubat or the Upper Primary School in Saigon thanks to scholarships, but few did this. Most of the children at the orphanage had great difficulties with their studies. When many of the children entered the institution, they had never been to school before, and they spoke little or no French. They were usually well behind their French and Vietnamese peers in the other schools in the city. Many schools would not admit Eurasian children from the orphanage because they were so poorly prepared.[75]

The orphanage maintained discipline through a variety of rewards and punishments. A studious and well-behaved child received cumulative rewards. For good behavior or school work a child received a "bon point" coupon; five "bons points" resulted in a testimonial of satisfaction; the name of a child who received ten such testimonials in a single month was added to the table of honor; and when he or she appeared on the table of honor five times, the orphanage deposited two piasters in a savings account in the child's name. In contrast, a poorly behaved child could have privileges progressively withdrawn: Children could be barred from leaving the orphanage on Thursdays and Sundays or be deprived of time for leisure and recreation. In the most serious cases an orphan could be ejected from the orphanage. The orphanage's regulations, progressive for the time, explicitly forbade the use of corporal punishment on the orphans as well as forced labor.[76]

Most of the time the children behaved well. The president of the society seldom remarked on disciplinary problems in his reports. But from time to time there were outbreaks of unruly behavior. In one instance, insubordination became a problem among many of the older girls who had become particularly "arrogant," as the phrase had it. On several occasions, the director of the orphanage had to summon the president of the society to restore order. The society expelled the nineteen-year-old leader of the disobedience, and many other girls were forbidden to leave the orphanage for a month.[77]

The orphanage regulated comings and goings. Surviving parents, guardians, and others could visit the orphanage on Sundays and holidays from three to five in the afternoon, provided the permission of the director had been received. On Thursdays, Sundays, and holidays, one of the caregivers led the children on a walk into the city. The children were also permitted to leave the orphanage on Sundays, from half past seven in the morning to seven in the evening, if they went with an adult known to the society—a parent, a sibling, a caregiver from the orphanage, or one of its administrators.[78]

The Society for the Protection of Childhood also ran a foyer for young women in Saigon. It opened in 1924 in a modest compartment on Espagne Street but moved the following year to a new building on the corner of Kitchener Boulevard and Marcel Parent Street. The new building was spacious: The director's apartment was on the ground floor, in addition to a large dining room, a small library, a toilet and washroom, and an office. On the second floor nineteen bedrooms came off a corridor, each with a bed, a dressing table, two chairs, and a small table. At the corridor's end were two bathrooms and sinks and toilets. There was a large kitchen, a pantry, and servants' quarters behind the main building. The foyer was home to young women who were too old to remain in the orphanage in Chợ Lớn but who lacked the means to fully support themselves. Its purpose was to protect the young women from isolation and from bad influences, chiefly the temptation to vice. The women worked in the city during the day—as typists, secretaries, store assistants, and seamstresses, among other jobs—and each month contributed half of their wages to the upkeep of the foyer. The society provided additional funds. The foyer was home to between ten and twenty women, most of whom eventually left it to marry. In 1933, the foyer opened an embroidery studio. During the Great Depression, which had buffeted the colonial economies of Southeast Asia, many of the young women who left the orphanage and entered the foyer were unable to find work in the city. They worked instead in the embroidery studio but learned very little there. With mounting expenses and a diminishing income, the foyer eventually closed.[79]

Many prominent figures in Saigon, both French and Vietnamese, supported the Society for the Protection of Childhood and its orphanage. The printer Claude Ardin and the eminent merchant Étienne-Jean Boy Landry both did so, as well as Henry Chavigny de la Chevrotière, the vice president of the Colonial Council and editor of the newspaper *L'Impartial,* who was himself of mixed parentage; the lawyer Henri Sambuc; and the presidents of the municipal commissions of Saigon and Chợ Lớn. Among the Vietnamese, the well-known engineer Lưu Văn Lang subscribed; and so did the director of the newspaper *Tribune Indigène,* Nguyễn Phú Khai; the prosperous printer Nguyễn Văn Của; the privy councilor Lương Khắc Ninh; and the wealthy landowners Lý Lập and Trần Trinh Trạch.[80] Through supporting the Society and its orphanage, they hoped that Eurasian children would become industrious and loyal residents of the colony when they went out to work.

Aimée left the orphanage of the Holy Childhood to seek work in 1905. It was a difficult time in the city after the typhoon and natural disasters of the previous year, which had led to the collapse of the export economy. Aimée drifted in and out of various jobs over the next several years. She seems to have avoided a life of vice: There is no record of any complaint against her, and the authorities considered her a woman of "good conduct." In July 1905, Aimée first went to work for Ngô Thị Hải, a pottery merchant on Ormay Street. Located in the most fashionable and commercial part

The Military Hospital. Photograph: Ludovic Crespin.

of Saigon, Ormay Street intersected three parallel streets: Paul Blanchy Street, Catinat Street, and Charner Boulevard. Aimée was probably helped by the French education she had at the Holy Childhood. In exchange for her labor, she received room and board. But at the beginning of 1907, Aimée left the employ of Ngô Thị Hải for reasons unknown. She had trouble finding work again. By August 1907, she was living off the charity of a Monsieur Tanays, who resided on Arfeuille Street in Tân Định. The area was then home to many Vietnamese coolies and laborers who often lived in makeshift huts and houses. The colonial government considered it a foyer of vice and disease.[81] After some time, Aimée left Monsieur Tanays to work in a millinery owned by Madame Gaubert on Norodom Boulevard. Aimée seems to have been a good employee. Madame Gaubert found that she lacked nothing "from the point of view of ability, as much as from the point of view of honesty." In May 1916, Aimée found new employment when she became an orderly at the French military hospital.[82]

The hospital occupied a large precinct and faced onto Lagrandière Street. There were separate buildings erected in iron and brick for surgery, general medicine, and ophthalmology as well as for children, female patients, and the mentally ill. There was also a pharmacy, a kitchen, a chapel, a mortuary, and housing for the hospital staff. Porticoes, supported by a cast-iron colonnade, linked the buildings to one another. They formed an impressive ensemble. Trees, plants, and flowers filled the gardens around them in which the patients could promenade.[83]

Aimée worked hard at the hospital. She spent her first two years there as an orderly, then three years as a laundress. The hospital administrator testified that "Miss Lahaye is intelligent, hardworking, and devoted."[84] According to the head doctor she "always accomplished her work to the complete satisfaction of her supervisors."[85] The work was physically demanding. Orderlies helped lift patients, make beds, and maintain the cleanliness of the wards. Laundresses cleaned and distributed sheets, blankets, and pillowcases in the hospital. Aimée probably spent many hours each day stirring sheets in a hot boiler filled with scalding water and astringent detergents. In 1921, after working at the hospital for five years, Aimée fell desperately ill and needed an operation and a long convalescence.

The French in Indochina had long believed that the torrid tropical heat and humidity of the colony was a source of illness and infirmity. They attributed to the ruinous climate diseases ranging from malaria, dysentery, and cholera to listlessness and the more general malaise that the French called "colonial anemia."[86] They sought refuge from the sultry lowlands in the higher elevations and cooler mountain temperatures of Đà Lạt in the south and Sa Pa in the north. The climate there was thought to be closer to that of France and to have a restorative, therapeutic effect. Yet instead of heading for the Vietnamese highlands, Aimée decided to go to France to recuperate and regain her strength. She left Saigon bound for Marseille with her friends the Merle family. Mr. Merle was a functionary in the Department of Public Works, and his purpose was to take his family back to France for a holiday; Madame Merle had been Aimée's friend since her childhood in the orphanage. After many years working, Aimée had scrupulously saved a substantial sum that she took with her in the form of a letter of credit for 13,000 francs, issued by the Industrial Bank of China.[87]

The French and Chinese governments had founded the bank as a joint venture in 1913 with an initial stake of forty-five million francs. The bank issued paper money in China and financed major public works in the fledgling republic. It also lent money to the Chinese merchants and millers in Hong Kong and Cochinchina to finance the regional rice trade that had made Saigon so affluent. It had opened its first Indochina office in Saigon in 1917 and a second in the port city of Hải Phòng the following year. In 1919, it opened branches in Guangzhou, Fuzhou, and Marseille.[88] By 1920, the bank was deeply entangled in East Asia and Southeast Asia and appeared remarkably prosperous: It had established twenty-two branches and was building five more; it had thirty thousand customers and one billion francs in deposits. At the beginning of the year, the board of directors accorded the director general of the bank, a Joseph Pernotte, a bonus of 200,000 francs to recognize his leadership. At the annual general meeting in the middle of the year, the bank announced that it would pay its shareholders a dividend of 14 percent.[89] But the bank soon began to falter. It had kept very limited cash assets and had made large loans to the Chinese government and other borrowers with little regard for its capital base. Pernotte attributed its difficulties to recent shocks to the regional rice trade. The price of rice had spiked in 1920 before plummeting back to earth in 1921.[90] Trouble for Chinese merchants and millers spelled trouble for the Industrial Bank of China and therefore trouble for its depositors, of whom one was Aimée.

On June 30, 1921, while Aimée was only four days out of Marseille, the bank collapsed. It shuttered its premises on Saint Lazare Street in Paris and filed a petition for liquidation. The bank suspended all payments. When Aimée arrived in Marseille on July 4, she found herself penniless, as the bank, now closed, was unable to honor her letter of credit. The collapse of the bank left Adèle Hennion, a supervisor at the orphanage of the Society for the Protection of Childhood in Chợ Lớn, similarly destitute. She had spent eleven years in Cochinchina and had returned to France for a holiday. But by the time she arrived in Marseille the bank had closed and would not honor the check it had issued her in Saigon.[91] Once responsible for orphans, she was now herself a type of orphan. And Aimée was also an orphan once more, an unwitting victim of the vicissitudes of the regional rice trade.

Monsieur and Madame Merle adopted the stranded woman, figuratively at least. Aimée lived with them at their home in Vence for more than two years. Unable to find work, she grew increasingly desperate. In 1923, a week before Christmas, she wrote a letter to the minister of colonies in Paris requesting his assistance. She wrote in simple, unadorned French. "Sir," she began:

> I have the honor of calling upon your very great and kind sympathy, to ask the favor of a free passage to Saigon (Cochinchina), my native land.
>
> In support of my request, please allow me to give you the following explanation of my present situation, in consequence of which I find myself in the necessity of asking you for my repatriation.

Born in Saigon in October 1887 of a French father (Mr. Lahaye was a forest warden) and a Vietnamese mother, both of whom died when I was young, I was raised at the Holy Childhood in Saigon.

After having worked at the Military Hospital in Saigon for two years as an orderly and three years as a laundress . . . I was exhausted to the point that I had to undergo a very serious operation at the hospital itself. To fully restore my health, I came to France with the family of Mr. Merle, a civil servant with the Public Works of Indochina, who was on holiday with his wife, a childhood friend, and his son.

With some small savings painfully amassed over long years of work, I thought of taking only a holiday in France for my health.

Unfortunately, four days before our departure, we took out, both Mr. Merle and I, a letter of credit with the Industrial Bank of China (my own letter for 13,000 francs).

Upon our arrival in Marseille, on July 4, 1921, we learned of the closure of the bank.

Without this money and always in the hope of being reimbursed, I had to stay with my friends Mr. and Mrs. Merle in Vence. Moreover, unable to heal as much as I needed to, I attribute to this loss, a relapse which forced me to undergo a new operation in Nice.

The little money that I kept in my possession was quickly exhausted and ever since I have been completely supported by the Merle family (as states the attached certificate from the mayor of Vence).

Seeing that despite all our efforts, the Bank has still given us nothing, I cannot continue to remain in this sad situation created solely by the bank.

For all these reasons, I hope, Minister, that you will receive my request favorably, for I must return to my country where I hope to find a job which will allow me to live and rebuild a situation, which is impossible to find in France.[92]

The recipient of this letter, the minister of colonies, was Albert Sarraut. Sarraut had been a journalist and a Radical-Socialist deputy in the French Chamber of Deputies. He had served as governor-general of Indochina from 1911 to 1914 and then again from 1917 to 1919. While idealistic and seemingly benevolent, Sarraut had made rather modest contributions to the improvement of Vietnamese health, welfare, and education.[93] As minister of colonies, he elaborated a policy that emphasized not only the economic exploitation but also the social development of France's overseas territories.[94] He was thwarted, however, by budgetary and political constraints. "The collapse of the Industrial Bank of China" had alarmed Sarraut, since it "could unleash a monetary crisis in Indochina." But there were potentially graver problems yet: "In the end it could be dangerous for the indigenous politics of the Union, by shaking the confidence of the natives," he noted. The collapse of the bank had surely shaken the confidence of poor Aimée.[95]

The Minister sent her letter on to the governor of Cochinchina who ordered an inquiry into Aimée's circumstances. Three months later, Superintendent Monnier confirmed for the authorities the miserable story that Aimée had relayed to Sarraut. He concluded his report affirming that "her conduct and morality are good and she is worthy of interest." After being stranded for almost three years in France, the colonial government paid for Aimée to return to Saigon.[96]

On returning to Saigon she promptly vanished. There is no trace of Aimée in the colonial archive for almost four years. When she finally reappears, she is no longer in Saigon but in Phnom Penh. Once again she has found work in a hospital laundry. She appears for the final time in a few lines of official correspondence from the governor-general of Indochina to the résident supérieur of Cambodia. The letter is dated March 6, 1928. "I authorize the extension, for a period of three months," the governor-general began, of "the contract of Miss Lahaye, laundress at the hospital of Phnom Penh, to permit her to benefit in the following May from a holiday of six months, at the expiration of which she can receive a new contract for a year on the same terms as the last one."[97] And that is the last official mention of Aimée Lahaye, orphan from Saigon.

Adults give childhood a pattern and a purpose. They determine the ways in which children grow up—in wealth or in poverty, in a loving home or a cruel one, educated or ignorant, among siblings or alone. To the child the pattern and purpose are seldom evident; they emerge only in retrospect, as part of a longer life. As a child, Aimée could not have known why the Sisters of Saint Paul de Chartres had taken her in. The rules at the orphanage probably seemed arbitrary and inscrutable; rules often seem that way to children. Aimée may have wondered about her parents' lives, but she probably never questioned the permanence of French rule in Indochina.

She may never have reflected on why this meant she had to speak French as a girl, to learn how to read and write and how to sew—so that she could provide for herself as an adult and take part in Saigon's urban economy. Only in light of her future adulthood does Aimée's childhood make sense.

Yet her lost adulthood makes sense only in light of her childhood. Aimée was the orphaned child of a French father and a Vietnamese mother. But she was also the recipient of charity. In the orphanage of the Holy Childhood in Saigon, she achieved fluency in French—language and mores—that enabled her to ascend, if only a short distance, the social and economic hierarchy in the city. It was this fluency that allowed Aimée to travel to France. It explains how, in conjunction with ill fortune, a woman born in Saigon found herself a pauper in Provence in 1921 and yet managed to find her way home again before disappearing into the hinterland of French Indochina.

In some ways, Aimée had a fortunate childhood. Although her birth was ignominious, she survived her infancy when many did not. She learned to speak French and to read and write when many did not. She learned a skill, grew up, found work, and traveled abroad. Many did not. It is only possible to uncover the plan and pattern of Aimée's childhood because she grew up in a colonial institution. The thousands of poor children who grew up in the orphanages of Saigon must have followed a similar pattern. Such children were spared a life of relentless misery and want. They did not have to hang about cafés and restaurants on Catinat Street or the stalls at the Central Market, like the ragged, grubby little cherubs hawking flowers, daily beseeching passersby for alms, ready to recite a litany of woes.[98] And their privileged childhood might have preserved them from the precarious adulthood of poor Vietnamese such as Lương Thị Lắm or Trần Văn Lang.

CHAPTER SIX

TRISTES TROPIQUES

The question mark surrounds a human life:
the snail gnaws on the heart—hushed drops of blood.
Today, the final examination point:
the answer's nailed—it's in the coffin now.
—*Vũ Hoàng Chương, "No More Anxiety"*[1]

In 1900, the American Jasper Whiting was an employee of the Illinois Steel Company. Alarmed by the Boxer Rebellion in China, he decided to become a war correspondent for the *Westminster Gazette,* an influential London newspaper, and made his way to the Far East. In 1902, Whiting arrived in Saigon and vividly described the city in his journal. "Were it not for the natives in the streets," he wrote, "the stranger might very easily imagine that he was in one of the smaller provincial capitals of La Belle France." In Whiting's estimation, Saigon was "Paris on a small scale. The streets and boulevards are broad and immaculate," he wrote. "The public buildings are handsome, dignified structures, standing well back from the thoroughfare, and surrounded by gardens laid out with great taste." Saigon had imitated Paris in almost every way, Whiting thought. "There is a miniature Champs Élysées, a miniature Bois de Boulogne, and a miniature Avenue de l'Opéra, and each is adorned with statuary such as only French artists can produce. There is, too," Whiting observed, "a twin-spired cathedral, the Notre Dame of the city, and a beautiful Opera House, of which every resident is justly proud."[2] But in the nineteenth century, Paris was known not only for its opulence and beauty. It was famous for its criminality, poverty, and disease as well. In *A Winter in Paris,* the French writer and critic Jules Janin documented the "frightful corners which Paris hides away behind its palaces and museums." In such places, he wrote, "there lurks a swarming and oozing population that is beyond comparison." Its denizens lived on "crusts and miserable remains." They inhabited a "vile Bohemian world, a frightful world, a purulent wart on the face of this great city."[3] If Saigon was "Paris on a small scale," then Saigon too had its Montmartre, its Île de la Cité, and its Marais—notorious slums, foyers of poverty and disease.[4] The incurable invalid Trần Văn Chinh knew such places well: By 1930 he had begged on the streets of Saigon for thirteen years.[5]

Trần Văn Chinh was born in the province of Gia Định in 1882. The province shared its name with the reign name of an emperor from the Song dynasty that meant "elegant fixity." It was bounded to the north by the province of Thủ Dầu Một; to the east by the provinces of Biên Hòa and Bà Rịa; and to the south and west by the provinces of Gò Công, Chợ Lớn, and Tây Ninh.[6] The Saigon River ran through Gia Định and gave shape to its physical geography, dividing the province into low-lying wetlands adjacent to the river and dry, elevated, sandy lands along the border with Tây Ninh and Biên Hòa. Gia Định encompassed the city of Saigon, which made it the most developed of the provinces of Cochinchina. It presented many economic opportunities for those who lived there.

Most of the residents of Gia Định during Trần Văn Chinh's youth made their living from the land. He too might have toiled for a time in the fields and forests of the province. The wet lowland part of Gia Định had been intensively planted. Cultivators raised areca trees, sugar cane, tea, coconuts, and mangosteens in addition to rice, but most of the white rice consumed in the province came from the fields of the Mekong Delta and the mills of Chợ Lớn. The forests of Gia Định were a valuable source of firewood for the hearths and industrial enterprises of Saigon and Chợ Lớn and for the vessels of the Messageries Fluviales that navigated the inland waterways of the colony. Woodcutters in the province made a little additional money from selling the bark of certain trees to make dyes for fabric. They used the bark from one tree in particular to color saffron the robes of monks. The dry and sandy regions of Gia Định had been minutely parceled out and the addition of manure and other fertilizers made the land arable. Rice grew less well in the dry region than the wet one, but it grew nonetheless, alongside other fruits and vegetables, around almost every dwelling and settlement. Cultivators planted maize, betel, beans, sweet potatoes, and tobacco for sale in the market towns. Sugar cane grew close to the Saigon river, and there were small sugar refineries in some of the larger villages. The tobacco grown around Hóc Môn, Gò Vấp, and Thủ Đức was renowned for the smoothness and flavor of its smoke. Cultivators had once grown peanuts in abundance too, but as Trần Văn Chinh grew older, they planted less and less of the crop: For several years, a disease had attacked the peanut fields and spoiled the harvest. Meanwhile Vietnamese were increasingly buying gasoline instead of peanut oil because it lighted their lamps more brightly and cleanly. Vietnamese also planted coconuts to make oil for lamps, to flavor Indian curries, and for the confection of traditional cakes and candies. They extracted oil from the fruit of the *mù u* or poon tree, which they used as an alternative source of fuel and to treat scabies. The wood of the poon tree was light and strong and was also useful for making camp beds.[7]

Trần Văn Chinh might have raised livestock or hunted wild animals to supplement his earnings. Animal husbandry, hunting, and fishing were all important to the economic life of the province. Indeed, Gia Định had the most domesticated animals of all the provinces of Cochinchina. The cutting of roads, the excavation of canals, and the planting of fields during Trần Văn Chinh's youth had led to substantial growth in the number of horses, cows, oxen, and buffaloes raised in the province. Vietnamese also reared dogs, pigs, goats, chickens, ducks, geese, guinea fowls, turkeys, pigeons, and rabbits on their plots. French and Vietnamese typically hunted the wild animals of the province for food, for their pelts, and for sport. There were highly prized tigers and panthers in the dense and flooded forests near the coast, which were also inhabited by large families of monkeys. Vietnamese hunted monkeys for their meat and for their bones. They liked to eat monkey meat less well than dog meat, and they used the bones to make medicine for the treatment of mental illness. They also used the tibia and the skull to fashion amulets for the protection of pregnant women. Vietnamese in Gia Định variously valued anteaters, pangolins, crocodiles, snakes, and tortoises for their meat and their skins. Rats infested nearly every rice field in the province and ravaged the young plants, while foxes and weasels threatened poultry and farm animals. The coast and many waterways ensured that the province was always provided with fish and prawns, which fetched handsome prices in the markets of neighboring provinces.[8]

There were many skilled artisans and craftsmen in Gia Định to whom Trần Văn Chinh might have apprenticed himself as a young man. The masons in the province had built its many pagodas and tombs. While he was young, they used the traditional tools of their trade: a trowel, a plumb line, a ruler, and a crudely fashioned square. They preferred to work with stone from Biên Hòa and with a mortar made from chalk, sand, and unrefined sugar, kneaded in water that had been made viscous and sticky with the macerated bark of the myrrh tree. The masons fashioned edifices of great durability, and many of the sepulchres on the Plain of Tombs had resisted the picks and sledgehammers of vandals and land prospectors. By the beginning of the twentieth century, the masons in Gia Định had adopted a number of European materials and tools, but they continued to use the Vietnamese trowel, which was shaped like a lotus leaf and which they wielded with great dexterity. Entrepreneurs in Saigon recruited masons from the largest settlements of Bình Hòa, Phú Nhuận, and Gò Vấp for work in the city. The same villages were also reputed to have skilled builders who erected houses and buildings that were rough-hewn but sturdy. The European residents of Gia Định and Saigon preferred to employ Chinese builders, whom they believed to work faster and with more skill yet. Carpenters in the largest villages, and those in Hóc Môn and Thủ Đức, fashioned coffers, camp beds, and tables; turners made boxes for betel, trays, and chandeliers; sculptors fashioned crossbow tips, exquisitely decorated panels, and ornate columns; and wheelwrights made carriages and carts. Boat builders, who produced many of the small watercraft that plied the waterways of Cochinchina, prospered in Gia Định. So too did the province's many coffin makers, who could be found in almost every village. The most elaborate coffins, fashioned from precious wood, could sell for $200, while more modest caskets sold for between $6 and $12. Artisans in Phú Nhuận and An Nhơn Tây produced lacquered statues, panels, and boxes upon request, but their craft was still in its infancy. Vietnamese from Tonkin who lived in Gia Định considered the local lacquerware inferior to that from the north. There were smiths throughout the province who shod horses and also fashioned knives, plowshares, lances, and other metal tools. The larger towns had specialists in dyeing and coloring fabric. They manufactured two different plant dyes, one yellow and one black, from the bark of one tree and the leaves of another. The dyes were well known for their solidity. Chinese silk merchants in Chợ Lớn used the dyes to color their fabrics, which they sold for prices comparable to finished cloth imported from China. The corporation of dyers even had a temple, the Miếu Bổn Thợ, consecrated to their craft in Gò Vấp. In all the other important centers, jewelers fashioned pins, rings, bracelets, necklaces, and other adornments from precious stones and metals. Potters used clay, especially from around Thủ Đức, to manufacture vessels for storage, cookware, and figurines. Miners in the province obtained scree and granite from open quarries for use in construction but mainly to cover roads and streets.[9]

If he had not labored in the fields or workshops of Gia Định, Trần Văn Chinh might have gone to work for a local merchant or trader. Commerce had flourished in Gia Định in the decades since the French conquest of Cochinchina. Each year, more and more land had been cleared and planted, and new roads and waterways linked settlements in the hinterland to Saigon. A steam tram operating between Saigon and Gò Vấp could cover twenty kilometers in an hour. The passengers were mainly ambulant merchants, who could transport their small and sundry wares on the tram for free, as well as the employees of various enterprises in Saigon. Peddlers and itinerant merchants sold small sundries in all the villages and hamlets of the province. More important commerce was in the hands of Chinese merchants and concentrated in the market towns of Phú Nhuận, Gò Vấp, Hóc Môn, and Thủ Đức. Vietnamese had begun to engage in commerce by opening shops in the vicinity of the markets, but they still preferred to trade from boats on the waterways of the province. Chinese traders exported commodities such as paddy; tobacco; tea; areca; betel; peanuts; fruits and other agricultural products; fish; fish sauce; furniture, such as ornate sets for preparing betel, laquered panels, and credenzas; jewelry; clogs and shoes; pottery; joss sticks; and animals and animal skins. They imported other items, such as silks, European wines and spirits, sugar, wheat, hardware, haberdashery, gasoline, paper, salt, milled rice, cows and buffaloes from Cambodia, horses from Annam, and silkworm manure from Phnom Penh for fertilizing betel trees.[10]

Trần Văn Chinh might have learned how to read and write in one of the schools in Gia Định. By the time he was eighteen years old, there were sixty-nine schools scattered throughout the province. The five communal schools, seventeen cantonal schools, the provincial school, the normal school, and the school run by the Christian Brothers all taught French. There were also fourteen other mission schools, which taught romanized Vietnamese, and there were thirty traditional schools, which taught Chinese characters. Each year, the best students in the cantonal schools attended the provincial school and the normal school with bursaries awarded through competitive examination.[11]

There were limited opportunities for the literate and learned in Gia Định, and Trần Văn Chinh did not remain in the province beyond his youth. He went instead to Saigon, where he found work as a coolie in the busy print shop of Nguyễn Văn Của, who paid him $30 each month for his labors. If he had learned to read and write, such skills would have been useful, but they were not essential. The printer of several newspapers and a wide variety of books, his employer Nguyễn Văn Của became one of the wealthiest and most influential figures in colonial Saigon. In 1917, he founded the widely read newspaper *Nam Trung Nhựt Báo* (*Daily News of the South and Center*) with the French chemist Louis Renoux. But Trần Văn Chinh did not work in the print shop long enough to gauge the full measure of his employer's growing prominence.[12] In the same year, the young migrant from Gia Định contracted a terrible disease that seems to have ravaged his body and left him completely unable to work. Trần Văn Chinh became a beggar.

Trần Văn Chinh sought alms on the streets of Saigon during the Roaring Twenties, a time of rapid economic growth in Cochinchina. The French called these years "les années folles"—the "crazy years." Between 1921 and 1930, rice exports averaged 1,370,000 tons annually, with more than one-third of that volume destined for the ports of Hong Kong and southern China.[13] At the beginning of the period, the best milled rice cost $8.70 per 100 kilograms; by the end its price had risen to $11.34.[14] The population of Saigon grew briskly: In 1921, 83,800 people lived in the city; by 1930, that number had risen to 125,600, an increase of almost 50 percent in just under ten years.[15] During the decade, a number of new companies established themselves in the city: Indochine film et cinéma, Brasserie et Glacière de l'Indochine, Compagnie de Caoutchoucs Mekong, Les Caoutchoucs de Phước Hòa, Société Indochinoise des Plantations Réunies de Mimot, Société des Plantations Mariani, Société Minière du Sud Annam, Union Electrique de l'Indochine, and the Société Hydraulique d'Asie, among others.[16] The prosperity and growing fame of Saigon attracted celebrity tourists and literary voyagers: André Malraux, W. Somerset Maugham, and Rabindranath Tagore all visited Saigon. Wealthy visitors could stay at the Continental Hotel in Saigon and then indulge themselves at one luxury hotel after another: the Grand Hôtel d'Angkor in Siem Reap, the Grand Hôtel in Huế, and the Metropole in Hà Nội. In 1920, 188 such travelers—Americans, English, French, and others—disembarked at the ports of Saigon and Hải Phòng; a decade later, more than a thousand visitors alighted at the same ports.[17] At the same time, the number of those who slept or begged on the streets of the city for charity and assistance blossomed too.[18] In such times of affluence, a beggar like Trần Văn Chinh might receive an extra piece of fruit or candy, one or two more *sous* in his alms bowl, or some other act of kindness from those who passed him on Catinat Street or Bonard Boulevard.

By 1930, Trần Văn Chinh could no longer rely on the kindness of strangers. Diseased and decrepit, he sought refuge at the hospice at Phú Mỹ. The Sisters of Saint Paul de Chartres had established the hospice in 1876 to care for the elderly and the incurable. The hospice was located just beyond the limits of the city, across the bridge at the eastern end of Chasseloup-Laubat Street, on the far side of the Avalanche Arroyo, and behind the Botanical Gardens. Half a dozen buildings and a small chapel comprised the hospice, which a high stone wall concealed from view. It also concealed the many unfortunate souls who suffered within.[19]

The hospice was a veritable Bedlam in Bến Nghé. Bedlam, otherwise known as Bethlem Hospital, had been founded in London in 1247, during the reign of Henry III. It provided care for the sick and the needy from its earliest days and for the insane and mentally ill from the early fifteenth century. It became notorious for the ceaseless "cryings, screechings, roarings, brawlings, shaking of chaines, swearings, frettings," and "chaffings" of the patients within.[20] In Paris, the Hôtel-Dieu also received the poor, the sick, and the mentally ill and was infamous throughout the city for its filth, overcrowding, and high mortality.[21] The hospice at Phú Mỹ was similarly meant to be a sanctuary for the miserable and misfortunate, the weakened and the woebegone. In 1928, it began to house the many beggars and vagrants arrested by the police in Saigon and Chợ Lớn and secluded from disapproving eyes the ragged and wretched who might have defiled the streets and sidewalks of the two cities.[22] In the words of one visitor, the hospice cared for the "true human wrecks" of the colony, those whom the city and the countryside had rejected as "useless and embarrassing." Its residents were a mournful medley of "the half mad, idiots, cretins, the crippled, paralytics, the malnourished, those with chronic rheumatism, beggars, cancer patients, epileptics, hysterics, inveterate opium addicts, the wasting, and those whom the hospitals reject." The hospice admitted "those who were weary of life but still clung to it desperately, and those whose bodies had entered a wasting state because death sat at their bedside to feast on their cruel agony."[23] More than fifty years after its founding, the hospice was an institution from a bygone era. Some of the residents were confined against their will: More than a hundred beggars were locked up in one building to prevent them from returning to the streets. Able-bodied residents had to care for the sick, the disabled, and the incompetent. The men who could work toiled in the garden, while the women embroidered and helped to cook and clean. The elderly and infirm were left to languish for hours, days, months, even years.[24] The hospice provided refuge, not treatment or cure. Trần Văn Chinh would have found little comfort in Phú Mỹ.

But what affliction had forced Trần Văn Chinh to give up work in 1917? What malady eventually made him seek sanctuary in Phú Mỹ? The records do not say. But some diseases were more prevalent in Saigon than others, some disorders more common. The years that Trần Văn Chinh lived in the city, from 1900 to 1930, were years not only of quickening economic and social change but of rapid epidemiological change as well. Among the different factors—the mobility of the poor, miserable sanitation, and the transmission of disease from abroad—poor sanitation played the greatest role in the spread of disease among the poor in Saigon. It contributed to the spread of tuberculosis and malaria, and it was crucial to outbreaks of bubonic plague and cholera. Among epidemic diseases in Saigon, only smallpox showed no prejudice and failed to discriminate between the tidy and the untidy, the clean and the unclean, the fair and the foul.

Most smallpox victims contracted the disease while in face-to-face contact with another victim, by breathing air infected with the smallpox virus. Sometimes clothing or blankets contaminated with pus or scabs transmitted the disease, as did the corpses of victims.

Smallpox ran a long and painful course in its victims. Typically, initial signs of the disease appeared twelve to thirteen days after contact with the virus. The symptoms were mild at first. They included headache, backache, fever, nausea, and vomiting. In some cases, the victim experienced convulsions and delirium. Then, they began to feel better. They might even return to their daily business—pulling a rickshaw, peddling various small wares, scavenging for old newspapers, hauling cement, or begging on Bonard Boulevard.

But the relief was fleeting. Four days after the first symptoms appeared, painful lesions began to form in the mouth, throat, and nasal passages, making the victim contagious. During the next twenty-four hours, the distinctive rash of flat, reddish spots appeared. In the days that followed, the rash turned into raised pustules. The pustules concentrated on the soles of the feet, the palms of the hands as well as the face, forearms, neck, and back. Victims could become unrecognizable. The rash also spread internally, to the throat, lungs, heart, liver, intestines, and other internal organs. As the rash progressed in the mouth and throat, many victims found drinking impossible. By the tenth day, the pustules began to soften and turn into blisters. Victims began to give off a sickly odor. Near the end of the second week, the blisters began to harden into scabs. For the most afflicted, movement became impossible. Large pieces of skin could simply slough off, which increased the risk of secondary infections. After two weeks, most victims began to heal. Scabs fell off, the fever abated, and scars began to replace the scabs and pustules. By the end of the third week, for those who lived through the ordeal, most of the lesions had healed, except for those on the soles of the feet and the palms of the hands. Victims remained contagious until the last scab dropped off, usually a month after contracting the disease.[25]

Smallpox claimed a number of victims in colonial Saigon, but not as many as malaria or cholera. Vietnamese had been inoculating against smallpox since before the French conquest.[26] After the conquest, the French introduced vaccinations against the disease on a wide scale. Colonial reports regularly boasted of the number of vaccinations delivered by the medical services.[27] The vaccinations reduced the number of smallpox victims in Cochinchina, but there were still four major epidemics in the colony between 1900 and the beginning of World War II.[28] The first outbreak occurred in 1908. In that year, thirteen cases of smallpox were declared in Saigon, and sixteen more were declared in 1909. Most of the victims were from Khánh Hội, a quarter of the city near the port.[29] After 1909, instances of smallpox in Saigon were rare. In 1916, there was only one case of the disease in the city. The municipal doctor declared in his annual report that "smallpox has almost completely vanished from our city since we regularly vaccinate all newborns and daily vaccinations are practiced at the polyclinic. The rare cases that we observe are almost all imported from outside the city."[30]

There was a bitter irony to the doctor's words. In the following year, another epidemic broke out, claiming many victims in Saigon. Some 2,081 cases of smallpox were declared in the colony, followed by a further 2,839 in 1918.[31] The provinces of Chợ Lớn, Tân An, and Bến Tre were the worst affected. In Saigon, there were eighty-four reported cases of smallpox in 1917, 139 in 1918. Almost half of those who contracted the disease in the city died. Most of the victims were migrants from neighboring provinces or had contracted it from migrants. The disease was particularly prevalent among the Chinese in Saigon.[32] In 1923, a smallpox epidemic spread across Asia, affecting Siam, Japan, British India, Canton, Shanghai, and Hong Kong. Cochinchina was not spared: There were 1,569 cases in 1923 and 2,133 in 1924.[33] The disease returned at the end of the decade in a fourth epidemic that lasted for several years. In 1929, there were 1,462 cases of smallpox reported in Cochinchina, but Saigon was spared a major outbreak, with only nine instances of the disease.[34] In 1930, there were only fifteen cases of smallpox in Saigon, of 2,701 cases counted in Cochinchina. In 1931, the number of cases listed for Saigon climbed to seventy-six, but exploded sevenfold in 1932, affecting almost a quarter of the 2,322 cases in all of Cochinchina that year. Of the city's 515 smallpox victims, 454 died.[35]

The resurgence of smallpox in Saigon was caused in part by neglect: A coincident cholera epidemic in 1929 had siphoned the resources of the medical services away from smallpox prevention.[36] After the many deaths of 1932, the medical services initiated a massive new campaign to vaccinate the residents of Saigon and Chợ Lớn. The campaign successfully halted the spread of the disease: Only four cases of smallpox were reported in 1933, and three in 1934.[37] After 1932, there were no significant outbreaks of the disease until World War II.[38] The reports of colonial doctors make clear that most instances of smallpox in Saigon were due to contagious migrants who brought the disease to the city.

The same was not true of cholera. The main reason for the spread of cholera in Saigon was the miserable sanitary conditions in which the poor of the city lived. Most migrants to Saigon did not settle in its center. Instead, they lived in adjacent villages that had been gradually annexed to the city. Although nominally part of Saigon, these former villages had few urban characteristics. In 1908, the residents of Phú Thạnh, Tân Định, and Chợ Đũi north of Chasseloup Laubat Street and of Khánh Hội and Cầu Kho near the Chinese Arroyo continued to live in thatched huts. There were no roads or streets in these quarters, only a maze of tangled paths. The huts faced in all directions. The residents raised vegetables in gardens scattered among thickets of bamboo and kept ducks, chickens, pigs, and cattle. There was no running water, so residents had to sink their own wells. There were no drains or sewers, so effluent ran off in channels and small streams or stood in stagnant pools. Residents disposed of household waste in nearby undergrowth and vacant areas, where they also buried their dead.[39] Coolies and other migrant laborers like Trần Văn Chinh settled in such quarters. In 1910, the municipal doctor complained that the edge of the city, "constituted by villages annexed in the past few years, is formed for the most part by a wasteland, which has not yet been cleared of brushwood, and which lacks a supply of drinkable water and a means of removing waste water."[40] The same observation was true nearly twenty years later. Cholera repeatedly broke out in these poor parts of Saigon because of the lack of clean water.

The disease, which the Vietnamese called *dịch tả*, moved with extraordinary speed. The incubation period could be as brief as twenty-four hours

A poor person's home. Photograph: Ludovic Crespin.

or as long as five days. As it began to grip the victim, cholera caused a vague feeling of being unwell and a slight deafness. The main symptoms of the disease, violent spasms of vomiting and watery diarrhea, appeared abruptly and were vast and prolonged in their extent. The vomit was a clear, watery, alkaline fluid. The stools, which the victim usually passed painlessly, resembled rice water and sometimes had a foul fishy odor. The victim could lose up to a quarter of his or her body fluids and experienced severe dehydration. The blood coagulated and stopped circulating properly; the pulse in the limbs became slow or absent altogether. The hands and feet became as cold as ice, the eyes sunken and dull, and the skin blue and wrinkled—as though the victim had taken a long, cold bath. As victims lost fluids, they became restless and extremely thirsty, but as their bodies went into shock, they became apathetic and sometimes lost consciousness. The breathing of many victims became labored, at first rapid and shallow and eventually deep, slow, and gasping. Half died from cardiac or renal failure brought on by acute dehydration and the loss of vital chemicals and electrolytes; the other half recovered, more or less rapidly. The whole progress of the disease could take as little as five to twelve hours, but it more often took around three to four days.[41]

A microscopic bacillus known as *Vibrio cholerae* caused the disease. It thrived in warm and humid conditions and above all in river water, although it could survive in colder temperatures. Saigon, with its tropical climate and river, arroyos, and canals, was an ideal home for the disease. *Vibrio cholera* could live on food, especially on fruits and vegetables that had been washed in infected water. Milk and eggs were also hospitable to the disease. But it could strike only if it entered the digestive tract: The victims had to put infected food or drink into their mouth or touch their mouth with infected hands. The bacillus could survive for up to two weeks on human excrement and up to a week on ordinary soil. Infected clothes and linens, especially bed linens, could transmit the disease if others touched them and later put their hands to their mouths. Flies could carry the disease over short distances. The best way to combat cholera was through fastidious personal hygiene, particularly frequent hand washing. The disease could be killed by heat: Boiling water and milk and baking other foodstuffs helped arrest its transmission. *Vibrio cholera* lasted for only a few minutes in wine or spirits and a few hours in beer. But it lasted for years among the poor and the sick of Saigon.[42]

There were several major outbreaks of cholera in Saigon between 1900 and World War II. The epidemics tended to occur in April and May, during the transition from the dry to the wet season. The first significant outbreak occurred in 1908. In that year, 5,940 instances of cholera and 3,777 subsequent deaths were reported.[43] Only eighteen of the instances were in Saigon, however. All of the rest occurred in Tân Định, Cầu Kho, or Cầu Ông Lãnh, former villages along the Avalanche or Chinese arroyos.[44] The next major outbreak of cholera occurred in 1912. In that year, 7,488 victims contracted the disease, but only a fraction, 125, lived in Saigon.[45] In 1915, a third epidemic claimed 3,807 victims in the colony, including fifty-six in Saigon. If this suggested that Saigon was not the center of this outbreak, the municipal doctor noted that it was necessary "to double the number of cases determined in order to get an exact idea of the extent of the epidemic." It was equally suggestive that eleven of the fifty-six cases occurred among rickshaw pullers. "This profession of the poor," the doctor wrote, "undertaken by men in poor physical health, exposed to bad weather, and who take their food in lodging houses, paid a heavy tribute to the disease."[46] They often made close contact with travelers from outside the city center.

Cholera always appeared in the same places in the city: "it is the quarters without roads and running water that are almost exclusively contaminated," the municipal doctor stated in his report. "The best way to prevent cholera," he said, was "to extend running water to the whole city" and to fill all of the private wells.[47] A cholera epidemic spread across Southeast Asia in 1926: There were 5,130 cases in Cochinchina.[48] There were several thousand cases of the disease in the colony each year for the next five years.[49] In 1930, there were 1,952 instances, only 110 of which were in Saigon.[50] But in the following year, there were 154 cases in the city—nearly half of the 325 cases in Cochinchina. In 1932, the instances of cholera reported in Saigon fell to eight, while the number in the colony dropped to 261. According to the municipal doctor, these cases occurred "almost exclusively in the quarters where there is no network for the distribution of drinkable water"—quarters located on the margins of the city and typically occupied by the poor. After 1932, there were no further epidemics of cholera in the city before the outbreak of World War II.[51] Doctors attributed the decline of the disease to a massive campaign of vaccinations and to improvements in the city, including the extension of water pipes and sewers to once-peripheral areas inhabited by the poor.[52]

The poor lived not only on the periphery of Saigon but also at its center. Many coolies like Trần Văn Chinh, as well as domestic servants and day laborers, inhabited dark, crowded, and filthy apartment buildings on Paul Blanchy, Hamelin, Adran, Pellerin, Ormay, and Mac Mahon streets, among others. Some of the worst apartment buildings were close to the old central market, at the end of Catinat Street opposite the municipal cathedral. In many cases, an apartment that was designed to house a single family had more than thirty individuals living in it. The residents usually left during the day to work and to attend to their affairs and returned at night just to sleep.[53]

Sometimes several families lived crammed into a single room, which was usually no more than three meters wide and eight meters long. Wooden planks divided the room into a number of smaller compartments, to give each family some privacy. But the compartments were dark, hot, stifling, and dirty. They usually opened onto a common area that the families used for cooking and storage. Few of the apartment buildings had lavatories, and the gutters and drains, when they existed at all, were usually in poor condition. The courtyards of many buildings housed enormous piles of rubbish and debris, such as old boxes, barrels, bottles, burned coals, rubble, and vegetation. The poor residents of one courtyard lived in a small shantytown that they had constructed entirely out of junk.[54] In 1910, the municipal doctor wrote that "there are lots of over-populated apartments, poorly ventilated, with inadequate plumbing, which are terribly unhealthy for the masses of Chinese and Vietnamese who pile into them, and for the European population who lives nearby." In the view of the doctor, the only way the municipality could sanitize certain buildings in the center of the city was to raze them to the ground, thus "producing total destruction, and leaving the area free for more hygienic buildings."[55]

When rats found a home in such cramped and dirty buildings, bubonic plague could spread quickly. The earliest outbreak of plague in Saigon occurred in 1906, close to the center of the city. It seems to have arrived via the burgeoning vectors of regional commerce and export trade. Doctors first diagnosed the disease among the South Asian inhabitants of Hamelin Street, not far from the Immigration Service. A careful investigation revealed that bundles belonging to Chinese migrants from Guangzhou and Hong Kong had contained rats that brought the disease to the colony. When the migrants opened the bundles at the Immigration Service, the rats escaped and made their way to insalubrious neighboring buildings.[56] The same steamships that carried products and people from port to port also carried plague. Starting in 1894, steamships carried plague from Hong Kong to the major seaports of the world.[57] In 1906, after the infected rats escaped into the city, the municipal authorities in Saigon registered twenty-seven cases of plague.[58]

Bubonic plague is primarily a disease of rodents. Fleas ingest the bacteria that causes plague from their rodent host and carry it from one animal to another. Rats can build up immunity to the disease, and the infecting bacteria can move among resistant animals, causing only an occasional death. If the bacteria enter a new population of susceptible rodents, a large number will die. This causes the fleas to abandon their dead hosts in search of other warm-blooded animals on which to feed.[59] In 1907, a large number of dead rats appeared in the Saigon Botanical Gardens, mainly in the corners and recesses of the seed store. Tests confirmed the presence of plague.[60] Shortly after, the disease broke out among residents of the city.

When an infected flea bites a person, plague bacteria invade the individual's lymphatic system.[61] Two or three days after infection, buboes appear in the groin, armpits, or neck. The victim also experiences high fever, shivering, vomiting, headaches, giddiness, and delirium. If the buboes drain on their own, the victim may recover. Otherwise, in the absence of treatment, death usually occurs in four to five days. In 1907, plague killed nearly five hundred people in Saigon.[62] Among these deaths, more than two hundred occurred in Tân Định and Dakao, former villages along the Avalanche Arroyo. In the following year, the city tabulated a hundred cases of plague and then twenty-five in 1909. The municipal doctor reported that "the epidemic chose to manifest itself in the most insalubrious dwellings, the most poorly kept, those in which overpopulation was the most accentuated."[63] According to his notes, the vast majority of plague victims again lived in Tân Định and Dakao and in thatched dwellings along the Chinese Arroyo.[64]

The worst outbreak of plague in Saigon occurred in 1911. That was also the worst year for Cochinchina, with documented 1,018 cases of the disease. Châu Đốc, Thủ Dầu Một, and Gia Định were the most affected provinces.[65] In Saigon, the authorities counted ninety-seven cases of plague.[66] Most victims came from the same poor parts of the city.[67]

Another, milder outbreak occurred in 1914. This time plague affected seventy-four people in Saigon. Reviewing the origins of the victims, the municipal doctor observed that "the urban areas of Dakao, Tân Định, and Chợ Đũi, are always the worst hit." The disease even broke out on the same streets as in 1907: Rousseau, Gallimard, and Martin des Pallières streets, Paul Bert and Luro boulevards, Fancault Street, and Legrand de la Liraye Street, all in Dakao. Arfeuille Street in Tân Định, where Lê Văn Bội had gone begging only a year earlier, had "the unhappy privilege of annually having the greatest number of cases," the doctor noted. Rats abounded in "these quarters of thatched huts and of wooden apartments, dotted with wasteland, covered in bushes, and without any underground plumbing." There were many fewer instances of plague in the center of the city, where there were fewer places for rats to nest, because of proper sewers and buildings constructed from masonry. There were many more cases of plague among the poor inhabitants of thatched dwellings alongside the Chinese Arroyo, however. The municipal doctor lamented that "constant efforts are made in the contaminated quarters to ensure the cleanliness of the empty lands, which their neighbors use to dispose of trash."[68] On the city's margins these efforts were not always successful. But two years later the doctor reported that "the central quarters of the city" were "almost completely immune" from plague, "with sewers, pavements and the evacuation of used and dirty water." In general, he concluded: "Our best course of action is to create a 'desert of stone,' that is a modern city with pavements and sewers, to try to ward off neighborhoods of thatched huts, and to ensure the constant maintenance of the wastelands and open ditches that serve as rubbish tips."[69] In the doctor's eyes, the homes of the poor were serving as incubators for disease as well as despair.

The mobility of the poor hindered efforts to control the spread of plague. The doctor complained that it was "impossible to establish an effective cordon around Saigon during times of epidemic. The Vietnamese take those they suspect to be ill beyond the city in order to evade the disinfection measures." These measures usually involved forced vaccinations, the razing of thatched huts, the incineration of private property, and the use of milk of lime and sulfur gas to clean apartments. Few Vietnamese wanted to endure such procedures.

Cochinchina and its capital, Saigon, endured their last major outbreak of plague in 1918. In that year there were 485 cases recorded in the colony and 64 in Saigon. The disease killed thirty-four people in the city. After 1918, the cases of plague in Cochinchina and in Saigon steadily diminished, a result of the combination of massive vaccination campaigns, the concerted effort to destroy rats, and the gradual improvement of sanitation in quarters on the edge of the city. Between 1930 and 1934, cases of plague in Saigon averaged slightly more than four each year.[70] By the end of the decade, the disease had completely disappeared from Cochinchina and its capital.[71]

Malaria was the most prevalent disease among the poor in Saigon. It was endemic to the city.[72] The name *malaria* comes from the Italian *mal'aria,* which means "bad air." In the early nineteenth century, the disease was thought to be caused by a "miasma" or a poisoning of the air. Some thought that the noxious brume originated from leaves, branches, and vines that had fallen into swamp water and then decomposed, releasing pestilential vapors into the air. Malaria, which the French called *paludisme,* from the Latin word *palus,* meaning "swamp," occurred when an individual inhaled the gases or absorbed them through his or her pores. Others believed that a "germ"—a microscopic plant or some kind of "animalcule"—produced the lethal swamp gases. Winds carried the germs away from swamps and seeded the ground that they passed over. Heat, humidity, and clay topsoil that retained moisture allowed the germs to ferment in the earth and release poisonous fumes. The susceptible became sick when they crossed contaminated "fields of death" and breathed in the poisonous vapors or when they drank infected swamp water.[73] At the end of the nineteenth century, some in the colonial administration still thought that the soils of Cochinchina emanated vapors and miasmas that were deadly to those with weakened or feeble constitutions.[74]

In 1880, under the lens of his microscope the French army physician Alphonse Laveran discovered the *Plasmodium* protist, the parasite that causes malaria, in the blood of malaria victims. In 1898, the Italian doctor Giovanni Grassi demonstrated that the *Anopheles* mosquito transmitted the parasite among humans. When an infected mosquito bit a victim, it injected him or her with the *Plasmodium* parasite. The parasite traveled to the victim's liver, where it penetrated the cells and multiplied. The circulatory system carried the parasites throughout the body. After seven to ten days, the classic symptoms of malaria appeared: fever, chills, profuse sweating, and violent headaches. Vomiting, diarrhea, and delirium were also common. The disease could also cause massive hemorrhages as well as premature births and miscarriages in pregnant women. In the worst cases, the victim exhibited profound anemia, respiratory distress, and coma before dying. Those who survived might continue to suffer from chronic disabilities, such as painful enlargement of the spleen, emaciation, anemia, and cachexia—total apathy and indifference to the world around them.[75]

The mosquitoes that carried malaria nested along the banks of the Saigon River and the Chinese and Avalanche arroyos, and in the brackish
standing water found in the poorest quarters on the margins of the city.
In 1911, the municipal doctor wrote that "malaria is severe in Saigon in
all of its forms. It is the most important cause of death." In his estimation,
thirty-five of every hundred Vietnamese in Saigon had malaria.[76] In 1916,
the municipal polyclinic saw 4,286 cases of the disease, an enormous number given that Saigon's population was only sixty-seven thousand.[77] Despite ongoing attempts to eradicate mosquitoes and their larvae, malaria
continued to sap the poor of their vitality and rob them of their lives. As
late as 1934, the municipal doctor wrote that "malaria remains the most
common endemic disease in the region." That year it killed 460 people in
Saigon, eighty-seven more lives than it had in 1933.[78]

At the beginning of the twentieth century, the quarter of Saigon most
notorious for malaria infections was known as the Marais Boresse. The
Marais, or "swamp," comprised a vast expanse at the end of Bonard Boulevard, in the direction of Chợ Lớn. It lay lower than other parts of the
city, and the Chinese Arroyo regularly inundated it. The inhabitants of the
quarter erected their thatched huts on a marshland amid grasses, rushes,
ditches, and pools of stagnant water. The municipal doctor recorded in
1910 that malaria is "manifest above all in low regions, that are wet, and
covered in brush. The Marais Boresse in Saigon is a quite classic example
of a malarial area."[79]

In 1914, the municipality completed a long program of public works intended to improve the Marais. It drained the marshland, filled the ponds
and ditches, and built a network of sewers. Sealed roads connected Saigon
to the Marais, where the municipality had also built a new railway station
and central market. The new market drew many people away from the
crowded tenements near the old market at the end of Catinat Street. The
city built new apartment buildings out of reinforced concrete to replace
the thatched huts that had once occupied the quarter. In 1914, the municipal doctor wrote in his sanitation report that "in the very near future, the
former 'Marais Boresse' will become the most beautiful quarter of Saigon,
as well as the most airy, and the most hygienically ordered and built."[80]
After 1914, malaria no longer plagued the inhabitants of the Marais, but
it did continue to afflict the poor inhabitants of quarters alongside the

river and arroyos. The municipal medical service registered 43,190 cases of the disease in 1937—almost one-third of all the illnesses in the city. Khánh Hội, Cầu Kho, Xóm Chiếu, Vĩnh Hội, Câu Ông Lãnh, and Tân Định continued to be the worst afflicted parts of the city.[81] Malaria gave the poor little relief.

After malaria, tuberculosis was the next most prevalent disease endemic to Saigon.[82] Indeed, the municipal doctor observed that the disease "is, by its essence, a sickness of towns and of poverty." The struggle against tuberculosis, he stated, was "tightly bound up with the question of insalubrious housing" in the city.[83] The poor occupied the most unsanitary housing in the villages that had recently been added to the city. Their resistance to tuberculosis had already been reduced by "poverty, inadequate nutrition, malaria, and syphilis." Their weakened bodies thus provided "a thoroughly prepared and favorable ground for the hatching and the evolution of the tuberculosis bacteria."[84] In 1916, the municipal clinic saw 304 cases of the disease.[85] In 1937, a clinic in Saigon dedicated to assisting those with tuberculosis saw 12,910 new patients. Among those, 1,822 tested positive for the disease.[86]

Tuberculosis bacteria are easily transmitted. When a person infected with tuberculosis speaks or coughs, his or her moist breath contains tiny droplets of water. These droplets carry the bacteria that cause tuberculosis. Within a foot or two of the speaker's mouth, the moisture of the tiny droplets evaporates, leaving dried droplet nuclei suspended in the air. If these nuclei contain virulent tuberculosis bacteria, they become infectious particles. Because they are so light, they can remain suspended in the air for many hours, and because they are so small, they can reach deep into the lungs when inhaled by an uninfected person. These factors made the tuberculosis bacteria quite virulent indeed.[87]

The infection did not always start immediately. The bacteria could lie dormant in the body for weeks, even years. During this time, victims showed no symptoms and were not contagious. The typical symptoms of the disease included fever, night sweats, weight loss, loss of appetite, fatigue, persistent cough, bloody sputum, and breathing difficulty. The disease killed by destroying lung tissue, which eventually caused respiratory failure.

Less commonly, the disease could enter the body through the digestive tract. "A practice of Vietnamese mothers, which I judge to be very pernicious," the municipal doctor declared, "consists of giving their infants rice that they have already chewed and salivated into. If the mother who feeds her child in this way has tuberculosis, it is almost always fatal for the child."[88] To help prevent the spread of disease, the doctor believed that the French needed to train Vietnamese school teachers more effectively. "The teacher, trained by us and penetrated by our ideas of hygiene," he wrote, "can train his countrymen of the need to improve his food, his clothing, his personal care, and his domestic architecture, which lacks air and light." Sunlight could kill the bacteria that caused tuberculosis. The doctor concluded that "it is by the improvement of well-being, and the suppression of inadequately aired and lighted housing, that the disease will be reduced."[89] Despite efforts at education and improved sanitation, and vaccination campaigns after 1924, tuberculosis remained endemic in Saigon and a constant companion of the poor.[90]

What disease crippled Trần Văn Chinh in 1917? What illness made begging the only profession he could practice? Perhaps he contracted malaria or tuberculosis—many of his contemporaries did. But both were wasting diseases: They seldom struck their victims down. Cholera and plague survivors eventually recovered. Smallpox maimed; it could cause disfiguring scars and left many survivors blind. In 1917 and 1918, smallpox swept through Saigon and infected hundreds of victims. Perhaps Trần Văn Chinh was one of them. While the coincidence is appealing, the likelihood is small. Many other illnesses might have afflicted Trần Văn Chinh: syphilis, typhoid, dysentery, measles, diphtheria, and beriberi were all prevalent in Saigon. Such diseases both diminished their victim's quality of life and, often, reduced its length.

The available sources do not allow for the construction of a life table or for an analysis of mortality by gender or social strata: The "crude death rate" is appropriately named. Even that measure can be calculated for only a few scattered years, from rather rough and approximate data. But the data that are available provide eloquent, if muted, testimony to how grim life in colonial Saigon must have been. By any reckoning, the crude death rate for Asians was very high. In 1907, it was 32.7, meaning that in that year, 32.7 out of every thousand Asian residents of the city died. In the same year, the crude death rate for Europeans in Saigon was already lower, at 29.5. In 1908, during the plague epidemic, the crude death rate for Asians climbed to 36, while the rate for Europeans, who were barely affected by the plague, fell to 24.2. Over the next several years, the crude death rate for Europeans in Saigon declined. By 1913, it had fallen to 16.9 and rarely rose again. In the same year, the rate for Asians remained almost twice as high, at 31.3.[91] During the plague epidemic of 1914, the crude death rate for Asians increased to 36.4. In 1916, the municipal doctor estimated that in Saigon it remained between 30 and 35.[92] The statistic became slightly less grim over the following years, but it still remained unacceptably high. By 1930, it had dropped to 27.4. The cholera and smallpox epidemics in the following years and the drop in the population due to the Great Depression pushed the figure up to 28.0 in 1931 and 31.0 in 1932. By 1934, when both epidemics had ended and migrants had returned to the city, the Asian crude death rate was around 24.3.[93] By World War II, the crude death rate for Asians in Saigon and Chợ Lớn remained well above 20.0. The rate for Europeans was significantly lower, at 16.4.[94] The different age structures of the two communities make comparison difficult, but it is clear is that Asians in Saigon—many of whom were poor Vietnamese—died in staggering numbers until the end of the colonial period.

If the lives of the poor in Saigon were highly varied, so too were the manners of their death. Many died on the very streets on which Trần Văn Chinh and other mendicants begged. Some passed away peacefully while they slept on the pavement beneath the awnings of shops; others died violently after being crushed by a horse-drawn carriage or a tram. Junks sometimes deposited the dying on the quay alongside the Chinese Arroyo, near Chợ Quán hospital. Others fell down dead without ever receiving assistance, having collapsed while pulling a rickshaw, carrying a load, or begging for alms on Norodom Boulevard, Catinat Street, or Charner Boulevard in the center of the city.[95]

When a policeman discovered a corpse on the street, he was supposed to alert the commissioner of police so that proper steps could be taken to remove it. In the meantime, he had to prevent family members, friends, and members of the public from attempting to move the body. The municipality allowed no burial to take place without prior written authorization. But the poor often died alone, and many bodies went unclaimed. The policeman had to keep onlookers and the curious away, and he had to ensure that nobody tried to remove anything from the body—coins, paper money, tax payment cards and other identifying documents, perhaps the tattered and faded photograph of a loved one, any of the sundry and sometimes precious items the poor kept about their persons.[96]

The corpse secured, the authorities then had to determine the cause of death. From the beginning of 1907, residents of Saigon had to report all deaths to the municipality, which sent a doctor out to inspect the corpse. The residents of Hà Nội had followed the same procedure for many years, and it had helped prevent the spread of disease. But during the first years of its implementation in Saigon, the doctor often found it difficult to determine the cause of death.[97] Sometimes it took up to three days for residents to notify the municipality of a death and for a doctor to examine the corpse. In those cases, moisture and heat, coupled with vermin, flies, and other pests, meant that the corpse had already achieved a state of advanced putrefaction by the time the doctor arrived. It was almost impossible for the doctor to identify signs of a contagious disease or other causes of mortality.[98]

If the doctor found evidence of plague or smallpox on the corpse, the municipality had to take special steps. If the cadaver was in an apartment, the municipality disinfected the dwelling with sulfur gas. But if the corpse was found in a thatched hut, the municipality razed it to the ground with fire and treated the ground with milk of lime or benzene vapor to kill any contagion. Police kept watch over the neighborhood for several days on the lookout for any further signs of death or disease. The corpse itself was thoroughly dowsed in antiseptic chemicals such as lime, calcium hypochlorite, or iron sulfate and quickly buried in a deep grave.[99]

Graves were scattered all over Saigon. Brick tombs and raised mounds, placed seemingly indiscriminately, littered the countryside and many of the villages that later became part of the city. Many neighborhoods had their own small cemeteries.[100] If a poor Vietnamese died in the hospital at Chợ Quán and there was nobody to claim the body, the hospital interred it in the adjacent burial ground. The municipality paid for a grave in Saigon's

Asian cemetery for the poor Vietnamese who died in his or her thatched
dwelling or on the streets of the city. It claimed the expense back from the
colony.[101]

Saigon established its first Asian cemetery in 1873, in the adjacent village
of An Hòa. But the burial ground quickly filled up. Before long, the municipality had to close it and acquire further land in which to bury the dead.[102]
Chinese and Vietnamese were reluctant to bury their dead in the Asian
cemetery, referring to it with disgust as *đất thánh Chà,* or the "Indian cemetery," because of the large number of South Asians buried there.[103]

Temples and churches kept their own cemeteries, but they soon filled
up as well. Usually located close to homes and businesses, they could become a public health hazard. The graves were often shallow, heavy rain
could strip away the soil, and wild animals sometimes dug up the bodies.
The stench of decomposition often lingered heavily in the air nearby. The
municipality had to close the cemetery belonging to the Catholic church
at Tân Định for these reasons in 1903. It set aside a special section in the
Asian cemetery where members of the parish could bury their dead.[104]

Europeans in Saigon had their own cemetery. It was located at the end of
Bangkok Street, later named Massiges Street. "See you on Bangkok Street"
was a morbid greeting the French in the city offered the ill and injured.
The French sometimes referred to the cemetery as the "garden of Old Man
d'Ormay," after Dr. Lalluyeaux-d'Ormay, the gregarious and well-liked former head of the health service who dispatched many French soldiers and
civil servants to the cemetery in the first years of French rule. The cemetery became a place for leisurely walks and promenades, and the graves
of Saigon's most celebrated and notorious French residents became sites
of veneration, or at least homage.[105]

Graves and funerals could be very expensive and were thus a special
concern for poor men and women like Trần Văn Chinh. They did not want
to suffer in death as they had in life, wandering the netherworld as hungry
ghosts, just as they had wandered the streets of Saigon as hungry men and
women. Churches and pagodas sometimes established mutual aid associations to help pay for funerals and burials. Members of one of the pagodas
to Mazu formed a mutual aid association in 1922. The Catholic employees
of Tân Định formed one in 1923. The Catholic Mutual Association of Cầu
Kho, founded in 1928, had members across the city. Nam Chơn Pagoda had

such an association in 1936, as did Cô Hồn Pagoda in 1939. Vietnamese also founded secular organizations to provide each other with assistance during the passing of a loved one and at other difficult times. The Mutual Association of the Native Employees of Trade and Industry of Cochinchina was one such society. The membership lists of these organizations are filled with printers, typists, secretaries, civil servants, merchants, and traders—the new middling ranks of Saigon society who rode to work in rickshaws. Listed more rarely are cooks, hairdressers, workers, and day laborers. The members of such mutual aid societies usually had to pay a modest fee to join as well as a monthly subscription to receive benefits.[106] These fees and subscriptions were often more than the poorest residents of Saigon like Trần Văn Chinh could afford to pay. In 1922, a number of philanthropic Vietnamese came together to form the Vietnamese Cemetery Association of Cochinchina. The society paid for the burial of its members in the cemetery it owned on Lefebvre Street. It also assumed the burden of paying for the burials of the many poor Vietnamese who died penniless and anonymous in Saigon.[107]

The records give no indication of what happened to Trần Văn Chinh after he entered the hospice in Phú Mỹ. If he died alone and without resources, he may have had to rely in death, as he had done in life, on the kindness of strangers.

CHAPTER SEVEN

A PRODIGAL SON

I float and drift, now near, now far —
jade sings ten thousand melodies, unheard.
In silence, pearls drop one by one
in a clear lake, pristine beside the steps.
Two nymphs come sliding down to lie —
two nymphs stand there with incense, on both sides.
Dark smokes ascend, dark smokes ascend —
the boat is bobbing: where're Peach Blossom Springs?
—*Thế Lữ, "Opium"*[1]

On December 19, 1921, Edouard Morin penned a plea to the governor of Cochinchina. His French was hesitant and sometimes broken. Penniless and desperately ill, he sought free passage back to France. Edouard suffered from several conditions: malaria, a double hernia, hemorrhoids, anemia, and a chronic liver disorder. He had lived on the streets of Saigon for almost two weeks without shelter, money, or medical care. He had failed utterly in his attempts to find work. His circumstances had become so wretched, he told the governor, that he was hoping for death.

Edouard was an incorrigible rogue. He had arrived in the colony twenty-six years earlier, and according to one policeman he was "one of the most

155

disreputable Frenchmen who have lived in Indochina." He had worked at several jobs in Cochinchina, Tonkin, and Siam as well as aboard various ships. Although he had once married and fathered a son, Edouard regularly kept the company of prostitutes. He was forever seeking alms, occupying a hospital bed or a prison cell, or appearing before a police officer or a magistrate: He had, at a minimum, five convictions. "Opium addict, drunk, trafficker in arms and morphine, delinquent parent, a man ready for every disreputable task because his age, his health, and his premature decrepitude now keep him from pimping—that is Edouard François Morin," wrote one policeman. "I have only one wish," the policeman continued, "which is that Morin, who is completely without any respectable income, leave the colony as soon as possible."[2] Edouard Morin was a burden to the colonial authorities. But worst of all, he was an embarrassing stain on the pristine picture of "la Belle Colonie."

Many visitors, like Jasper Whiting, had described Saigon as "the Pearl of the Orient" or "the Paris of the Far East." But others thought it less grand. When Somerset Maugham stopped in the city in 1922, he thought it had "all the air of a little provincial town in the South of France."[3] Whether more like Paris or Aix-en-Provence, Saigon's urban design—with its broad, tree-lined streets, opera house, cathedral, and city hall—was meant to engender admiration of French civilization in visitors and inhabitants alike.[4] Another prominent English traveler, Osbert Sitwell, made this point vividly after visiting Saigon in 1934. "In Paris the Colonial Exhibition had but recently finished," he remarked, "and the general effect of Saigon was that it had been constructed as its antithesis; a French Imperial Exhibition arranged for the Colonies, or, even, something larger and more important, a Western Exhibition organized for the benefit of the peoples of the Extreme East."[5] But some poor whites, such as Edouard Morin, made spectacles of themselves. One French official in Tonkin deemed the poor French in the colony "a disgrace to the good name of our nationality." Reduced to begging and vagrancy, they were given charity out of "a feeling of pity among Europeans, and mockery among the Vietnamese, happy to deride French prestige."[6] The colonial authorities feared that such degrading exhibitions would undermine French superiority in the eyes of the Vietnamese.

The threat of being undermined by poor whites was a source of constant anxiety for colonial administrations throughout South and Southeast Asia.

There were thousands of poor Englishmen in British India. By the middle of the nineteenth century, officials considered European vagrants a "shame and inconvenience" and "a serious stigma on the character of our government, which must suffer in Native eyes accordingly." By the end of the century, nearly half of the 150,000 Europeans living in India were poor whites.[7] In British Malaya, colonists worked hard to remain aloof from the small number of poor Britons in the colony. In 1919, one European train driver reminded the government that it had a responsibility to pay drivers a salary which could "enable them to live in a manner as befits a European without exposing him to danger of ill-health and an early death."[8] In the Netherlands East Indies, European pauperism had become a concern to the authorities as early as the middle of the eighteenth century. By the early twentieth century, the colonial government had identified tens of thousands of Eurasians and Europeans as dangerously impoverished.[9] Edouard Morin was not only dangerously impoverished; he was a danger to the dignity of the French in Saigon.[10]

The colonial authorities seldom counted or questioned the poor French who lived in the city. But in 1937, the administration ordered an inquiry into the conditions of all the French indigents living in Cochinchina.[11] The provincial and municipal authorities delegated the task to the colonial police who conducted investigations and wrote brief reports on each poor Frenchman living in their jurisdiction. The police reports described each man's name, age, marital status, family circumstances, and occupation (if working) and gave a brief account of how he had become poor. Altogether, the police in Cochinchina submitted seventy such reports. Twenty-eight were from provinces neighboring Saigon: ten from Gia Định, eleven from Biên Hòa, four from Rạch Giá, and three from Thủ Dầu Một. Forty-two reports were from Saigon-Chợ Lớn. They included reports on seven men from France or men with two French parents, ten Eurasians, twenty-three French citizens of South Asian origin from the French possessions on the Coromandel coast, and two naturalized French citizens. The reports also included additional information on twenty-four wives and seventy-nine children, or 145 individuals in total. Taken together they cast a brief and lurid light on the lives of the poor French in the city in 1937. Some reports provided only brief accounts of miserable, squalid lives, summarized and condemned in a few brief lines. But several recorded their subjects' lives in rich detail: some were a catalogue of misfortune, others a litany of misbehavior.

One report reveals a life which, like a bold weft thread, ducked under and over the many warp threads of colonial society: a Corsican youth, military service, a position in the colonial administration, private employment, a failed entrepreneurial venture, unemployment, opium addiction, scandal and dishonor, and finally dependence on public charity. The report narrates the life of Félix Colonna d'Istria, the son of a noble Corsican family who went to Indochina to seek his fortune but who found poverty and ignominy instead. His story illustrates the role of roguery and of diminishing occupational opportunity in making the poor French citizenry of colonial Saigon. The police report described Félix as "a true human wreck." He lived a life, it lamented, that did nothing to enhance the prestige of the French in Cochinchina.[12] He was a disgrace. Even his birth had been sordid.

Félix was a bastard. He was born in Avignon in 1878, the illegitimate son of Laurence Emélie Knoll and Alexandre Ignace Colonna d'Istria, a local landowner and descendant of a noble Corsican family. His grandfather, the Viscount François Marie Pierre Hugues Colonna d'Istria, was a lawyer at the Cour Royale in Bastia, and his grandmother, the Viscountess Marie Magdelaine, was the daughter of an aristocratic Corsican family. The shame that his birth must have brought upon his family was mitigated when his parents finally wed in 1880.[13]

Félix had an unremarkable youth. He attended school in Avignon and in Bastia, his paternal home on the island of Corsica. In 1897, at the age of nineteen, he volunteered for military service. He spent the next four years in the Second Regiment of the Chasseurs d'Afrique, stationed at Oran on the coast of Algeria. The Chasseurs were a light cavalry corps, the mounted equivalent of the Zouave infantry. Volunteers or French settlers in Algeria manned the Chasseurs, as they did the Zouaves. The Second Regiment had taken part in the French conquest of Algeria, fought at the Crimea, in Italy, in China during the Second Opium War, in Mexico during the French Intervention, and in Lorraine during the Franco-Prussian War. After 1870, the regiment was stationed along the Moroccan frontier.[14] While Félix was in Oran, one of the few notable events was the arrival of the first electric trams in 1899. When he demobilized in 1901, he returned to Corsica. But his time in Oran had enlivened in him, it seems, a taste for empire, for adventure, and for the exotic. Early in 1903, Félix set sail for Hà Nội.

Hà Nội had supplanted Saigon as the capital of French Indochina in 1902. The relocation of the colonial administration coincided with a massive campaign of public works: The governor general ruled from a grand new palace adjacent to the city's botanical gardens; a broad new wrought-iron bridge spanned the Red River, welding the city together; and improved roads and new railway lines linked Hà Nội with Lạng Sơn and Lào Cai in the north and the city of Vinh to the south.[15] The government paid for these new works from the recently implemented general budget, which was supported by indirect taxation. The Customs and Excise Service, founded in 1898, was the main contributor to the government coffers. It collected duties on various imports and exports as well as excise taxes on three principal goods: salt, alcohol, and opium.[16] After arriving in Hà Nội, Félix joined the Customs and Excise Service in Biên Hòa.

The Customs and Excise Service was the largest department in the colonial administration, dwarfing all others. In 1899, the service employed 1,915 personnel, 828 of whom were European. By 1913, the service had increased in size by more than 70 percent and employed 3,311 personnel, including 1,246 Europeans. While the Government General expected the service to supply 91 percent of its revenue in 1913, the operation of the service also absorbed 31 percent of the central government's budget that year. From its inception, the service remained one of the largest, and costliest, branches of the colonial administration.[17]

The agents of the service were among the most visible embodiments of the colonial state, hated and feared throughout French Indochina. They were present in every province. Their main tasks were to ensure the payment of customs duties and to prevent the evasion of excise taxes through the manufacture and sale of contraband salt, opium, and especially alcohol. The service had armed brigades endowed with broad powers of search and seizure. They combed the countryside for moonshine and bootleggers. The brigades acted brutally and arbitrarily, often with impunity.[18] The service recruited its agents heavily from among former military men, men with experience using violence, men just like Félix.

Félix soon found that living in the Far East could be enervating. Colonial officials were entitled to six months of leave in France every three years to ameliorate the hardship of living in the tropics. In November 1907, Félix returned to Bastia, his home in Corsica, to rest and recover. When his leave came to an end, he applied to prolong it. Two military doctors certified that he was suffering from tropical anomie and chronic diarrhea, so the colonial administration granted him another three months in Bastia. When that extension expired, Félix sought yet further leave. The doctors declared that Félix still had chronic diarrhea, and he spent another month in Bastia.

Félix sought six extensions to his original period of leave in all. Each time, he obtained a certificate that testified to his poor health: diarrhea, gastroenteritis, and tropical or colonial anomie. The malady the colonial administration seemed to worry about most, however, was sheer fecklessness. Many officials sought to prolong their leave when in France by claiming a spurious convalescence, at great cost to the French treasury.[19] While on leave, Félix received a promotion. He finally returned to Indochina at the end of 1909. But whether malingering or still unwell, he resigned from his position at the Customs and Excise Service, citing poor health, in 1915.[20]

Félix still needed to work and to make a wage. He eventually found a position with the Société française des distilleries de l'Indochine in the province of Biên Hòa. At the Customs and Excise Service, Félix had policed the consumption of contraband alcohol. In Biên Hòa, he worked for the only company that had been licensed to sell alcohol in Cochinchina, a monopoly.[21] It had a warehouse in Biên Hòa as well as dozens of wholesale traders and hundreds of retail merchants. In the other territories of French Indochina, the monopoly also controlled the production of alcohol, but in Cochinchina Chinese entrepreneurs owned almost all of the distilleries. A Chinese merchant had been the proprietor of the only distillery in Biên Hòa for decades. It could produce up to five hundred liters of rice alcohol each day, which it sold through monopoly merchants locally, as well as in the neighboring provinces of Thủ Dầu Một, Bà Rịa, and Gò Công.[22] Félix stayed with the monopoly for fifteen months.

He then took up work logging the forests of Tây Ninh and Biên Hòa, where the rickshaw puller Trần Văn Lang had once worked as a woodcutter. Félix must have made an adequate living—he worked in the forests for nine years. He even prospered enough to briefly launch a commercial newspaper in Saigon. But then, perhaps fatigued or possibly bored by the isolation of rural life, Félix settled in Saigon permanently in 1928.

By the time Félix moved to the capital of Cochinchina, the Jazz Age in the Far East was drawing to a close. In the second half of 1928, the Vietnamese residents of Saigon began to show signs of disquiet and unrest. Festivals and public holidays, such as the Vietnamese New Year celebration Tết, Bastille Day, Armistice Day, and the death anniversary of the revered scholar and patriot Phan Châu Trinh, had all passed without protest. But in August, rumors of the end of the world began to spread throughout the city, as they had done almost every year. Pamphlets with the title *Lưu Bá Ôn Will Save the Fate of the Three Countries* appeared in Saigon and throughout the countryside. Lưu Bá Ôn was the Vietnamese name of the famous medieval Chinese scholar and military strategist Liu Bowen (劉伯溫); the three countries were Cochinchina, Annam, and Tonkin. While official biographies credited Liu Bowen with an important role in founding the Ming dynasty and portrayed him as an exemplary imperial advisor, popular fiction transformed him into an illustrious Daoist mystic and prognosticator.[23] The Vietnamese pamphlets bearing his name proclaimed that during the approaching winter, terrible calamities would befall the people of Vietnam. Those calamities would portend the end of the world and the almost complete destruction of the Vietnamese people. Only the virtuous—those who followed the prescriptions in the tracts— would survive. The prescriptions were simple: Readers had to reprint the tracts and further distribute them, they had to take a special potion described in the tract, and they had to redouble their Buddhist fervor and virtue. Such predictions and admonitions had appeared in Saigon many times before but always on flyers written in Chinese characters; in 1928, they appeared for the first time in romanized Vietnamese.[24] They augured troubles to come.

Such troubles were not immediately evident to Félix upon arriving in Saigon. The European community in the city seemed prosperous. Since 1923, the French population of 8,400 had grown by 50 percent, to 12,600 in 1928.[25] The cost of living for Europeans in the city had increased steadily since 1910. It had risen sharply during the economic crisis in 1920 and 1921 and then continued to increase, despite some fluctuations, until the end of the decade.[26] But colonial officials, military officers, and French business-men were all handsomely compensated. A French businessman working for a large company in Saigon or a colonial administrator of the third rank might receive an annual salary of 14,000 francs, a colonial supplement of 5,115 piasters, and an annual indemnity of 2,600 piasters, giving a monthly salary of 740 piasters in sum. A man with a wife and child who rented a fur-nished home in the city, paid school fees, and employed two domestic ser-vants could live in comfort and still save sixty-eight piasters each month for frivolity. In contrast, the monthly wages such a man usually paid his Vietnamese domestic servants, a cook and a boy, might amount to only fifty piasters for the pair. A single French man working in Saigon, such as Félix, had very few expenses. He might spend 160 piasters for room and board in a hotel each month, twenty piasters on laundering his clothes, and a further 120 piasters on various distractions, such as tobacco, club memberships, and newspapers.[27]

It was with just such colonists in mind that Félix had launched a news-paper in Saigon in 1924 called *L'Express du Commerce et de l'Industrie.*[28] It was only one of the many newspapers, journals, and magazines available by subscription or at bookstores and kiosks throughout the city. Indeed, a vibrant colonial Grub Street had developed in Saigon after World War I. French and Vietnamese intellectuals, entrepreneurs, and hacks published a bewildering number of periodicals, magazines, and newspapers. French-language newspapers, such as *L'Impartial* or *Tribune Indigène,* circulated as many as 1,200 copies, while Vietnamese-language newspapers such as *Đông Pháp Thời Báo* (*Indochina Times*) and *Thần Chung* (*Morning Bell*) circulated nearly 10,000 copies, while the widely read *Trung Lập Báo,* the Vietnamese edition of *L'Impartial,* circulated 15,000 copies each day. Some newspapers carried reports from other parts of the colony, the empire, or the world, while various scandal sheets advanced radical critiques, sometimes veiled, sometimes not, of French colonialism in Cochinchina. The press in Cochin-china enjoyed greater liberty than it did in the protectorates of Tonkin and Annam, and newspapers published in French had more freedom than those that appeared in Vietnamese.[29] Almost all the publications, whatever their political differences and whether published in French or Vietnamese, exhorted readers to smoke Job cigarettes, to give their children Nestlé condensed milk, to drink Larue beer, or to shop at the Solirène pharmacy or the Denis Frères department store on Catinat Street. The columns devoted to advertising in many newspapers sometimes equaled or dwarfed the columns assigned to news and editorial comment.[30]

Félix hoped that his magazine, *L'Express du Commerce et de l'Industrie*, would play an important role in the commercial life of Cochinchina. The boom in rice exports during the 1920s had led to the flourishing of retail trade in the colony. The magazine was devoted almost entirely to advertising. Its bold red cover depicted a boat taking goods to be loaded on a steamer. In the first issue, dated June 1924, Félix declared that the magazine would "become a truly indispensable guide to buyers and an indispensable agent for sellers." Its essential purpose was "facilitating business; its role that of intermediary."[31] After the second issue appeared in July 1924, however, the paper vanished. It reappeared five years later with the publication of three further issues in April and May 1929 and then ceased altogether. Félix had initially intended for the magazine to appear once a month and for readers to pay an annual subscription of ten piasters; a thousand copies of each issue were published. Advertising was meant to generate the rest of the magazine's revenue. Notices for Perrier bottled water, Elcké pianos, Citroën automobiles, Michelin tires, the Quang-Hap café-restaurant, Chiêu Nam Viên gentleman's outfitters, and Cheong Seng jewelers and goldsmiths appeared alongside many others on the twenty-five pages of the first issue. But they also appeared next to many blank spaces, or spaces marked "for rent." There were even more blank spaces in the magazine's second issue. For want of advertisers, and probably subscribers as well, Félix stopped publishing *L'Express du Commerce et de l'Industrie* almost as soon as he began. Its existence had been evanescent.

Five years later, after he had settled in Saigon permanently, Félix resumed publication of *L'Express du Commerce et de l'Industrie*. Despite retaining its title, the magazine no longer focused on advertising. Each copy was four pages long and cost ten centimes. The three issues he released in April and May of 1929 coincided with the municipal elections that were being held that year. Félix devoted several columns in each issue to supporting an electoral bloc led by Jules Béziat and Hippolyte Ardin. Béziat was a prominent Saigon attorney who had defended André Malraux in

1924 against charges of stealing Khmer statues from the ruins at Banteay Srei. Hippolyte Ardin was the owner of the largest printing house in Saigon, a publisher of the newspaper *Saigon Républicain,* and a member of the Radical-Socialist Party.[32] Béziat and Ardin, both liberals, were opposed to an electoral bloc affiliated with the conservative and corrupt Eurasian journalist Henry Chavigny de la Chevrotière. The two men campaigned for improved public health and public works in the city. In an open letter in his magazine, Félix declared that Béziat and Ardin were among the "intellectual, commercial, and industrial elite of Saigon."[33] But their status seemed to make little difference: The ballot on May 5 failed to produce a clear winner. On May 11, Félix renewed his plea for his readers to cast their vote for Béziat at the ballot on the following day. His entreaty met with success when, on May 15, the attorney general declared Béziat the mayor of Saigon, with Ardin and the former municipal councillor Léon Lefèbvre to be his deputies.[34] "Now the task that was assigned to *The Express* can be considered completely fulfilled," Félix wrote in a triumphant editorial after the election. "It is in this oasis of calm," he concluded, "that we will withdraw to devote our efforts henceforth to the economic development of this country."[35] But that calm was about to become a clamorous din.

After rice exports from Saigon reached a *crescendo* in 1928, the *subito forzando* of the Great Depression quickly followed.[36] The demand for rice on the Saigon market collapsed. In 1929, the port moved 27 percent less rice than the previous year. In 1930, it dropped a further 12 percent. Throughout the Great Depression the harvests in Cochinchina were abundant; until 1934, the ports of Hong Kong and southern China bought almost a third of that rice annually. But new tariffs and protective measures, introduced on the eve of the Depression and elaborated throughout it, began to redirect rice from Saigon toward France.[37] In 1928, France bought 17 percent of the rice that Saigon exported; by 1931, it bought 31 percent of the export crop; and by 1933, 47 percent.[38] But French demand could not maintain the price of rice. From 1930 to 1934, the price of paddy dropped from $6.90 to $1.88; the price of the best milled rice dropped comparably, from $11.34 to $3.26. The sharpest drop occurred in 1931 when the price of the best milled rice fell by 40 percent.[39] The drop in the price of rice had profound consequences for the residents of Saigon. A grim parade of figures and official statistics describes the contraction of the urban economy and the growing misery of the city's residents.[40]

Figures recorded by the Court of Commerce reveal that the drop in the value of exports led to the liquidation and bankruptcy of many firms in Saigon. In 1928, the court liquidated thirteen companies and declared seventy-nine firms bankrupt, forty more such actions than it had taken in the previous year. In 1929, the court liquidated 6 firms and declared 112 bankrupt; in 1930, it liquidated 12 and made 92 bankrupt. Company failures peaked in 1931 when the court liquidated 41 firms and declared a further 108 bankrupt. Reflecting the extent of their involvement in the colonial economy, most of the firms that went bankrupt were Chinese: between 1928 and 1931, 64 percent of the bankrupt firms were Chinese; 16 percent were Vietnamese; 10 percent were European; and the remaining 10 percent were Indian firms.[41] The drop in the price of rice and other commodities had ruined the income of many Chinese exporting firms, leaving them unable to pay their debts. The failure of so many firms put many out of work.

There was much less work in the construction industry than there had been before the Depression. A tally in 1933 of the building permits issued in Saigon showed a sharp decline in construction. During the 1920s, carpenters, masons, plumbers, electricians, painters, and decorators built thousands of new apartments, houses, and commercial buildings as the city expanded. In 1929, Saigon issued permits for 829 apartments, 130 houses, and 10 other buildings, more than twice the number of permits it had issued only four years earlier. The city also sanctioned the erection of 56 wooden buildings and the repair of 246 others. But the Depression quickly halted the growth of construction. In 1931, the city authorized only 336 apartments, 21 houses, and 35 other new buildings. In neighboring Chợ Lớn, the construction contracted even more tightly. Between 1929 and 1931, the number of permits for new brick buildings fell by 82 percent, and the number for new wooden buildings fell by 69 percent. Few people had enough money to purchase land, buy building materials, and pay tradesmen.[42]

The municipal administration also had less money to pay its personnel. In April 1931, the cities of Saigon and Chợ Lớn fused to form a single region governed by an administrative council and presided over by a prefect. The reorganization allowed the new region to reduce the number of people it employed. In 1930, Saigon and Chợ Lớn spent $1,530,000 on personnel. After dismissing several employees, the new region spent only $1,370,000.[43] The region saved almost $100,000 by laying off fifteen European personnel. In 1931, the city of Saigon alone spent $112,000 on administrators. After further reductions, the new region spent only $96,000 on its administrative staff in 1933. According to the new prefect, the region had "a significantly reduced management personnel to administer a territory and perform an amount of work three times larger than that corresponding in the past to the city of Saigon alone."[44]

Companies also laid off workers throughout the new region. A survey in 1937 of thirty-eight companies with several thousand workers painted a bleak picture. It revealed an overall decline in available jobs between 1931 and 1936, with employment at its lowest in 1933. Workers with special skills, such as mechanics, electricians, fitters, turners, and machinists, usually retained their positions: Their number declined by only 13 percent between 1931 and 1936. Unskilled laborers were not as fortunate. During the same period, their number declined by 57 percent. Most of the unskilled laborers laid off were men: Their number fell by 66 percent. But the number of unskilled female laborers at work increased by 62 percent.[45] At $0.42, the average daily wage of an unskilled woman was almost a third less than that of an unskilled man. With fewer workers to supervise, the firms needed fewer foremen and overseers: Their number fell by 36 percent between 1931 and 1933, when hiring began again. But even when companies did start to hire again, they had many fewer positions to fill.[46]

Companies in Saigon not only reduced their workforce, they also reduced the wages they paid their male and female workers. In 1930, the average daily wage for skilled laborers in the city—which included carpenters, masons, painters, mechanics, fitters, turners, plumbers, and electricians—was $1.49. Between 1931 and 1936, their wage declined by 26 percent, to only $1.10. The wages of unskilled male laborers—those who carried rocks, moved earth, and hauled lumber—fell even more dramatically. In 1930, such laborers earned $0.78 each day, on average. But in 1936, they earned an average wage of only $0.53, having lost almost one third of their income. The wages of female laborers fell from $0.46 to $0.38 during the same period. Foremen and overseers also saw their wages decline, from $2.00 in 1931 to $1.85 in 1936.[47] Workers had much less money to spend.

So they spent less. In 1931, the governor of Cochinchina observed that "the holidays of the first day of the year," meaning Tết, "have, on the whole, been less splendid than in previous years." He explained that "without doubt, this lack of enthusiasm among the population for engaging in their traditional celebrations is uniquely due to the general stagnation of business, to the lack of money resulting from the poor sales of rice, and to concerns about preparation for the next rice season."[48] There was little money for fêting and feasting with family. But Vietnamese not only spent less lavishly on festivals, they partook in fewer daily pleasures too: They drank less alcohol, smoked fewer cigarettes, and consumed less opium. They even cut back on essential household items: They cooked with less salt, bought fewer matches, and let their lamps burn less brightly and for shorter periods to conserve kerosene.[49] They also ate less meat. In 1931, the municipal abattoir slaughtered fewer pigs, cows, calves, buffaloes, and goats than it had in 1930. Between 1932 and 1935, the abattoir butchered many more buffalo than it had in previous years, as more Vietnamese consumed this cheaper meat.[50] Consumption changed among the wealthy too. Between 1931 and 1934, electricity use in Saigon declined by 19 percent. Even though the utility company reduced the price of electricity in 1932, its use did not increase until 1935.[51] The wealthy also bought fewer cars: The number of cars imported into Indochina fell from 1,378 in 1930 to 773 in 1931 to 416 in 1932.[52] People traveled less. Annual revenues from the trains on the southern network between Saigon and Mỹ Tho and between the city and Nha Trang diminished for the five years between 1929 and 1933.[53] During the Depression, consumption of almost every kind declined in Saigon.

As did the cost of living. The colonial administration studied the cost of living for workers in Saigon over several years. It recorded the cost of rent and housing expenses, such as water, firewood, and charcoal, as well as the prices of items in a basket of goods, including rice, seasonal dry vegetables, chicken eggs, beef, pork, poultry, fresh fish, and rice alcohol, calico, soap, the cost of a third-class railway ticket, and the price of a trip in a rickshaw. From 1930 to 1931, workers' cost of living dropped by more than 13 percent, with the cost of food falling the most. From 1930 to 1936, their cost of living fell by 35 percent.

The streets became sclerotic. The city had problems removing household waste and keeping the streets clear; many alleys became veritable dumping grounds, piled high with rubbish. Few houses in the city were connected to the municipal sewage system. With fewer municipal employees, the night soil workers struggled to make their rounds each evening, leaving containers of ordure to be warmed by the morning sun in front of many houses. There was also a perennial water shortage. It was particularly acute during the dry season from December to April, when residents seldom had enough to drink, bathe, and clean. Buildings went unwashed and municipal swimming pools unfilled.[54] The city was also short of funds. There was enough money to undertake only the most essential public works. To save money on construction costs in 1932, the city used building materials from a recently demolished market to help build new roads.[55] Those roads were increasingly choked with vehicles: cars, buses, trams, rickshaws, and horse-drawn buggies known as "match boxes" whose number in Saigon alone grew from 328 in 1931 to 1,119 in 1935.[56] If vehicles crowded the roads, mendicants congested the pavements—police raids in 1930 led to the arrest of 427.[57] Also hoping to avoid arrest, many workers who had deserted the rubber plantations to the east sought refuge in the city, as Trần Văn Lang had. Between 1929 and 1934, more than half of them evaded capture.[58] Saigon had become dirty, stagnant, and poor; with few opportunities, it became uninhabitable for many.

And so many of its inhabitants abandoned the city. The population of Saigon had peaked at 126,000 in 1931. After the economy collapsed in 1931 with the drop in the price of rice, the population fell to 117,000 in the following year. By 1935, it had dropped to 105,000. In 1931, the Vietnamese population of the city was 75,800; by 1935, it was down to 67,500. Many migrants who had come to the city in search of work abandoned it for the countryside. Many Chinese also left the city: Their number fell from 28,700 in 1931 to 17,300 in 1933. The city of Chợ Lớn became a ghost town, its population peaking at 193,000 in 1929 before falling to 88,000 in 1933.[59] During the Depression, the floating population of the poor in Saigon withdrew from the city to the countryside when the opportunities for work vanished.

As the Great Depression gripped Saigon, Félix found himself jobless and steadily going broke. He entreated the colonial authorities to return him to his former position at the Customs and Excise Service. He petitioned the head of the service, the governor general, the minister of colonies, and even his cousin, the chief constable in Paris, to intercede on his behalf. But the administration rebuffed his requests: The Customs and Excise Service had been forced to reduce the number of its employees during the economic crisis and to suspend its recruitment of all European personnel.[60]

After the military, the colonial administration was the largest employer in French Indochina. At the end of the nineteenth century, aspiring French civil servants like Félix could join the administration without difficulty. After they were decommissioned, many soldiers from the Tonkin campaign entered the civil service to help govern the new territory. Between 1900 and 1905, the administration expanded dramatically following the reforms of Governor General Paul Doumer, with the establishment of the Customs and Excise Service; the Departments of Public Works, Agriculture, and Trade; and the Post and Telegraph as well as the elaboration of the colonial bureaucracy. The administration recruited hundreds of French functionaries to its lower levels, functionaries who often had little education, experience, or aptitude for their new positions, French functionaries like Félix.[61]

But from the first decades of the twentieth century, a growing number of Vietnamese in Cochinchina had begun to receive a French education. After World War I, the number of schools teaching French and modern subjects in the colony expanded rapidly. In 1920, there were 916 elementary schools, 33 full primary schools, and 4 upper primary schools in the colony educating 56,568 students. By 1929, there were 1,350 elementary schools, 112 full primary schools, and 5 upper primary schools teaching 127,211 students. While expansion was greatest at the lowest levels and only a small proportion of the total number of children attended such schools, a growing number of Vietnamese students in Cochinchina received a modern education. The primary school leaving examination was the minimum necessary qualification for a job as a teacher or as a secretary in the colonial administration. It tested fluency in both French and romanized Vietnamese as well as ability in history, geography, mathematics, and science. In 1921–1922, 814 students in Cochinchina passed the examination; in 1928–1929, 2,351 students passed.[62]

Many of these educated Vietnamese took up work in the colonial administration, displacing French functionaries from its bottom rungs who were costlier to employ.[63] In 1915, Vietnamese, Cambodians, and Laotians occupied 80 percent of the positions in the colonial administration, but by 1932, that figure was 87 percent. Although the number of positions occupied by Europeans grew in absolute terms between 1915 and 1932, such positions comprised a diminishing proportion of the total administrative personnel. During the Great Depression, the number of Europeans in the civil service fell by 20 percent overall. Vietnamese employees took their place.[64] Similar trends no doubt prevailed in private employment: French-educated Vietnamese increasingly occupied positions that had once been held exclusively by Europeans. By the 1920s and 1930s, there were fewer and fewer positions in Saigon for French colonists of modest means and abilities such as Félix. The humble French inhabitants of Saigon had little capital to invest in private commerce and insufficient education to enter the liberal professions. Many of those who arrived in the city and were unable to join the administration—or later lost their positions in it—struggled to maintain a European lifestyle. Some, like Félix, faced genuine poverty and destitution.

Unable to return to the civil service or to find permanent work, Félix tried his hand at various jobs to scratch out a living, seldom staying for long at any one of them: He trafficked in narcotics, he managed a newspaper, he acted as an intermediary between Vietnamese who wanted to buy and sell property, and he even collected and sold old newspapers. And like many of the poorest inhabitants of the city, he sometimes turned to crime. The first time the authorities prosecuted him it was for using false documents, but the court eventually found him not guilty after the statute of limitations on the charge had expired. The second time that Félix appeared before the court he had to pay a fine of one hundred francs for operating an illegal gambling den, although the court eventually suspended the fine on appeal. But crime and intermittent joblessness appear to have been symptoms of a more chronic problem.

Félix had become addicted to opium. Many Europeans in Saigon used the drug from time to time. There were probably close to a thousand occasional opium smokers among Europeans in the city in 1937. Fewer seem to have smoked opium habitually, however—only two or three hundred in the same year. The proportion of Europeans who used the drug in Saigon had gradually declined as living conditions in the city improved, from 25 percent in the years immediately after the conquest to less than 10 percent at the end of the 1930s. The typical consequences of opium addiction were usually fairly mundane: The time spent smoking and its ill effects—numbness, a sense of euphoria and detachment, a loss of appetite, drowsiness, vomiting, profuse sweating, increased urination, and difficulty seeing—all made it difficult for addicts to seek a permanent wage and to provide for themselves. The colonial government forbade Europeans to enter opium dens.[65] But there were other ways to obtain it.

Félix went to pathetic, even perverse, lengths to secure a supply of opium. In April 1929, he had recognized Jean André Colonna d'Istria as his son. But Félix was not Jean's father. Jean had been born Diệp Ngọc Danh in the province of Gia Định on December 15, 1927. His father was Diệp Ngọc Huồn, a merchant in Gò Vấp and friend of Félix. Diệp Ngọc Huồn wished the benefits of French citizenship for his son, and Félix desired a supply of opium. The two made an exchange—the legal recognition of Diệp Ngọc Danh for a quantity of opium. Félix gave the name Jean to his newly recognized son—"Jean" in French and "Danh" in Vietnamese can sound alike. Félix does not seem to have played the role of father to young Jean, who remained with Diệp Ngọc Huồn, which was probably for the best.[66]

Opium could also help palliate the chafing of intimate entanglements between Europeans and Vietnamese. The Vietnamese author and journalist Vũ Trọng Phụng related the story of one Corporal Dimitov, a "hero of the Karenski government" following the February Revolution in Russia. Dimitov had eventually become a legionnaire and had lived in Tonkin for five years. As Vũ Trọng Phụng told the tale, among the three hundred legionnaires posted at Thị Cầu, in Bắc Ninh province, "one man might have poked a knife in the soft white neck of a faithless woman. Another might have shot his mother in the chest for cuckolding his father. And another might have stabbed a few guys to death who were against the party." Like Dimitov, they had enlisted and arrived in Indochina "in order to look for what remained of life or to forget" the life they had left behind. According to Vũ Trọng Phụng, "A legionnaire who had been a petty murderer in days gone by had at least been a tiger. He usually had guts and remarkable gall. But when he married a Vietnamese woman, the mighty and exalted tiger fell upon evil times." Such unions were often miserable and they were frequently violent: Vietnamese women had made an "industry of marrying Europeans" not out of love but lust for money.[67] Dimitov had had fourteen wives since he arrived in Tonkin. "All fourteen of them cheated on me, in different ways, and under different circumstances," he complained dejectedly to Vũ Trọng Phụng. Desolate and dissolute, Dimitov had turned to opium, and the grisly monotony of his romantic life gradually gave way to the tragic monotony of opium addiction.[68]

Opium had also been a tragedy for François Gevin, a poor Frenchman who lived on the streets of Saigon with Félix. François worked at several jobs after leaving school at the age of sixteen: as a student draughtsman in Marseille, as an apprentice cook at a hotel in St. Cyr de Mer, as a pastry chef aboard the ships of several lines, and as a cook for the Messageries Maritimes. In 1932, François left his position aboard the SS *Général Metzinger* to become a chef at the Palace Hotel in Saigon. He kept his new job for only seven months; after a short time in Saigon, François had become addicted to opium. François spent four short months at his next job, stocking shelves at a bar called La Pagode on the corner of Catinat Street and Bonard Boulevard. For nearly two years, François managed the restaurant of the Committee for Assistance to the Unemployed, but he was eventually dismissed for misusing the committee's funds. In 1936, he worked at the Majestic Hotel for a single month. He lived unmarried with Mademoiselle Louise Marchand, who was also without work. The pair was homeless.[69] And so was Félix.

Many of the poorest French citizens in Saigon in 1937 were not Europeans like Félix and François. They were South Asians. In 1881, France had granted the inhabitants of its South Asian territories—Pondicherry, Karaikal, Chandernagor, Yanaon, and Mahé—a means of obtaining French citizenship through renouncing their native laws and submitting to the French civil code. Only a small number ever did so. Some among them, mainly Tamil speakers from Pondicherry and Karaikal, migrated to Cochinchina, although they probably never comprised more than a fifth of one percent of the population of the colony.[70] In 1937, fewer than one thousand lived in Saigon.[71] The French referred to them as "les Français de l'Inde," and the Vietnamese called them "Tây Đen"—"black Westerners." In the colony they worked in the colonial administration, especially the Customs and Excise Service; in the municipal police force; in clerical positions in French firms; in communal banking; and in the army.[72] But they also figured prominently among the indigent French citizens of the city: More than half of the forty-two police reports filed during the 1937 inquiry into the poor French described *Français de l'Inde* and their families.

Once they lost their jobs, many of the *Français de l'Inde* found it difficult to find work again, especially in the years of the Great Depression. Educated Vietnamese could fill most of the positions they had traditionally occupied. André Aroule, for instance, lived with his Vietnamese wife in a grass hut in an alley opposite the Cầu Kho cemetery on Nguyễn Tấn Nghiệm Street. He had worked at several jobs: at the printing house of André Portail, at a dredging company, and at a French firm where he worked as a clerk. By 1937, he had been out of work for three years. André and his wife lived from the meager proceeds of her sales as a wandering merchant on the streets of Saigon. The authorities had twice prosecuted André for swindling, finding him not guilty on one occasion but fining him 500 francs on another. Paquiry Conjandassamy, however, had no record of criminal conviction. Born in Pondicherry in 1885, he arrived in Saigon at the age of sixteen and established a jewelry business. It went bankrupt in 1928. Despite many efforts, Paquiry was unsuccessful finding work elsewhere. His burden was made all the heavier by the family he had started: In 1937, he had three children aged ten, eight, and four. Joseph Hilaire had two children. He and his family lived on the Chemin des Dames, close to one of the city's "reserved quarters" where prostitution was authorized. Joseph had studied at the Colonial College in Pondicherry before arriving in Saigon in 1905. He had held several responsible positions working as a bailiff and as a clerk until he lost his job in 1926. Joseph had injured his left arm, which made many physical tasks difficult, and his advanced years— he was born in 1879—made it difficult for him to find work. Despite being a year older than Joseph, Sandanassamy Samou never stopped looking for work after losing his job in 1931. He had twelve children: Four were old enough to provide for themselves, but eight under the age of seventeen still lived with their parents; the youngest child was only ten months old. Sandanassamy had arrived in Saigon in 1903. Like Félix, he had worked in print and publishing, first for the newspaper *Le Courrier Saïgonnais* and then for the publisher André Portail in Phnom Penh. He managed another printing house in that city before returning to Saigon where he became the co-proprietor of a printing works that closed in 1929. Sandanassamy spent a short time keeping accounts for the electricity company in the province of Cần Thơ in the Mekong Delta but then did not work after 1931. To feed his family, Sandanassamy relied on the aid of a municipal charity—the Committee for Assistance to the Unemployed.[73] Like many of the other homeless and jobless French residents of Saigon, Félix relied on the committee too.

Each day, the Committee for Assistance to the Unemployed distributed provisions to the jobless at its refectory in the Botanical Gardens. The committee disbursed rice, soup, vegetables, and sometimes a little meat. It had once allotted a ration of bread to the French, until it became too expensive. The French complained when they too started to receive a ration of rice, but not too ardently. Most Vietnamese expressed a preference for receiving uncooked rice, so for reasons of economy, the committee distributed uncooked rice to everyone. It allocated sufficient rations for two meals for its European patrons, but only enough for one meal for the Vietnamese who sought its help. In 1937, the committee budgeted 1,500 piasters each month for provisions: It cost four piasters to feed a European, and two piasters to feed a Vietnamese.[74] The committee always had many mouths to feed: According to its statutes, it provided assistance to "every person, man or woman, citizen, subject, or French protégé, without sufficient resources, who can prove that they are unemployed."[75]

The committee required the unemployed, such as Félix, to conform to few regulations. They needed to have worked in Saigon for at least one year and to have been without work for more than three months before they were eligible for assistance. The committee supported their wives too if they could show that they were legally married or that they had lived in a marital relationship for at least two years. It also provided for their children if the children were legitimate, if they were illegitimate but recognized, or if they had been in the applicant's care for at least two years. The committee published a list in the local press each week of the unemployed who were able to work, organized by skill or specialty. If the unemployed secured a paying job, refused a paying job without good reason, or quit a job without good reason the committee would refuse to provide them with further assistance.[76]

The committee assisted the greatest number of unemployed people during the Great Depression. It helped more than eight hundred individuals in 1933, its first year, including 120 French citizens and almost seven hundred Vietnamese. Four years later, with the economy improved, those numbers had diminished considerably: The committee supported only eighty-six French citizens and 230 Vietnamese in 1937. The committee expected most to find work again, but many were not able to. Of the eighty-six French citizens whom the committee helped, only seven were born in France, fifteen were naturalized Vietnamese, twenty-five were French Indians, and thirty-nine were Eurasian. The committee supposed that there were many more than seven Frenchmen looking for work in Saigon but that they did not yet want to prevail upon the committee for assistance. Of the seven whom the committee did assist, it deemed three capable of eventually finding work, but the other four were too old or too sick to do so. All the naturalized Vietnamese were under forty years of age and had held jobs as mechanics, controllers on the tramway, and toll collectors, among other positions. Many left the ranks of the unemployed from time to time and found work. Fewer than half of the French Indians receiving aid were deemed employable, most being much too old, but the committee considered all its Eurasian patrons young, fit, and able to work. Among the 230 jobless Vietnamese, fifty-two had previously been coolies, forty-one had been cooks, and another thirty had been "boys," or household domestic servants. Several others had been secretaries, mechanics, or drivers as well as guards, stone cutters, carpenters, and boiler men. Sixty were too old, and another twenty were too ill to work.[77]

The committee came to the aid of many poor French citizens, like Félix, who might never work again. Pierre Durand arrived in the colony as a soldier in 1931. He married in 1933, and the military decommissioned him in 1935. Pierre took up work on the tramways but was laid off in 1936 when the company was forced to reduce its personnel. He was physically weak and lacked any kind of special skills, making it difficult to find a job. With two small children to provide for, he turned to the committee for assistance. René Boyer d'Eguilles also had to find some way to feed his Vietnamese wife and his four children. René arrived in Indochina in 1922 and worked as a fitter and turner for several companies: the railways in Yunnan, a tanning company, a distillery, a forestry enterprise, and a plantation in Biên Hòa, and an automobile sales company in Central Annam. When René lost his job at the beginning of 1937, he turned to the committee for assistance. So did Joseph Trang. Unlike René and Pierre, Joseph had grown up in Cochinchina. His name suggests that he was probably Chinese and also Catholic. He was born in Mỹ Tho in 1908 and studied in Saigon at the Institution Taberd until the age of twenty. After graduating, he worked first as a secretary for an automobile and agriculture company and then as a typist for the colonial agricultural service. But he was soon laid off. By 1937, he had been out of work for six years. By then, Ponnoussamy Ponnou had not had a job in eight years. Born in the French *comptoir* of Karaikal in 1886, Ponnoussamy arrived in Saigon at the age of nineteen. He worked as a salesman at various companies in the city, ending up at the Maison Jules Berthet in 1910, which later became Carrière-Dufourg and Garriguence. He worked there for eighteen years, except for the years from 1915 to 1919, which he spent in the army. In 1928, Ponnoussamy left for Karaikal for a year and discovered when he returned to Saigon in 1929 that Carrière-Dufourg and Garriguence had gone bankrupt. Despite a record of excellent service, he was unable to find work. As the years went by, Ponnoussamy found it harder and harder to support his wife and five children in their house on Farinolle Street, just a short distance from the municipal park and the governor's palace. There were fewer jobs for French citizens that educated Vietnamese could not also do for lower wages. The Committee for Assistance to the Unemployed provided the family with food and clothing while Ponnoussamy looked for work.[78]

The committee was a late addition to the institutions in Saigon. At the turn of the twentieth century, characters such as Pierre Durand, René Boyer d'Eguilles, and Félix Colonna d'Istria would have found food and lodging at the Saigon Central Prison. There were few other places for indigent Europeans to shelter in Saigon, only a pavilion in the municipal gardens, beneath the canopy of the Central Market, or under the generous eaves of a colonial store front. In 1902, the municipal authorities set aside a room in the Central Prison to house poor Europeans while they looked for work or waited for the next steamer to take them home. The prison fed and housed them, and the indigents were free to come and go

as they pleased. The prison was meant to provide them with only temporary accommodation, but many stayed for weeks or even months. Some,
for instance, deliberately missed their boats home. Others who had been
former inmates in the prison could not find work and had no money and
nowhere else to go after being released, so they returned to the prison.
Despite being jobless and penniless, the poor Europeans in the prison were
often drunk, and they quarreled, argued, shouted, and sang at all hours of
the day and night. They regularly came to blows and had to be disciplined
by the guards. In 1906, the prison housed thirty-seven European indigents;
by 1907, the number had reached eighty-nine.[79]

The poor Europeans came from across the continent: They were Dutch
from the Netherlands East Indies, Britons from Malaya, or fortune seek-
ers from some other part of Europe who had traveled to Southeast Asia.
Some had been expelled from Indochina's neighboring colonies for various crimes and misdemeanors, but many others arrived with genuine as-
pirations to work. Two masons, a Serbian named Zvetan Yvetokovitch and
a Montenegran named Laboudy Mirovitch, landed in Saigon in 1907 on a
Norwegian steamer from Vladivostok. Their attempts to find work proved
fruitless, and they eventually found themselves destitute. Both ended up
at the Central Prison.[80]

The jailers considered poor Europeans a nuisance, while the other European residents of Saigon regarded them as an embarrassment. It was vital,
a colonial official maintained in 1907, for the Vietnamese inhabitants of
the city to avoid any "view of these Europeans, true vagabonds, whose
scenes of drunkenness and scandal, can only strike a disastrous blow at the
prestige of the white population." That year the administration considered
establishing a refuge for indigent Europeans in the city gardens or at the
municipal dispensary. But the city already had other plans for the gardens,
and the ten beds at the dispensary were meant only for the sick and the
truly needy. And as one official noted, the nurses at the dispensary could
not be expected to guard the rowdy and unruly indigents when jailers at
the prison had difficulty doing so.[81]

The municipal authorities struggled over what to do about the growing
number of poor Europeans in the city. Private charity remained deeply
personal—a few *sous* given to a beggar on the streets or room and lodging
to a homeless friend. The city paid for the hospitalization of the weakest

and the sickest Europeans, and it met the costs of repatriating those exhausted by the climate or in a state of extreme destitution.[82] But the city took such steps only in exceptional circumstances. For the more mundane needs of indigent Europeans, Saigon had an annual discretionary fund of only four thousand piasters to distribute. While there had been poor Europeans in Saigon in the past, by 1913 the poverty had become endemic. The city found that ad hoc disbursements from its discretionary fund had little palliative effect. First, once divided among the many Europeans who sought assistance, the fund proved too meager. Second, the city knew very little about those needing assistance. When it received a request, the city charged the police with gathering further information about the poor. But the details the police collected were often sketchy or incomplete. It was difficult to sort out the facts from the distortions, evasions, and fabrications. And the city did not keep meticulous records of those it had helped from one year to the next. When confronted by a Frenchman complaining of hunger, such inquiries seemed callous and unnecessary. Third, many indigent Europeans did not use the money they received wisely. Some spent it at the theater or at the casino, while all too many used it to get drunk. The city often dispensed alms to those it considered undeserving. By 1913, the disbursements had become expensive, haphazard, and ineffective.[83] But Saigon had a model it could emulate: In France, each town or city had a municipal office of charity that assisted the poor and the needy. It raised funds, identified the truly needy, and distributed alms among them. In 1914, Saigon established its own office of charity.

The Office of Charity changed the way the city assisted poor Europeans and those with French citizenship. When such a needy individual applied for assistance, the office investigated to establish their particulars and the degree of their need. If they were found deserving, the office then determined the quantity and duration of the assistance it would provide and entered the name of each indigent into a register. The register had three categories: those the office would assist continuously, such as the chronically ill and the elderly; those it would help temporarily, such as the bereaved, the sick, and the unemployed; and those it would repatriate to their country of origin. The office distributed alms in the form of food, medicine, clothing, and blankets. It very rarely provided monetary assistance. The office had several sources of revenue: the interest on investments; subventions from the budgets of Saigon and Cochinchina; gifts from donors, annual collections, subscriptions, bequests, and other donations; proceeds from the sale and rental of property; and loans from banks and the colonial government.[84] Over the next thirty years, the Office of Charity used this revenue to assist thousands of needy French people in Saigon.

The number of needy rose and fell with the economic fortunes of the city and the colony. In its early years, many poor French in Saigon were ignorant of the office's existence. The long application process and investigation into the cause of their want discouraged many poor French from seeking help. In 1915, the office received forty-eight requests for assistance. It rejected two because the applicants had not resided in Saigon for at least a year and a further eight because it judged the applicants to be insufficiently needy. The office repatriated thirty-two people: eight to France, nineteen to Pondicherry, and five to the island of Réunion. In the following year, the office received twenty-seven requests, of which it rejected four. At the end of 1915, it was providing continuous assistance to twenty-two residents of Saigon. Twenty-four people had applied to the office to be repatriated that year, and twenty were successful: Eight went to Marseille, four to Colombo, and eight to Pondicherry. Over the next five years, the number of requests for assistance grew steadily and peaked during the slump in 1920 and 1921. In 1920, 171 poor French applied for aid or repatriation; 146 were successful. The office repatriated four people to Marseille and twenty-four to Pondicherry. At the end of the year, it listed 107 people in its registers, of whom sixty-four received long-term or temporary relief. In 1922, the year after the slump, the number of people seeking assistance fell to 112, sixteen of whom sought repatriation. But by year's end the total number of people receiving aid from the Office of Charity on a long-term basis had grown to 133. Then, during the Roaring Twenties, as the rice export economy boomed, the number of poor French who received long-term assistance declined. In 1928, on the eve of the Great Depression, the office received only fifty-nine new applications for assistance. It listed 150 people in its register at the end of the year, along with fifty-nine children. But it gave long-term relief to only 104 people. As the Great Depression shook the colony over the next several years, the Office of Charity assisted a growing number of distressed French families. In 1930, 130 people applied to the office for relief or repatriation. A total of 198 men and women, the parents of 157 children, were receiving help at the end of the year. The number of poor French did not diminish as trade began to expand again and the economy improved after the initial slump. At the end of the decade the figures were discouraging: In 1939, another 138 poor French people requested assistance from the Office of Charity. In total, it helped 288 adults and 448 children that year. Of the adults, fully 275 were women. Only seven people applied to be repatriated in 1939, none of them to France. The available documents record no request for repatriation from Félix Colonna d'Istria.[85]

Félix's story has an almost picaresque quality. He was the illegitimate son of a Corsican noble family and was naturally endowed with seemingly modest talents. After serving in the French army in Algeria, he went to Indochina to seek his fortune. He worked for the colonial administration and for various private companies, and he even started his own newspaper. But Félix became an opium addict and a scoundrel. Unable to keep a permanent job, he moved from one disreputable pursuit to the next, fell afoul of the law, and ended up as a recipient of public charity. His story is best understood in the changing context of the colonial situation.[86] Many Vietnamese migrants, like Lương Thị Lắm and Trần Văn Lang, sought better opportunities in the expanding export economy of colonial Saigon but ended up doing makeshift work of one kind or other. But after World War I, a small but growing number of educated Vietnamese entered the colonial administration and private employment. This left fewer positions for Frenchmen of limited abilities such as Félix to occupy, and during the Great Depression the situation became acute. The documents do not record a happy homecoming for this prodigal son of Corsica. After 1937, Félix no longer appears in any archival documents. The thread of his story frays at the end.[87]

On the eve of World War II, poor French made up some several hundred of the city's residents. But they were still comparatively few: in 1939, they made up not more than 5 percent of the French population of Saigon/Chợ Lớn and only 0.1 percent of its total population.[88] Poor Frenchmen like Félix were a tiny minority among an already small group. But that tiny minority could still pose a large threat to French prestige. Figures such as Félix illustrate the diversity and complexity of the French community in colonial Saigon, which was deeply divided by competing cultural allegiances, political frictions, and varying levels of prosperity.[89] Frenchmen in positions of political or economic power have figured prominently in the historical record: governors of Cochinchina such as Charles Le Myre de Vilers, Ernest Outrey, and Maurice Cognacq; writers and publishers like Paul Monin, J. A. Marx, and André Portail; and traders such as the merchants Alfred, Emile, and Gustave Denis; the importer Louis Ogliastro; and the rice exporter Eugène Ville. But the colonial archives also preserve the stories of the many poor and powerless French people who struggled to make ends meet in Saigon in a rapidly changing colonial situation: the criminal and uncorrectable Edouard Morin; the unemployed and unemployable Mademoiselle Marcelle Fix; the suicidal and senescent Monsieur Lacquement; and the weak and convalescent Ernest Costa, among many others.[90] No statues were built in their honor, their names never adorned any of the streets or squares of the city, and they were never feted for their bravery or their achievements—like so many others who spent their lives down and out in Saigon.

EPILOGUE

It blows and rains enough to make you sick.
And thinking of the world, you feel damn sad.
Dung stinks in baskets—lasses carry it.
Coins smell like garbage—fellows covet them.
Chinks grope in girlies' pants and paw soft thighs.
Bushmen, amid green woods, climb cassia trees.
What's going on in cities that's great fun?
Some farces—comics don their caps and gowns.
—*Tản Đà, "The State of the World"*[1]

In 1940, the northern Vietnamese journalist Vũ Xuân Tự went to Saigon to report on economic and social life in the city.[2] Saigon was renowned in the north for its prosperity, but few there knew very much else about it. It had been home to rich men such as Lê Phát Đạt, a wealthy landowner; the administrator, landlord, and comprador, Đỗ Hữu Phương; Lý Tường Quan, who had made his fortune as a comprador; and the affluent proprietor, Trần Trinh Trạch, who owned vast tracts of land in Cochinchina. Saigon attracted those with commercial talents who came to the city to make their fortunes. But it also beckoned to the poor and the ragged, who sought to make their lives in the city in countless different ways.[3] The travelogue *One Month in Cochinchina,* by the journalist Phạm Quỳnh, and *The*

Influence of the Chinese and the Problem of Migration, by the journalist Đào Trinh Nhất, described life in Saigon for northern audiences, but they had both been written many years earlier.[4] Since then, the Great Depression and the outbreak of war in Europe yet again had shaped the city. And so Vũ Xuân Tự wanted to discover for his readers if the "Pearl of the Orient" continued to retain its luster. His discussion of southern manners and mores is sometimes piquant and at other times facetious, but his pointillist description of Saigon on the eve of the Pacific War is vivid and arresting.

The rice trade had made Saigon wealthy and attracted migrants from near and far. The city reached the height of its prosperity in the years between 1926 and 1930, when the price of rice peaked. There was plenty of work in the city, but too few workers to do it, Vũ Xuân Tự recorded. Even fashionable department stores on Charner Boulevard had to fill positions with barely literate applicants and appoint clerks who had hardly any education. In those years, proprietors had to treat workers well because they were in such great demand. The supply of labor was so short that employers in some professions had to request that workers be recruited to Saigon from the north. The competition for workers was so intense that one proprietor had taken to meeting workers arriving from Tonkin at the port to prevent them from being poached by rival employers.[5] But that was before the Great Depression. In 1930, the prices of rice and rubber, the main exports from the port of Saigon, dropped precipitously. "The scene in Saigon suddenly became shabby. Businesses could not find customers, despite specially lowering their prices," Vũ Xuân Tự noted. Many people lost their homes, especially on Sabourain and Hamelin streets, where twenty or thirty houses in a row had been consistently empty for five or six years during the slump. Prosperity finally returned in 1938 when rice and rubber fetched high prices again on the world market.

Saigon attracted migrants from the length of French Indochina, across the Bay of Bengal, and from the coast of southern China. Vietnamese from Cochinchina initially worked in industrial and commercial enterprises owned by Chinese and South Asians, and they dominated the professions in Saigon, working as civil servants in the colonial administration, as clerks in private companies, or as medical doctors. Over time, a growing Vietnamese commercial class established banks, soap factories, and rice mills and erected impressive buildings in the city.[6] Migrants from

northern Annam, who began to arrive in the city around 1920, were com-
monplace by 1930. They labored assiduously so that they could send regular sums of money home.[7] Hardship in densely populated Tonkin led many
northern Vietnamese to seek their fortunes in the south during the 1920s
and in the years following the Great Depression. After the completion of
the railroad linking Hà Nội to Saigon in 1936 their number grew considerably. According to Vũ Xuân Tự, "Saigon became a second province of
Hà Nội." Northern Vietnamese engaged in every kind of commerce, licit
and illicit: from selling northern embroidery, French lace, and silk from Hà
Đông to smuggling, trafficking in persons, and prostitution. Vietnamese
from Tonkin owned nearly all of the stationery stores, tailor's shops, mil-
liner's shops, luggage suppliers, and furniture stores in colonial Saigon.
They also sold delicacies to hungry northern workers, such as pig's tripe
soup and curdled duck blood, which had yet to seduce the palates of those
from the center and the south. Far from their native place, they established a number of mutual aid associations to provide assistance to one
another in times of need and want. Southern Vietnamese knew little of
the literature and journalism written in the north before the appearance
of periodicals such as *Phụ Nữ Tân Văn* (*Women's News*), *Thần Chung* (*Morning
Bell*), and *Đuốc Nhà Nam* (*Torch of the Southern Homeland*). The first northern
journal to attract the attention of readers in the south was the newspaper
Phong Hóa (*Mores*), which featured a cartoon presenting the misadventures
of the hapless rustic Lý Toét in the rapidly changing capital.[8] There were
also South Asians who lived in Saigon separately from the Vietnamese,
worshipped their own gods in their own temples, ate their own food, and
often trucked, bartered, and traded among themselves. There were those
from the French concessions in India who had taken French citizenship,
joined the military, and enjoyed the same rights as the French; migrants
from Bengal who worked as wardens and guards over administrative offices and private homes; cloth merchants, clad in dhotis and fezzes, who
sold their wares in stores on the main commercial streets of the city and
in bazaars; merchants from Bombay who sold silk near the central market;
and Chettiars from Tamil Nadu who lent money to Vietnamese at sometimes extortionate rates.[9] Additionally, there were Chinese capitalists
who had become extraordinarily wealthy through industry, commerce,
and real estate; petty Chinese merchants who sold small goods and sun-

dries, such as Chinese medicine, canned goods, and fruits and vegetables, in their stores or market stalls; secondhand merchants and rag and bone men who bought and sold scrap and junk; Chinese restaurateurs who prepared traditional dishes for the wealthy and those of more modest means; those who provided roadside drinks and refreshments for the busy populace; those who sold cigarettes, tobacco, and opium to the poor and working masses; and those who worked as clerks and secretaries in banks and French and Chinese commercial houses, large and small.[10] The rice trade had helped make colonial Saigon a colorful mosaic of peoples.

The city was also a "paradise of the poor," according to Vũ Xuân Tự. It attracted the down and out from the north, the center, and the south of French Indochina. It was easier than elsewhere to earn a living in Saigon. In the north, the poor typically had two enemies: hunger and, in the winter, cold. But in Saigon, people only had to combat hunger because it was warm throughout the year. In the south, "the masses never attach too much importance to what people wear," Vũ Xuân Tự noted. "There are many people with a simple outward appearance but who have a lot of money in their pocket," he wrote.[11] There was no shortage of food in the south as there was in the north, so the deeper one's pockets, the more one could eat one's fill. In Saigon, labor was expensive, but many goods were cheaper than in other parts of French Indochina. This meant that the working poor were comparatively well off. The poor could have coffee at breakfast, tea at lunch, and iced water in the evenings—libations they could never have expected elsewhere. Even the police in Saigon were more lenient, Vũ Xuân Tự thought.[12]

At the beginning of September 1939, France declared war against Germany. "Saigon was somewhat shaken," Vũ Xuân Tự observed. But compared with Hà Nội in the north and Huế in the center, Saigon stood steadfast. People were alarmed, but they did not abandon commerce or industry. "Little by little they returned to spending vast sums of money with little regard for tomorrow," the journalist wrote.[13] At the beginning of the war, as much as half of the trade of French Indochina was with France. In 1939, Cochinchina had exported 1.6 million tons of rice, and in the following year it exported a little over 1.4 million tons.[14] But at the end of 1941, the war in Europe severed trade between Cochinchina and France, which had been the main destination for rice from Saigon since the beginning of the

Great Depression. Saigon had to turn once again to the markets of East and Southeast Asia for the sale of its products and for its provisioning, but this time it turned to Japan rather than southern China. Japanese forces had advanced into southern Indochina in July 1941. A military agreement in December made Japan responsible for the defense of the south. By that time, Saigon had become the headquarters of Japan's Southern Expeditionary Army Group, commanded by General Terauchi Hisaichi. In March 1941, the French and Japanese had signed treaties that governed trade and shipping and the role of Japanese firms in Indochina, which were supplemented by later agreements. During the Pacific War, Japan was Saigon's most important market. As the war progressed, transportation between Cochinchina and Japan became increasingly difficult, and rice exports plummeted. In 1941, Saigon sent 870,000 tons of paddy, rice, and flour abroad, the smallest quantity in decades, with 585,000 tons destined for Japan; in 1942, it exported 990,000 tons; and in 1943, 1,048,000 tons.[15] As the economy deteriorated, the combined population of Saigon and Chợ Lớn grew from 449,000 in 1941 to 498,000 in 1943, as safety and security rather than economic opportunity became a growing concern for migrants to the city.[16] If the regional rice trade had once set the rhythms of economic life in colonial Saigon, those rhythms would become scarcely audible beneath the cacophony of violence, war, and disorder that marred French Indochina and then Vietnam in the decades after 1940.[17]

The history of colonial Saigon—part personal, part political, part economic, and part social—does not flow like the Đồng Nai River catching up its tributaries as it heads toward Gành Rái Bay, but as larger and smaller streams, canals and arroyos winding across Gia Định province, merging in one place and dividing again in another. It is not a single history but many histories, not a single story but many stories. There is order to the colonial past, but not regularity; patterns but not predictability: it is the order of the traffic circle on Rigault de Genouilly Square, continuously traversed by rickshaws, carriages, and automobiles headed in *toutes directions,* or of the Central Market, filled with customers cutting paths among jostling crowds, heckling merchants, and buckling tables burdened with merchandise.[18]

The stories of the poor are necessarily short stories. The documentary trail typically ends unceremoniously, even abruptly. On February 10, 1907, the prostitute Lương Thị Lắm rejoined her father after spending two hundred days in the municipal dispensary in Saigon. The Hakka mason Trần Dưỡng boarded the steamer *Kimchow* on September 14, 1916, forced to return to China. The colonial government expelled the rickshaw puller who called himself Nguyễn Văn Thủ from Cochinchina in December of 1922 and sent him back to Bình Định province. The twice-orphaned Aimée Lahaye had her contract at the hospital in Phnom Penh extended by three months on March 6, 1928. On November 21, 1930, the invalid Trần Văn Chinh languished in the hospice at Phú Mỹ after spending many years begging on the streets of Saigon. And in July 1937, the poor Frenchman, Félix Colonna d'Istria, received ongoing help from the Committee for Assistance to the Unemployed. Brief, fragmentary sources cut short the stories of these poor residents of colonial Saigon.

Such stories as can be told are melancholy and often grim, but they do not depict uniform misery or privation. The colonial past is not sepia-toned or monochromatic, and the urban poor were much more than an anonymous crowd. The stories in this book testify to the ingenuity and individuality of the poor in colonial Saigon: a prostitute from Biên Hòa who tried to evade the colonial authorities and confinement in jail and the municipal dispensary; a Chinese mason in Saigon's hinterland who used the judicial system to fight against calumny and exploitation by his former employers; a migrant from Bình Định who sought work in the Mekong Delta, cut wood, labored on a rubber plantation, and went by an alias so that he could pull a rickshaw through the city and eke out a living; a Eurasian woman who grew up in an orphanage, became orphaned again as an adult, and was forced to rely on the bonds of friendship to survive and the benevolence of the minister of colonies to return to her home; a laborer from Gia Định who worked in a print shop, became an incurable invalid, and begged on the streets of Saigon for more than a decade before convalescing in a hospice run by the Sisters of Saint Paul de Chartres; and a French civil servant who worked for the Customs and Excise Service, started a newspaper, and adopted a Vietnamese son to help satisfy an opium addiction, before living off of public charity. Such stories illustrate above all just how rich and varied, how dappled and piebald, were the experiences of poverty and colonial rule in Saigon.

NOTES

Abbreviations

Annales	*Annales de l'Oeuvre de la Sainte Enfance*
ANOM	Archives Nationales d'Outre-Mer, Aix-en-Provence
ASMEP	Archives de la Société des Missions Etrangères de Paris, Paris
EE II	Dossiers de Personnel
GGI	Fonds du Gouvernement Général de l'Indochine
GOUCOCH	Fonds du Gouvernement de la Cochinchine
GOUCOCH DIVERS	Fonds du Gouvernement de la Cochinchine Divers
GUERNUT	Fonds de la Commission d'Enquête dans les Territoires d'Outre-Mer (Commission Guernut)
INDO AF	Indochine, Ancien Fonds
INDO NF	Indochine, Nouveau Fonds
RST NF	Résidence Supérieure du Tonkin, Nouveau Fonds
SL	Services Locaux
TTLTQG-I	Trung Tâm Lưu Trữ Quốc Gia I [Vietnam National Archives Center I, Hà Nội]
TTLTQG-II	Trung Tâm Lưu Trữ Quốc Gia II [Vietnam National Archives Center II, Hồ Chí Minh City]

Prologue

1. Huỳnh Sanh Thông, ed. and trans., *An Anthology of Vietnamese Poems: From the Eleventh through the Twentieth Centuries* (New Haven, Conn.: Yale University Press, 1996), 356.

2. André Baudrit, *Guide historique des rues de Saigon* (Saigon: S.I.L.I., 1945), 85–87.

3. "Mr. E Chenieux, Propriétaire, 92 rue d'Arfeuille à Saigon, à Monsieur Lecoeur, Commissaire Central de Police," February 2, 1913; "Monsieur le Commissaire Central de Police à Monsieur le Gouverneur de la Cochinchine," February 10, 1913. GOUCOCH, V.10/04.02, TTLTQG-II.

4. See *Affaire du Complot de Saigon: Acte d'Accusation* (1913), 7–8, GGI 65527, ANOM; INDO NF 28(1), ANOM.

5. See the valuable press account in *Courrier Saïgonnais*, November 5, 1913. For archival documentation on the rebellion, see GGI 65527, ANOM; INDO NF 28(1), ANOM; and INDO NF 606, ANOM. The rebellion also quickly entered into popular verse. See, for example, the long Vietnamese poem telling the story of the rebellion based on newspaper reports: Đặng Lễ Nghi, *Thơ Phan Xích Long* [The poem of Phan Xích Long] (Saigon: Imprimerie de l'Union, 1914).

6. For Vietnamese-language accounts of the rebellion, see Trần Huy Liệu, *Lịch Sử Tám Mươi Năm Chống Pháp*, vol. 1, [A history of eighty years opposing the French] (Hà Nội: Văn Sử Địa, 1957), 180; Vương Hồng Sển, *Sài Gòn Năm Xưa* [Saigon in the past] (Saigon: Khai Trí, [1969]), 252–253; Việt Lâm, "Một Ít Tài Liệu Về Cuộc Khởi Nghĩa Phan Xích Long Ở Nam Kỳ Năm 1913," [A few documents on the Phan Xích Long uprising in Cochinchina in 1913] *Nghiên Cứu Lịch Sử* [Historical research] 38 (1962): 19–21, 30. For Western-language scholarship on the rebellion, see Georges Coulet, *Les sociétés secrètes en terre d'Annam* (Saigon: C. Ardin, 1926), 49–73, 202–207, 216–217, 265–270; R. B. Smith, "The Development of Opposition to French Rule in Southern Vietnam 1880–1940," *Past and Present* 54 (1972): 104–107; David G. Marr, *Vietnamese Anticolonialism, 1885-1925* (Berkeley: University of California Press, 1971), 221–223. Hue-Tam Ho Tai, *Millenarianism and Peasant Politics in Colonial Vietnam* (Cambridge, Mass.: Harvard University Press, 1983), 69–76.

7. On the political history of Vietnam, particularly during the French colonial period, see, *inter alia*, Joseph Buttinger, *Vietnam: A Political History* (New York: Praeger, 1968); William Duiker, *The Rise of Nationalism in Vietnam, 1900-1941* (Ithaca, N.Y.: Cornell University Press, 1976); idem, *The Communist Road to Power in Vietnam*, 2nd ed. (Boulder, Colo.: Westview Press, 1996); idem, *Ho Chi Minh* (New York: Hyperion, 2000); Huỳnh Kim Khánh, *Vietnamese Communism, 1925-1945* (Ithaca, N.Y.: Cornell University Press, 1982); Marr, *Vietnamese Anticolonialism*; Sophie Quinn-Judge, *Ho Chi Minh: The Missing Years, 1919-1941* (Berkeley: University of California Press, 2002); Hue-Tam Ho Tai, *Radicalism and the Origins of the Vietnamese Revolution* (Cambridge, Mass.: Harvard University Press, 1992); Alexander Woodside, *Community and Revolution in Modern Vietnam* (Boston, Mass.: Houghton Mifflin, 1976). Van Nguyen-Marshall has examined dif-

ferent discourses on poverty during the colonial period, primarily in what is now northern Vietnam, in *In Search of Moral Authority: The Discourse on Poverty, Poor Relief, and Charity in French Colonial Vietnam* (New York: Peter Lang, 2008). This book focuses instead on the experiences of poverty in what is now southern Vietnam.

8. For a general narrative of the history of Saigon during the colonial period, see Trần Văn Giàu, "Lược Sử Thành Phố Sài Gòn Từ Khi Pháp Xâm Chiếm (1859) Đến Tháng 4 Năm 1975," [A brief history of Saigon from the French invasion (1859) to April 1975] in *Địa Chí Văn Hóa Thành Phố Hồ Chí Minh* [Encyclopedia of Hồ Chí Minh City], vol. 1, ed. Trần Văn Giàu and Trần Bạch Đằng (Hồ Chí Minh City: Thành Phố Hồ Chí Minh, 1998), esp. 312–407. Perhaps the most important work on the history of Saigon published in the Republic of Vietnam is Vương Hồng Sển, *Sài Gòn Năm Xưa.* See also his subsequent addition to that work, *Sài Gòn Tạp Pín Lù* [Saigon hodge-podge] (Biên Hòa: Tổng Hợp Đồng Nai, 2005). Other useful works include Huỳnh Minh, *Gia Định Xưa* [Gia Định in the past] (Hồ Chí Minh City: Văn Hóa-Thông Tin, 2006); Sơn Nam, *Đất Gia Định-Bến Nghé Xưa & Người Sài Gòn* [The lands of Gia Định and Bến Nghé in the past and the people of Saigon] (Hồ Chí Minh City: Trẻ, 2004); Nguyễn Đình Đầu, *Tổng Kết Nghiên Cứu Địa Bạ Nam Kỳ Lục Tỉnh* [Summary of research on the cadastral registers of the six provinces of Cochinchina] (Hồ Chí Minh City: Thành Phố Hồ Chí Minh, 1994); idem, *Nghiên Cứu Địa Bạ Triều Nguyễn: Gia Định* [Research on the cadastral registers of the Nguyễn Dynasty: Gia Định] (Hồ Chí Minh City: Thành Phố Hồ Chí Minh, 1994). The most important Western study of the history of Saigon focuses on radical politics during the 1930s. See Daniel Hémery, *Révolutionnaires vietnamiens et pouvoir colonial en Indochine: Communistes, trotskystes, nationalistes à Saigon de 1932 à 1937* (Paris: François Maspero, 1975). On the history of Hà Nội, see Philippe Papin, *Histoire de Hanoi* (Paris: Fayard, 2001); idem, *Histoire des territoires de Hà Nội: Quartiers, villages et sociétés urbaines du XIXe au début du XXe siècle* (Paris: Indes Savantes, 2013); William S. Logan, *Hanoi: Biography of a City* (Seattle: University of Washington Press, 2000). And on the history of Đà Lạt, see Eric T. Jennings, *Imperial Heights: Dalat and the Making and Undoing of French Indochina* (Berkeley: University of California Press, 2011).

9. On the poor, particularly the unemployed, as members of a reserve army of labor, see Karl Marx, *Capital,* vol. 1, trans. Ben Fowkes (London: Penguin, 2004), ch. 25. On the "road to revolution," see Nguyễn Ái Quốc, "Đường Kách Mệnh" [The road to revolution], in *Các Tổ Chức Tiền Thân Của Đảng* [Organizational Predecessors of the Party], ed. Đảng Cộng Sản Việt Nam (Hà Nội: Ban Nghiên Cứu Lịch Sử Đảng Trung Ương, 1977), 15–81. For examples of the appropriation of the history of the poor by Vietnamese communist historians, see Trần Văn Giàu, *Giai Cấp Công Nhân Việt Nam: Sự Hình Thành Và Sự Phát Triển Của Nó Từ Giai Cấp "Tự Mình" Đến Giai Cấp "Cho Mình"* [The Vietnamese working class: Its appearance and development from a class "in itself" to a class "for itself"] (Hà Nội: Sự Thật, 1961); and Ban Sử Liên Hiệp Công Đoàn Thành Phố Hồ Chí Minh, *Công Nhân Sài Gòn Trong Sự Nghiệp Giải Phóng Dân Tộc* [Saigon workers in the task of national liberation] (Hồ Chí Minh City: Thành Phố Hồ Chí Minh, 1986).

10. The published memoirs of the revolutionary Nguyễn Trung Nguyệt, also known as Bảo Lương, have illustrated the value of a "biographical" approach to Vietnamese social history. See Hue-Tam Ho Tai, *Passion, Betrayal, and Revolution in Colonial Saigon: The Memoirs of Bao Luong* (Berkeley: University of California Press, 2010). The emphasis in this book on the ability of the poor to creatively adapt has been shaped by John R. W. Smail, "On the Possibility of an Autonomous History of Modern Southeast Asia," in *Autonomous Histories, Particular Truths: Essays in Honor of John Smail*, ed. Laurie Sears (Madison: Center for Southeast Asian Studies, University of Wisconsin-Madison, 1993), 39–70.

11. The relationship in this book between Southeast Asia and the littoral of the South China Sea has been much influenced by Denys Lombard, "Une autre Méditerranée dans le Sud-Est asiatique," *Hérodote* 88 (1988): 184–193. On the significance of the regional rice trade for social change in Southeast Asia, see Christopher Baker, "Economic Reorganization and the Slump in South and Southeast Asia," *Comparative Studies in Society and History* 23, no. 3 (1981): 325–341; and Paul H. Kratoska, "Commercial Rice Cultivation and the Regional Economy of Southeastern Asia, 1850–1950," in *Food and Globalization: Consumption, Markets, and Politics in the Modern World,* ed. Alexander Nützenadel and Frank Trentmann (Oxford: Berg, 2008), 75–90. On the rice trade in colonial Saigon, see Nguyễn Phan Quang, *Thị Trường Lúa Gạo Nam Kỳ, 1860-1945* [The rice market of Cochinchina] (Hồ Chí Minh City: Tổng Hợp TP. Hồ Chí Minh, 2004), which relies on some of the colonial-era studies cited later in this book. On the study of economic lives, see William H. Sewell Jr., "A Strange Career: The Historical Study of Economic Life," *History and Theory* 49, no. 4 (2010): 146–166. On the term *makeshift,* see the discussion in Olwen Hufton, *The Poor of Eighteenth-Century France, 1750-1789* (Oxford: Clarendon Press, 1974), esp. 69-127.

12. The approach to documentary evidence discussed here is adapted from Clifford Geertz, *Local Knowledge: Further Essays in Interpretive Anthropology,* 3rd ed. (New York: Basic Books, 2000), 156. On studying groups of people who "grow up together," see Alfred Schutz, "The Problem of Social Reality," *Collected Papers,* vol. 1, ed. M. Natanson (The Hague: Martinus Nijhoff, 1962), 15–17.

13. For examples of these templates, see A. Belland, *Guide des agents de police de la ville de Saïgon* (Saigon: Impr. Claude, 1897); A. Mouchonière, *Guide des agents de police de la ville de Cholon* (Saigon: Impr. Nguyen-Van-Cua, 1921). For an account of police work in colonial Saigon, see Henri Vermeren, *Un gendarme aux colonies: Madagascar-Indochine, 1895-1907* (Paris: Albin Michel, 2003), 152–165.

14. For some of the problems with using police records as sources for the history of the poor, see Richard Cobb, *The Police and the People: French Popular Protest, 1789-1820* (Oxford: Oxford University Press, 1970), 3–81. The transcripts of Inquisitorial interviews, which have many similarities to police depositions, have been an important source for European historians of the medieval and early modern periods. Two prominent works based on such sources are Carlo Ginzburg, *The Cheese and the Worms: The Cosmos*

of a Sixteenth-Century Miller, trans. John and Anne Tedeschi (Baltimore: Johns Hopkins University Press, 1980); and Emmanuel Le Roy Ladurie, *Montaillou, village occitan de 1294 à 1324* (Paris: Gallimard, 1975). For a discussion of some of the difficulties involved in using Inquisitorial sources, see Carlo Ginzburg, *Clues, Myths, and the Historical Method,* trans. John and Anne Tedeschi (Baltimore: Johns Hopkins University Press, 1989), 156–164; Renato Rosaldo, "From the Door of His Tent: The Fieldworker and the Inquisitor," in *Writing Culture: The Poetics and Politics of Ethnography,* ed. James Clifford and George Marcus (Berkeley: University of California Press, 1986), 77–97. See also Edward Muir and Guido Ruggiero, eds., *History from Crime,* trans. Corrada Biazzo Curry, Margaret A. Gallucci, and Mary M. Gallucci (Baltimore: The Johns Hopkins University Press, 1994). For an influential but problematic approach to using comparable sources produced in the colonial context, see Ranajit Guha, "The Prose of Counter Insurgency," in *Subaltern Studies II: Writings on South Asian History and Society,* ed. Ranajit Guha (Delhi: Oxford University Press, 1983), 1–42. On the "graphic" power of the colonial state and the role its affective anxieties played in shaping the colonial archive, see Ann Laura Stoler, *Along the Archival Grain: Epistemic Anxieties and Colonial Common Sense* (Princeton: Princeton University Press, 2009); and Antoinette Burton, ed., *Archive Stories: Facts, Fictions, and the Writing of History* (Durham, N.C.: Duke University Press, 2005).

15. On the history of the archives of the Government of Cochinchina, now preserved at Trung Tâm Lưu Trữ Quốc Gia II in Hồ Chí Minh City, see Trần Văn Kỳ, *Les archives du Gouvernement de la Cochinchine: Organisation—Méthode de Classement* (Hà Nội: Imprimerie Tonkinoise, 1915); Direction des Archives et les Bibliothèques, *Manuel de l'Archiviste* (Hà Nội: Imprimerie d'Extrême-Orient, 1934); Nha Văn Khố và Thư Viện Quốc Gia, Sở Lưu Trữ Công Văn và Thư Viện, "Lược sử văn khố Việt Nam" [A brief history of Vietnamese archives], unpublished typescript, General Sciences Library, Hồ Chí Minh City, Vietnam; Nguyễn Hùng Cường, "Văn khố Việt Nam" [Vietnamese archives], *Sử Địa* [History and geography] 26 (1974): 157–174. On the fate of the police archives until 1961, see E. H. Adkins and Hoang Kham Sen, *Survey of the National Records System of the Police and Security Services of Viet Nam* (Saigon: Michigan State University Viet Nam Advisory Group, 1961).

16. On the value of paying attention to such small events, see Edward Muir, "Introduction: Observing Trifles," in *Microhistory and the Lost Peoples of Europe,* ed. Edward Muir and Guido Ruggiero, trans. Eren Branch (Baltimore: Johns Hopkins University Press, 1991), vii–xxviii.

Chapter 1. Paulatim Crescam

1. Huỳnh Sanh Thông, ed. and trans., *An Anthology of Vietnamese Poems: From the Eleventh through the Twentieth Centuries* (New Haven, Conn.: Yale University Press, 1996), 91.
2. "Chef Bureau Gouvernement Général à Chef Cabinet Gouverneur Général, Hanoï," May 3, 1904; "Lieutenant Gouverneur à Gouverneur Général, Hanoï," May 3 1904;

"Résident Supérieur à Gouverneur Général, Hanoï," May 3, 1904; "Lieutenant Gouverneur à Gouverneur Général, Hanoï," May 5, 1904; "Directeur général Postes à Gouverneur Général, Hanoï," May 5, 1904; "Procureur Général à Gouverneur Général, Hanoï," May 5, 1904; "M. Ch. Guillemoto, Ingénieur en Chef des Ponts et Chaussées, Directeur Général des Travaux publics à Monsieur le Gouverneur Général de l'Indo-Chine," May 6, 1904, GGI 4819, ANOM; "Rapport au Gouverneur Général: Rapport d'ensemble sur la situation politique et économique de la Cochinchine pour les mois de mai et juin 1904," GGI 64326, ANOM.

3. "Rapport au Gouverneur Général: Rapport d'ensemble sur la situation politique et économique de la Cochinchine pour les mois de mai et juin 1904," GGI 64326, ANOM.

4. "Rapport au Gouverneur Général: Rapport d'ensemble sur la situation politique et économique de la Cochinchine pour les mois de janvier et février 1905," GGI 64327, ANOM.

5. Gouvernement Général de l'Indochine, *Rapports au Conseil Colonial (Session Ordinaire de 1905)* (Saigon: Imprimerie Commerciale Ménand and Rey, 1905), viii.

6. "Rapport au Gouverneur Général: Rapport d'ensemble sur la situation politique et économique de la Cochinchine pour les mois de janvier et février 1905"; "Rapport au Gouverneur Général de l'Indochine"; "Rapport au Gouverneur Général: Rapport d'ensemble sur la situation politique et économique de la Cochinchine pour les mois de septembre et octobre 1905," GGI 64327, ANOM; Gouvernement Général de l'Indochine, *Rapports au Conseil Colonial (Session Ordinaire de 1905)* (Saigon: Imprimerie Commerciale Ménand and Rey, 1905), viii.

7. "Rapport au Gouverneur Général: Rapport d'ensemble sur la situation politique et économique de la Cochinchine pour les mois de septembre et octobre 1905," GGI 64327, ANOM.

8. On the drop in rice prices, see Direction des Services Economiques, *Résumé statistique relative aux années 1913–1940* (Hanoi: Imprimerie d'Extrême-Orient, 1941); and Albert Coquerel, *Paddys et riz de Cochinchine* (Lyon: A. Rey, 1911), Appendix (Tables VI, VII, IX, X). Both the nominal and the real price of rice sold in Indochina increased in 1905 (in 1899–1903 piasters). The real value of exports dropped sharply that year, however, and showed only moderate improvement in 1906. See F. Leurence, *Etude statistique sur le développement économique de l'Indochine de 1899 à 1923* (Hanoi: n.p., 1925), 7, 14.

9. *Rapports au Conseil Colonial (Session Ordinaire de 1905)*, 35.

10. Gouvernement Général de l'Indochine, *Rapports au Conseil Colonial (Session Ordinaire de 1906)* (Saigon: Imprimerie Commerciale Ménand et Rey, 1906), xv.

11. Ville de Saigon, *Statistique Municipale: Année 1907* (Saigon: F.-H. Schneider, 1908), 3.

12. Ville de Saigon, *Statistique Municipale*, 3.

13. *Rapports au Conseil Colonial (Session Ordinaire de 1906)*, 28.

14. "Vicariat Apostolique de la Cochinchine," September 20, 1904, 757.108, ASMEP.

15. On the increase in rice exports in 1907, see *Statistique commerciale de la Cochinchine* (Saigon: Chambre de Commerce, 1938), table after 452; and Coquerel, *Paddys et riz,*

Appendices (Table VII). On the price of rice, see Direction des Services Economiques, *Résumé Statistique*, 43.

16. In 1907, the population grew to fifty-four thousand. See Ville de Saigon, *Statistique Municipale*, 3.

17. Lê Quý Đôn, *Phủ Biên Tạp Lục* [Miscellaneous chronicles of the pacified frontier], quyển I, 34a. For the Vietnamese translation see Lê Quý Đôn, *Phủ Biên Tạp Lục,* trans. Lê Xuân Giào, vol. 1 (Saigon: Phủ Quốc Vụ Khanh Đặc Trách Văn Hóa, 1973), 95. More recent translations such as Lê Quý Đôn, *Phủ Biên Tạp Lục* (Hanoi: Văn Hóa-Thông Tin, 2007) appear to be mistaken, giving the year 1672 instead. This is inconsistent with the reign years and the years of the zodiac calendar cited within the text. The characters for Saigon must be *Hán Nôm*, not *Hán Việt*, since the Hán Việt pronunciation would be "Sài Côn." On this point, see Nguyễn Quốc Lộc and Nguyễn Đình Đầu, "Cư dân, địa danh, địa bàn TP. Hồ Chí Minh" [The population, place name, and area of Hồ Chí Minh City] in *Địa Chí Văn Hóa Thành phố Hồ Chí Minh* [Cultural encyclopedia of Hồ Chí Minh City], ed. Trần Văn Giàu and Trần Bạch Đằng, vol. 1 (Hồ Chí Minh City: Thành phố Hồ Chí Minh, 1998), 592–593.

18. Pierre du Puy du Fayet, Jean de Antoine de la Court, and Charles Gouge, to the Directors, Missions Etrangères de Paris, July 26, 1732, ASMEP vol. 739, 925–930. Translation by Nola Cooke. Quoted in Ben Kiernan, *Blood and Soil: A World History of Genocide and Extermination from Sparta to Darfur* (New Haven, Conn.: Yale University Press, 2007), 159.

19. For identification of the cities in travelers' accounts, see George Finlayson, *The Mission to Siam, and Hue the Capital of Cochinchina in the Years 1821* (London: John Murray, 1826), 312–314; John Crawfurd, *Journal of an Embassy from the Governor-General of India to the Courts of Siam and Cochinchina; Exhibiting a View of the Actual State of those Kingdoms,* 2nd ed., vol. 1 (London: Henry Colburn and Richard Bentley, 1830), 343; John White, *History of a Voyage to the China Sea* (Boston: Wells and Lilly, 1823), 218ff. The name Chợ Lớn (literally "Big Market") refers to the eighteenth-century Tân Kiểng market in what is now the Chợ Quán area of Hồ Chí Minh City. See Lê Trung Hoa, *Địa Danh ở Thành Phố Hồ Chí Minh* [The place names of Hồ Chí Minh City] (Hà Nội: Khoa Học Xã Hội, 1991), 59. On this point, Lê Trung Hoa cites Trịnh Hoài Đức, *Gia Định Thành Thông Chí,* quyển VI, 17a. See Trịnh Hoài Đức, *Gia Định Thành Thông Chí* [Gazetteer of Gia Định], trans. Lý Việt Dũng (Biên Hòa: Tổng Hợp Đồng Nai, 2006), 228. *Bến Nghé* literally means "port for young buffaloes." One explanation for this name is that the caymans that lived on the banks of the river made a noise resembling that made by young buffaloes. See Lê Trung Hoa, *Địa Danh,* 62; Jean Bouchot, *Documents pour servir à l'histoire de Saïgon, 1859–1865* (Saigon: Albert Portail, 1927), 69. Another explanation is that the area was once a port for buffaloes that were brought downstream from Cambodia to Cochinchina. See Lê Trung Hoa, *Địa Danh,* 62; Li Tana, "The Late-Eighteenth- and Early-Nineteenth-Century Mekong Delta in the Regional Trade System," in *Water Frontier: Commerce and the Chinese in the Lower Mekong Region, 1750–1880,* ed. Nola Cooke and Li Tana (Lanham, Md.: Rowman and Littlefield, 2004), 80–81.

20. See Trịnh Hoài Đức, *Gia Định Thành Thông Chí*, quyển II, 17b. For the Vietnamese translation, see Trịnh Hoài Đức, *Gia Định Thành Thông Chí*, 39. Trịnh Hoài Đức writes, "[T]he people of the place usually call the land of Phiên An [a province of Gia Định], Sài Gòn or Bến Nghé." By the middle of the nineteenth century, Saigon had become a semi-formal place name, and became an administrative name only after the French conquest. For a semi-formal usage, see Quốc Sử Quán Triều Nguyễn, *Đại Nam Thực Lục Chính Biên Đệ Nhất Kỷ* [Primary compilation of the veritable records of the first reign of Đại Nam], quyển 1 in vol. 1 (Hà Nội: Giáo Dục, 2007), 204–205. On the vernacular versus administrative usage of place names, see Nguyễn Quốc Lộc and Nguyễn Đình Đầu, "Cư dân, địa danh, địa bàn," 590–591.

21. Nguyễn Quốc Lộc and Nguyễn Đình Đầu, "Cư dân, địa danh, địa bàn," 600–602.

22. On the possible Khmer origins of the name *Saigon*, see Vương Hồng Sển, *Sài Gòn Năm Xưa* [Saigon in the past] (Saigon: Khai Trí, 1960), 84–89; on the possible but improbable Chinese origins of the name, 89–91. As should be clear from the preceding discussion, the Vietnamese use of the name *Saigon* predates Chinese settlement in the area, which occurred in 1778 during the Tây Sơn rebellion. On the location of Prei Nokor, on part of what became Chợ Lớn, see Louis Malleret, "A la recherche de Prei Nokor," *Bulletin de la Société des Etudes Indochinoises*, New Series 17 (1942): 19–33. See also Nguyễn Quốc Lộc and Nguyễn Đình Đầu, "Cư dân, địa danh, địa bàn," 598–599.

23. See P. Trương Vĩnh Ký, *Souvenirs historiques sur Saïgon et ses environs* (Saigon: Imprimerie Impériale, 1885), 4. There are, however, objections to this explanation on linguistic grounds. See Bùi Đức Tịnh, *Lược Khảo Nguồn Gốc Địa Danh Nam Bộ* [A brief study of the origins of place names in southern Vietnam] (Hồ Chí Minh City: Văn Nghệ, 1999), 42. In neither Sino-Vietnamese nor Nôm is "củi gôn" a possible reading of Sài Gòn (柴棍).

24. Léonard Aurousseau, "Sur le nom Cochinchine," *Bulletin de l'Ecole française d'Extrême-Orient* 24 (1924): 563–579.

25. On the history of the port of Saigon, see Paul Texier, *Le port de Saïgon* (Bordeaux: Imprimerie du Midi—E Trénit, 1909); Jean Rondepierre, *Le port de Saïgon* (Paris: Les Presses Modernes, 1934); Charles Robequain, *The Economic Development of French Indo-China*, trans. Isabel A. Ward (London: Oxford University Press, 1944), 120–123.

26. L.I., *Saïgon Souvenir: Petit Guide Saïgonnais à l'Usage des Passagers et des Débutants dans la Colonie* (Saigon: Imprimerie et Librairie Nouvelles, 1907), 1.

27. L.I., *Saïgon Souvenir*, 3–4.

28. André Baudrit, *Guide historique des rues de Saigon* (Saïgon: S.I.L.I., 1945), 147–153.

29. André Baudrit, "Contribution à l'histoire de Saïgon: Extraits des registres de délibérations de la Ville de Saïgon (Indochine Française), 1868–1916," I, *Bulletin de la Société des Etudes Indochinoises*, New Series 10, nos. 1–3 (1935): 283–335. See also Gwendolyn Wright, *Politics of Design in French Colonial Urbanism* (Chicago: University of Chicago Press, 1991), 178.

30. Baudrit, *Guide historique*, 497.

31. Baudrit, *Guide historique,* 107–108.

32. R. Castex, *Les Rivages Indo-Chinois: étude économique et maritime* (Paris: Berger-Levrault, 1904), 61–65.

33. Louis Malleret, "Eléments d'une monographie des anciennes fortifications et citadelles de Saïgon," *Bulletin de la Société des Etudes Indochinoises,* New Series 10 (1935): 5–108.

34. L.I., *Saïgon Souvenir,* 8.

35. Auguste Chevalier, *Catalogue des plantes du Jardin botanique de Saïgon* (Saigon: Nouvelle Albert Portail, 1919), 5.

36. Chevalier, *Catalogue des plantes.*

37. Milton Osborne, *The French Presence in Cochinchina and Cambodia: Rule and Response, 1859-1905* (Ithaca, N.Y.: Cornell University Press, 1969), 175–205.

38. *Saïgon Souvenir,* 9; André Baudrit, "Contribution," 329. On Gambetta and French Indochina, see J. P. T. Bury, "Gambetta and Overseas Problems," *English Historical Review* 82 (1967): 277–295.

39. Georges Dürrwell, *Ma chère Cochinchine* (Paris: La renaissance du livre, 1911), 109.

40. Paul Doumer, *L'Indo-Chine française (souvenirs)* (Paris: Vuibert et Nony, 1905), 70.

41. "Vicariat Apostolique de la Cochinchine," October 10, 1880, 756.658, ASMEP; "Exposé de la situation de la Cochinchine pour 1877," INDO AF 5, ANOM; L.-E. Louvet, *Cochinchine religieuse,* vol. 2 (Paris: Librairie de la Société Asiatique, 1885), 444–446.

42. On the life of Pigneau de Béhaine, see Frédéric Mantienne, *Monseigneur Pigneau de Béhaine* (Paris: Editions Eglises d'Asie, 1999).

43. "Vicariat Apostolique de la Cochinchine Occidentale. Compte rendu, 1901–1902," 757.95, ASMEP.

44. René Despierres, "Le service des P.T.T. en Indochine (des origines à 1940)," *Bulletin des Amis du Vieux Hue* 31, no. 1 (1944): 3–61. On the overseas submarine telegraph network, see Comité agricole et industriel de la Cochinchine, *La Cochinchine française en 1878* (Paris: Callamel Ainé, 1878), 22–23. Private traffic quickly exceeded official traffic on the telegraph network. See, for example, the figures in *Etat de la Cochinchine* (1885): 82–83.

45. Baudrit, *Guide Historique,* 134–138.

46. L.I., *Saïgon Souvenir,* 11.

47. Dürrwell, *Ma chère Cochinchine,* 94; A. Eggers-Lura, "The Danes in Siam: Their Involvement in Establishing the Siam Commercial Bank Limited at the End of the Last Century," *Journal of the Siam Society* 81 (1993): 137.

48. Jann Pasler, "Friendship and Music in Indochina," in *Camille Saint-Saëns and His World,* ed. Jann Pasler (Princeton, N.J.: Princeton University Press, 2012), 189–190.

49. Dürrwell, *Ma chère Cochinchine,* 91–92.

50. Baudrit, *Guide historique,* 504–511; Baudrit, "Contribution à l'histoire," II, 326–328. On Francis Garnier, see Milton Osborne, "Francis Garnier (1839-1873), Explorer of the Mekong River," in *Explorers of Southeast Asia: Six Lives,* ed. Victor T. King (Kuala Lumpur: Oxford University Press, 1995), 51–107. On the Black Flags, see Bradley Camp

Davis, *Imperial Bandits: Outlaws and Rebels in the China-Vietnam Borderlands* (Seattle: University of Washington Press, 2017).

51. A. Brebion and A. Cabaton, *Dictionnaire de bio-bibliographie générale, ancienne et modern de l'Indochine française* (Paris: Société d'éditions géographiques, maritimes et coloniales, 1935), 159.

52. L.I., *Saïgon Souvenir,* 13.

53. L.I., *Saïgon Souvenir,* 14.

54. Baudrit, *Guide historique,* 153–158.

55. Chemins de fer de l'Indochine, *Historique et Construction* (Hanoi: Bureau de Travaux publics, 1940), 13–16.

56. Castex, *Rivages Indo-Chinois,* 54.

57. Castex, *Rivages Indo-Chinois,* 54–55.

58. Castex, *Rivages Indo-Chinois,* 56–57.

59. Castex, *Rivages Indo-Chinois,* 57; *Bulletin économique de l'Indochine* 11 (1908): 126. The names of the mills are recorded according to the conventions of the Chinese in the Straits Settlements.

60. Coquerel, *Paddys et riz,* 88–89; Etienne Denis, *Bordeaux et la Cochinchine sous la restauration et le second empire* (Bordeaux: Imprimerie Delmas, 1965), 230–231.

61. Tan Keong Sum, "Récit d'un voyage au Vietnam," *Archipel* 43 (1992): 152, 155; Song Ong Siang, *One Hundred Years' History of the Chinese in Singapore* (Singapore: University of Malaya Press, 1967), 92.

62. Song, *One Hundred Years' History,* 100–101.

63. His name, 郭琰 (Guo Yan), was pronounced "Quách Đàm" according to the Vietnamese convention. See Nguyễn Phú Xuân, "Quách Đàm: Người Xây Chợ Bình Tây" [Quách Đàm: The man who built Bình Tây Market], *Xưa Và Nay* [Past and present] 214 (2004): 29. Quách Đàm became a French citizen and died in 1927 a Chévalier de la Légion d'Honneur. His son succeeded him in his business. See "Gouvernement de Cochinchine. Rapport annuel de la Sûreté. 1er juillet 1926–1er juillet 1927," GGI 65475, ANOM.

64. *Bulletin économique de l'Indochine* 11 (1908): 126.

65. See Inspection Générale des Travaux Publics, *Dragages de Cochinchine: Canal Rachgia-Hatien* (Saigon: n.p., 1930), 11–20. For a detailed narrative of the colonial dredging of Cochinchina, see David Biggs, *Quagmire: Nation-Building and Nature in the Mekong Delta* (Seattle: University of Washington Press, 2010), 53–90, 91–126. See also Pierre Brocheux, *The Mekong Delta: Ecology, Economy, and Revolution, 1860-1960* (Madison: Center for Southeast Asian Studies, University of Wisconsin-Madison, 1995), 17–22; Robequain, *Economic Development,* 110–112.

66. These figures are from Yves Henry, *Economie agricole de l'Indochine* (Hanoi: Imprimerie d'Extrême-Orient, 1932), 272–274. As dredging continued after 1905, the region south of the Hậu Giang River was increasingly opened up and settled. On the settlement of the west, see Brocheux, *Mekong Delta,* 22–29. Vietnamese made up the largest number

of landowners. For most of the colonial period, landowners with French citizenship possessed only a very small proportion of the rice lands in Cochinchina (less than 10 percent in 1931). French citizens from France, rather than naturalized Vietnamese, owned an even smaller proportion of such land (approximately 5 percent in 1931). See Robequain, *Economic Development,* 192–193.

67. In the years after the typhoon, one-third of Saigon's rice exports came down the Tonlé Sap and Mekong river from Cambodia. See Martial Dupuy, "Le Cambodge et ses ressources," *Bulletin de la Société de géographie et d'études coloniales de Marseille* (1906): 252–264, esp. 253.

68. On the role of the Chinese in the domestic rice trade, see René Dubreuil, *De la condition des Chinois et de leur rôle économique en Indo-Chine* (Bar-sur-Seine, France: Imprimerie V.C. Saillard, 1910), 98; Nguyên Van Nghi, *Etude économique sur la Cochinchine française et l'infiltration chinoise* (Montpellier: Imprimerie Firmin et Montane, 1920), 47–48, 53–56; Wang Wen-Yuan, *Les Relations entre l'Indochine Française et la Chine: Etude de géographie économique* (Paris: Editions Pierre Bossuet, 1937), 37–42; Luong Nhi Ky, "The Chinese in Vietnam: A Study of Vietnamese-Chinese Relations with Special Attention to the Period 1862-1961" (Ph.D. diss., University of Michigan, 1962), 83–93; Victor Purcell, *The Chinese in Southeast Asia,* 2nd ed. (London: Oxford University Press, 1965), 195–197; Denis, *Bordeaux et la Cochinchine,* 211–244. Other useful studies of the Chinese in French Indochina include Nguyen Quoc Dinh, *Les congrégations chinoises en Indochine française* (Paris: Recueil Sirey, 1941); Tsai Maw-Kuey, *Les Chinois au Sud-Vietnam* (Paris: Bibliothèque Nationale, 1968); Tracey C. Barrett, *The Chinese Diaspora in South-East Asia: The Overseas Chinese in Indo-China* (New York: I.B. Tauris, 2012).

69. Castex, *Rivages Indo-Chinois,* 59–61; Coquerel, *Paddys et riz,* 118–130.

70. Previous analyses of rice exports have mainly relied on figures in the *Annuaire statistique de l'Indochine.* These are aggregate figures for the whole of French Indochina (including Annam, Tonkin, Cochinchina, Laos, and Cambodia). They are not useful, therefore, for gauging changes in the exports of Cochinchina and exports from Saigon. The figures in this paragraph are based on data presented in the appendices to Coquerel, *Paddys et riz* and are confirmed, for the most part, by *Etat de la Cochinchine Française* (1879–1905) and the *Statistique Commerciale de la Cochinchine* (Saigon: Chambre de Commerce, 1924–1938). Rice was always the most valuable commodity exported from Saigon, but it was not the only commodity. The port also exported pepper, copra, cotton, coffee, maize, and rubber in notable quantities. Among these, maize and rubber ranked second and third in export value after World War I. The port began to export maize, mainly grown in the provinces of Châu Đốc and Long Xuyên, to France at the beginning of World War I. The export of maize grew rapidly during the 1930s as its price increased. In 1930, the port exported 120,000 tons and by 1938, it was exporting 404,000 tons of maize annually. In that year, for the first time rubber became the second-most valuable export from Cochinchina. Rubber plantations in Cochinchina, located predominantly in the eastern provinces of Biên Hòa,

Tây Ninh, and Thủ Dầu Một, also began to export rubber at the beginning of World War I. The volume of rubber exported increased steadily, reaching fifty-eight thousand tons in 1938, although its price varied wildly. Rubber was vastly more valuable by weight than rice or maize, but it was exported in comparatively small quantities. Neither maize nor rubber ever rivaled rice as the most important export from the port of Saigon. For export volumes for maize and for rubber, see *Statistique commerciale de la Cochinchine* (Saigon: Chambre de Commerce, 1938), 473, 480. For the price of maize, see Direction des Services Economiques, *Résumé statistique,* 30. For a general account of the exports of French Indochina, see Robequain, *Economic Development,* 311–319. The *Résumé statistique* at 28 gives a table of the relative significance of the exports of French Indochina in the first half of the twentieth century. It is clear that rice absolutely dominated those exports. Before 1935, rubber never accounted for more than 10 percent of exports. In 1938, it accounted for more than 20 percent. Rice never accounted for less than 35 percent throughout that period.

71. Coquerel, *Paddys et riz,* 187–200.

72. Direction des Douanes et Régies, *Administration des douanes et régies en Indochine* (Hanoi: Imprimerie d'Extrême-Orient, 1930), 17; Direction des Finances, *Histoire budgétaire de l'Indochine* (Hanoi: Imprimerie d'Extrême-Orient, 1930), 96.

73. For figures from 1865 to 1910, see the appendices to Coquerel, *Paddys et riz.* These figures are confirmed, with slight variations, in appendices to *Etat de la Cochinchine française* (1879–1905). For the period after 1910, see *Statistique commerciale de la Cochinchine* (Saigon: Chambre de Commerce, 1924–1938).

74. Junks carried back cloves, nutmeg, pepper, black and blue silk, green velvet, and glassware from Batavia to Saigon. See Isodore Hedde, "Notice of Cochin-China, Made During a Visit in the Spring of Eighteen Hundred and Forty-Four," *Chinese Repository* 15 (1846): 120. On the junk trade with Singapore, Penang, and Melaka, see "Eugène Chaigneau Ministre des Affaires Etrangères, June 20, 1832," in *La geste française en Indochine,* vol. 1, ed. Georges Taboulet (Paris: Adrien-Maisonneuve, 1955), 319. On trade with Bangkok, see John Crawfurd, *Journal of an Embassy from the Governor-General of India to the Courts of Siam and Cochinchina; Exhibiting a View of the Actual State of those Kingdoms,* 2nd ed., vol. 2 (London: Henry Colburn and Richard Bentley, 1830), 164; on trade with Chinese ports, including Xiamen and Guangzhou, 317–318; on Singapore and the Straits Settlements, 320–321. For a detailed discussion of the place of Cochinchina in regional trade from 1750 to 1880, see the essays in Cooke and Li, ed., *Water Frontier.*

75. Hedde, "Notice of Cochin-China," 119–120.

76. Wong Lin Ken, "The Trade of Singapore, 1819–1869," *Journal of the Malayan Branch of the Royal Asiatic Society* 33, no. 192 (1960): 240–241. The missionary Charles-Emile Bouillevaux recounted his journey on a junk from Singapore to Saigon in 1849. See C.-E. Bouillevaux, *Voyage dans l'Indochine, 1848-1856* (Paris: Victor Palmé, 1858), 34.

77. Ellen A. Tsao, "Chinese Rice Merchants and Millers in French Indo-China," *Chinese Economic Journal* 11, no. 6 (1932): 459–461.

78. *Statistique commerciale de la Cochinchine* (Saigon: Chambre de Commerce, 1938), 506.

79. Serge de Labrusse, *Politique du cabotage en Indochine* (Saigon: Imprimerie Française d'Outre-Mer, 1950), 72–83, 94–95.

80. See David Faure, "The Rice Trade in Hong Kong Before the Second World War," in *Between East and West: Aspects of Social and Political Development in Hong Kong,* ed. Elizabeth Sinn (Hong Kong: Centre of Asian Studies, University of Hong Kong, 1990), 216–225; Ho Ping-yin, "A Survey of China's Trade with Hongkong," *Chinese Economic Journal* 16, no. 4 (1935): 331–359; Seung-joon Lee, *Gourmets in the Land of Famine: The Culture and Politics of Rice in Modern China* (Stanford: Stanford University Press, 2011), 1.

81. See David Faure, "The Plight of the Farmers: A Study of the Rural Economy of Jiangnan and the Pearl River Delta, 1870–1937," *Modern China* 11, no. 1 (1985): 3–37; idem, *The Rural Economy of Pre-Liberation China: Trade Expansion and Peasant Livelihood in Jiangsu and Guangdong, 1870–1937* (Hong Kong: Oxford University Press, 1989), 41–58; Lillian Li, *China's Silk Trade: Traditional Industry in the Modern World, 1842–1937* (Cambridge, Mass.: Council on East Asian Studies, Harvard University Press, 1981), 96–129.

82. For rice import figures for the Chinese province of Guangdong from 1875 to 1937, see Alfred H. Y. Lin, *The Rural Economy of Guangdong, 1870–1930: A Study of the Agrarian Crisis and Its Origins in Southernmost China* (London: Macmillan, 1997), 50–52. The figures Lin gives are from the annual statistical reports of the Imperial Maritime Customs for the ports of Guangdong.

83. "Le Commerce du riz en Colombie," *Bulletin économique de l'Indochine* 25 (1922): 487.

84. Christopher Baker, "Economic Reorganization and the Slump in South and Southeast Asia," *Comparative Studies in Society and History* (1981): 330–337; Paul H. Kratoska, "Commercial Rice Cultivation and the Regional Economy of Southeastern Asia, 1850–1950," in *Food and Globalization: Consumption, Markets, and Politics in the Modern World,* ed. Alexander Nützenadel and Frank Trentmann (Oxford: Berg, 2008), 75. The most comprehensive study of the Asian rice economy during the colonial period is V. D. Wickizer and M. K. Bennett, *The Rice Economy of Monsoon Asia* (Stanford: Stanford University Press, 1941). See also Randolph Barker, Robert W. Hardt, and Beth Rose, *The Rice Economy of Asia* (Washington, D.C.: Resources for the Future, 1985).

85. John Larkin, *The Pampangans: Colonial Society in a Philippine Province* (Berkeley: University of California Press, 1972), 45–47; idem, *Sugar and the Origins of Modern Philippine Society* (Berkeley: University of California Press, 1993), 34.

86. See Marshall S. McLennan, "Changing Human Ecology on the Central Luzon Plain: Nueva Ecija, 1705–1939," in *Philippine Social History: Global Trade and Local Transformations,* ed. Alfred W. McCoy and Ed. C. de Jesus (Quezon City: Ateneo de Manila University Press, 1982), 63; see also idem, *The Central Luzon Plain: Land and Society on the Inland Frontier* (Manila: Alemar-Phoenix, 1980).

87. On agricultural diversification on Java before 1830, see R. E. Elson, *Javanese Peasants and the Colonial Sugar Industry: Impact and Change in an East Java Residency, 1830–1940* (Singapore: Oxford University Press, 1984), 8–10.

88. On rice exports from Burma, see Cheng Siok-Hwa, *The Rice Industry of Burma, 1852–1940* (Kuala Lumpur: University of Malaya Press, 1968); Michael Adas, *The Burma Delta:*

Economic Development and Social Change on an Asian Rice Frontier, 1852-1941, 2nd ed. (Madison: University of Wisconsin Press, 2011). On rice exports from Thailand, see James C. Ingram, *Economic Change in Thailand, 1850-1970,* 2nd ed. (Stanford: Stanford University Press, 1971), 75-92; idem, "Thailand's Rice Trade and the Allocation of Resources," in *The Economic Development of Southeast Asia,* ed. C. D. Cowan (London: George Allen & Unwin, 1964), 102-126. On rice exports from Cochinchina, see Coquerel, *Paddys et riz*; Brocheux, *Mekong Delta;* Robert L. Sansom, *The Economics of Insurgency in the Mekong Delta of Vietnam* (Cambridge, Mass.: M.I.T. Press, 1970), 18-52, 258-267. For an examination of rice exports from mainland Southeast Asia before World War I, see Norman G. Owen, "The Rice Industry of Mainland Southeast Asia, 1850-1914," *Journal of the Siam Society* 59 (1971): 75-143. On the decline of rice cultivation and the beginnings of a tea plantation economy on Ceylon, see Roland Wenzlhuemer, *From Coffee to Tea Cultivation in Ceylon, 1880-1900: An Economic and Social History* (Leiden: Brill, 2008). On the plantation economy of Sumatra, see Karl J. Pelzer, *Planter and Peasant: Colonial Policy and the Agrarian Struggle in East Sumatra* ('s-Gravenhage: Martinus Nijhoff, 1978). On tin in Malaya, see Wong Lin-Ken, *The Malayan Tin Industry to 1914* (Tucson: University of Arizona Press, 1965). On plantations in Malaya, see Lim Teck Ghee, *Peasants and their Agricultural Economy in Colonial Malaya, 1874-1941* (Kuala Lumpur: Oxford University Press, 1977). On the early history of the rubber industry in Malaya, see J. H. Drabble, *Rubber in Malaya 1876-1922: The Genesis of the Industry* (Kuala Lumpur: Oxford University Press, 1973).

89. All contemporary and subsequent scholarly studies agree on the importance of the rice trade to the colonial economy of rural Cochinchina, but none acknowledges its significance for the economy and society of Saigon. See Henry, *Economie agricole,* 256–272, 302–320, 360–363; Robequain, *Economic Development,* 220–222, 308–311; Pierre Gourou, *L'utilisation du sol en Indochine Française* (Paris: Centre d'études de politique étrangère, 1940), 265–296; Nguyen Xuan Giac, *Le régime économique de la Cochinchine* (Paris: Ernest Sagot & Cie, 1920), 27–42; Inspection Générale de l'Agriculture de l'Elevage et des Forêts, *Riziculture en Indochine* (Hanoi: Imprimerie d'Extrême-Orient, 1931); Nguyen Tan Loi, *L'économie commerciale du riz en Indochine* (Paris: Les éditions Domat-Montchrestien, 1938); H. Brenier, *Note sur le développement commercial de l'Indo-Chine de 1897 à 1901* (Hanoi: F.-H. Schneider, 1902), 7–12; Paul Estebe, *Le problème du riz en Indochine* (Toulouse: Imprimerie F. Boisseau, 1934), 30–62, 109–146; Robert Sansom, *The Economics of Insurgency in the Mekong Delta of Vietnam* (Cambridge, Mass.: M.I.T. Press, 1970), 18–52; Irene Nørlund, "Rice Production in Colonial Vietnam," in *Rice Societies: Asian Problems and Prospects,* ed. Irene Nørlund, Sven Cederroth, and Ingela Gerdin (Copenhagen: Scandinavian Institute of Asian Studies, 1986), 203–229.

90. See *Annuaire colonial: agriculture, commerce, et industrie* (Paris: Comptoirs des intérêts coloniaux, 1891), 565ff; *Annuaire de l'Indochine française pour l'année 1893* (Saigon: Imprimerie Coloniale, 1893), 308ff.

91. "Cochinchine. Direction de l'Intérieur. Renseignements demandés par la Dépêche du 25 Avril 1870 pour servir à la rédaction de l'Exposé Général de la Situation de l'Empire," INDO AF 20(11), ANOM.

92. Baudrit, "Contribution à l'histoire," II, 289–290.

93. Baudrit, "Contribution à l'histoire," I, 46. The motto employs the first-person future active indicative form of the third-conjugation Latin verb *crescere*, meaning "to grow."

94. *Etat de la Cochinchine Française* (1880): 164.

95. In 1885 the population of the city was recorded as 30,300. See *Etat de la Cochinchine Française* (1885): 117. Two facts explain this surge in population. First, the area bordering Saigon had become insecure. Rebellion broke out in several adjacent villages and there was an abortive attack on the city. See Tribunaux de Binh Hoa, *Affaire d'Hoc-Mon* (Saigon: Imprimerie Coloniale, 1885); R. B. Smith, "Development of Opposition to French Rule in Southern Vietnam, 1880–1940," *Past and Present* 54 (1972): 97–100. Second, in 1885, the Hàm Nghi Emperor fled the capital, Huế, and launched the Cần Vương or "Save the King" Movement. This led to violence against the scholar-gentry and Catholics in Annam. See David G. Marr, *Vietnamese Anticolonialism, 1885-1925* (Berkeley: University of California Press, 1971), 59–60. Many Catholics and presumably others fled south and sought refuge in Saigon. The Apostolic Vicar for Western Cochinchina, Mgr. Isidore Colombert, reported 3,600 Catholic refugees from southern Annam in Saigon in 1885. See Letter, November 30, 1885, 756.723, ASMEP. According to Mgr. Colombert, the Catholic refugees returned to Annam in 1887. See Letter, November 25, 1887, 756.740, ASMEP. In 1888, the population of Saigon returned to earlier levels, not exceeding 16,200. See *Etat de la Cochinchine Française* (1888): 130.

96. For the debate over the addition of these villages to the city, see Baudrit, "Contribution à l'histoire," II, 292–298.

97. See *Etat de la Cochinchine Française* (1893): 124; *Etat de la Cochinchine Française* (1896): 78.

98. See *Etat de la Cochinchine Française* (1899): 77.

99. On the addition of the villages to the city, see Baudrit, "Contribution à l'histoire," II, 298; André Landron, "Notes sur le XXème arrondissement (1880–1888)," *Bulletin de la Société des Etudes Indochinoises*, New Series 19, no. 3 (1944): 37. On the population of the city in 1905, see Ville de Saïgon, *Statistique Municipale*, 3.

100. For the population in 1907, see *Statistique Municipale*, 3. For the population in later years, see André Baudrit, *Guide historique*, table after 80. The table is reprinted in Nguyễn Phan Quang, *Góp Thêm Tư Liệu Sài Gòn Gia Định Từ 1859-1945* [A contribution to data on Saigon—Gia Định from 1859 to 1945] (Hồ Chí Minh City: Trẻ, 1998), 52–53.

101. The rate of natural increase was low. Mortality in the city was very high, with the crude death rate in the first decade of the twentieth century between 30 and 40 per 1000. See Georges Montel, *La ville de Saïgon: Etude de démographie et d'hygiène coloniales* (Bordeaux: Imprimerie Moderne, 1911), 27–29. The crude death rate in Indochina remained very high throughout the colonial period. See Magali Barbieri, "Health and Mortality in Early 20th Century Vietnam: A Demographer's Perspective," Unpublished manuscript (2010).

102. Thái Văn Kiểm, "Curiosités Toponymiques et Folkloriques du Sud Viet-Nam," *Bulletin de la Société des Etudes Indochinoises*, New Series 35, no. 3 (1960): 15; Lê Trung Hoa,

Từ Điển Địa Danh Thành Phố Sài Gòn—Hồ Chí Minh (Hồ Chí Minh City: Trẻ, 2003), 104, 339, 411.

103. Orders for the expulsion of vagrants and petty criminals from Cochinchina suggest that many migrants came from the provinces of southern Annam. See GOU-COCH V10/03.05, GOUCOCH V10/04.01, GOUCOCH V10/04.02, GOUCOCH V10/04.03, GOUCOCH V10/04.06, GOUCOCH V10/06.07, GOUCOCH V10/07.01, TTLTQG-II.

104. Rickshaw pullers often returned to the countryside during the transplanting season. See "Note pour Monsieur le Chef local des services de Police et Sûreté," June 11, 1935, GOUCOCH VIA.7/192(14), TTLTQG-II. Railway income on the southern network usually peaked in January and July. See Statistique Générale de l'Indochine, *Indices économiques indochinois,* Second Series (Hanoi: n.p., 1937), 145. These circular migration patterns are very poorly documented.

105. On the role of such "invisible paths" in shaping the history of labor migration, see Paul-André Rosental, *Les sentiers invisibles: espaces, familles et migrations dans la France du 19e siècle* (Paris: Ecole des hautes études en sciences sociales, 1999). The sometimes circuitous routes that Vietnamese migrants took to Saigon will be evident in later chapters.

106. The suggestion here is that over the long run the expected gain from migration to the city makes migration reasonable, even though in the short term the difficulty of finding stable wage employment is high. See John R. Harris and Michael P. Todaro, "Migration, Unemployment, and Development: A Two-Sector Analysis," *American Economic Review* 60, no. 1 (1970): 126–142. Contemporary Hồ Chí Minh City faces similar issues today: rapid, export-led economic growth and high levels of rural-urban migration, unemployment, and urban poverty. See Hy V. Luong, ed., *Urbanization, Migration, and Poverty in a Vietnamese Metropolis* (Singapore: NUS Press, 2009).

Chapter 2. A Woman Who Ran Away

1. Huỳnh Sanh Thông, ed. and trans., *An Anthology of Vietnamese Poems: From the Eleventh through the Twentieth Centuries* (New Haven, Conn.: Yale University Press, 1996), 214.

2. The average annual rainfall in August in Saigon in 1907–1923 was 284 millimeters. Compare this to 3 millimeters in February during the dry season. See P. Bruzon and P. Carton, *Le climat de l'Indochine et les typhons de la mer de Chine* (Hanoi: Imprimerie d'Extrême-Orient, 1930), 73, ch. 6.

3. Perhaps the most famous account of time spent in the Maison Centrale is Phan Văn Hùm, *Ngồi tù khám lớn* [Sitting in the Maison Centrale] (Saigon: Dân Tộc, 1957). For a penetrating analysis of the colonial prison system, see Peter Zinoman, *The Colonial Bastille: A History of Imprisonment in Vietnam, 1862-1940* (Berkeley: University of California Press, 2001).

4. This and all subsequent dialogue between Lương Văn Sang and Inspector Léonardi is taken from the transcript of the interrogation. "Rapport du 21 au 22 août, 1907," GOUCOCH IB.37/257(7), TTLTQG-II.

5. Société des Etudes Indochinoises, *Monographie de la Province de Bien-Hoa* (Saigon: Imprimerie L. Ménard, 1901), 55. The exact figures for Biên Hòa in 1901 are: Vietnamese, 98,519; Cambodians, 443; Hill People, 2,581; Chinese, 1,305; French, 50; Indians, 8; Tagal, 5.

6. The monograph from 1901 gives an area of 560,000 hectares. Two later provincial monographs, however, give a figure of over a million hectares. The borders of the province do not seem to have changed significantly in the years between the publication of these works and techniques for gauging surface are likely to have improved, so the later, higher figure has been chosen. See M. Robert, *Monographie de la Province de Biênhoa* (Saigon: Imprimerie du Centre, 1924), 8; "Monographie de la Province de Bienhoa en 1930," Unpublished typescript, National Library of Vietnam, Hanoi, 3. The planted area for 1901 is, however, from the monograph for that year.

7. "Monographie de la Province de Bienhoa en 1930," 3.

8. Société des Etudes Indochinoises, *Province de Bien-Hoa*, 5.

9. Société des Etudes Indochinoises, *Province de Bien-Hoa*, 19–20.

10. Société des Etudes Indochinoises, *Province de Bien-Hoa*, 20.

11. Société des Etudes Indochinoises, *Province de Bien-Hoa*, 20, 22–23.

12. On the economic hierarchy in Southeast Asian villages and villagers' relative susceptibility to subsistence crises, see James C. Scott, *The Moral Economy of the Peasant: Rebellion and Subsistence in Southeast Asia* (New Haven, Conn.: Yale University Press, 1976).

13. For the location of Chánh Mỹ Trung, see the map at the end of Robert, *Monographie de la Province de Biênhoa.*

14. On the construction of small water craft in Tân Ba, see Société des Etudes indochinoises, *Province de Bien-Hoa*, 45. The existence of a market is indicated on page 13; the detail of potters in other villages getting kaolin from Tân Ba, 44.

15. See the multiple studies on the homes of poor villagers in "Cochinchine: à l'enquête no. 2 sur l'habitat (classement par provinces)," GUERNUT 88, ANOM. Although these studies were carried out in 1937, there is little indication that the poor constructed their homes any differently in 1905. The provincial monograph for 1901, for example, indicates that Nipa palm (*dừa nước* in Vietnamese, or "palmier d'eau" in the monograph) was used for covering houses then.

16. "Rapport au Gouverneur Général: Rapport d'ensemble sur la situation politique et économique de la Cochinchine pour les mois de janvier et février 1905," GGI 64327, ANOM; Gouvernement Général de l'Indochine, *Rapports au Conseil Colonial (Session Ordinaire de 1905)* (Saigon: Imprimerie Commerciale Ménand and Rey, 1905), vii–viii; David G. Marr, *Vietnamese Anticolonialism, 1885-1925* (Berkeley: University of California Press, 1971), 158.

17. Nguyen Huu Khang, *La commune Annamite: étude historique, juridique et économique* (Paris: Tepac, 1946), 204–208.

18. P. Kresser, *La commune Annamite en Cochinchine: le recrutement des notables* (Paris: Les Éditions Domat-Monchrestien, 1935), 29. Kresser quotes a speech by Governor General Paul Beau from August 28, 1903.

19. Gouvernement Général de l'Indochine, *Rapports au Conseil Colonial (Session Ordinaire de 1902)* (Saigon: Imprimerie Coloniale, 1902), vii–viii.

20. "Rapport de l'Inspecteur des services civils chargé de l'enquête sur les événements qui se sont déroulés au village de Vinh-Cửu (Province de Bien Hoa) le 12 Mai 1905," INDO NF 447, ANOM.

21. On the history of venal sex in French Indochina, see Marie Corine Rodriguez, "'L'administration de la prostitution': Réglementation et contrôle social au Vietnam pendant la période coloniale" and Annick Guénel, "Prostitution, maladies vénériennes et médecine coloniale au Vietnam de la conquête française à la guerre d'indépendance," both in *Vietnamese Society in Transition: The Daily Politics of Reform and Change,* ed. John Kleinen (Amsterdam: Het Spinhuis, 2001), 223–232, 233–249; Frank Proschan, "'Syphilis, Opiomania, and Pederasty': Colonial Constructions of Vietnamese and French) Social Diseases," *Journal of the History of Sexuality* 11 (2002): 610–636; idem, "Eunuch Mandarins, Soldats Mamzelles, Effeminate Boys, and Graceless Women: French Colonial Constructions of Vietnamese Genders," *GLQ* 8, no. 4 (2002): 435–467; Isabelle Tracol-Huynh, "The Shadow Theater of Prostitution in French Colonial Tonkin: Faceless Prostitutes under the Colonial Gaze," *Journal of Vietnamese Studies* 7, no. 1 (2012): 10–51; Shaun Kingsley Malarney, "Introduction," in Vũ Trọng Phụng, *Lục Xì: Prostitution and Venereal Disease in Colonial Hanoi,* trans. Shaun Kingsley Malarney (Honolulu: University of Hawai'i Press, 2010), 1–43.

22. See Jill Harsin, *Policing Prostitution in Nineteenth-Century Paris* (Princeton, N.J.: Princeton University Press, 1985); Alain Corbin, *Women for Hire: Prostitution and Sexuality in France after 1850,* trans. Alan Sheridan (Cambridge, Mass.: Harvard University Press, 1990).

23. The explication of these terms is from Harsin, *Policing Prostitution,* 6.

24. "Monsieur Girard, Commissaire central de police, à Monsieur le Secrétaire Général de la Cochinchine," January 24, 1888, GOUCOCH IB.38/171, TTLTQG-II.

25. "Le Gouverneur Général de l'Indo-Chine à Monsieur le Lieutenant-Gouverneur à Saigon," March 28, 1893, GOUCOCH IB.37/237(5), TTLTQG-II.

26. "Monsieur F. Drouhet, Secrétaire Général des Colonies, Maire de la Ville de Chợ Lớn, à Monsieur le Lieutenant-Gouverneur," June 24, 1904, GOUCOCH IB.38/172, TTLTQG-II.

27. André Baudrit, *Guide historique des rues de Saigon* (Saigon: S.I.L.I., 1945), table after 80.

28. Ville de Saigon, *Statistique municipale: année 1907* (Saigon: F.-H. Schneider, 1908), 3.

29. Société des Etudes Indochinoises, *Province de Bien-Hoa,* 8–10.

30. The distance from Tân Ba to Chợ Lớn is over 40 kilometers.

31. On naming in Vietnam, see Pierre Huard and Maurice Durand, *Connaissance du Viet-Nam* (Paris: Ecole française d'Extrême-Orient, 2002), 92–93.

32. Vietnamese midwives are mentioned in Médecin-Inspecteur Clavel, *L'Assistance médicale indigène en Indo-Chine* (Paris: Librairie Maritime & Coloniale, 1908), 256.

33. On domestic servants see Solène Granier, *Domestiques Indochinois* (Paris: Vendémiaire, 2014).

34. The work of Vietnamese nuns in Saigon and Chợ Lớn is mentioned in the discussion of medical assistance in those two cities in Clavel, *L'Assistance médicale indigène,* 255–281.

35. Arrests increased from 299 in 1905 to 746 in 1906 and 606 in 1907. See Ville de Saïgon, *Statistique Municipale,* 17.

36. "Une punition de 15 jours de prison est infligée à la femme Tran Thi Thanh, maîtresse de la maison de tolérance n°11 à Chợ Lớn," 1884, GOUCOCH IB.38/171, TTLTQ-GII.

37. "M. Renauld, Maire de la ville de Chợ Lớn à Monsieur le Directeur de l'Intérieur, Saïgon," April 18, 1886, GOUCOCH IB.38/171, TTLTQG-II.

38. "Monsieur Albertini, Commissaire Central, à Monsieur le Secrétaire Général de Police," July 1, 1891, GOUCOCH IB.38/172, TTLTQG-II.

39. "M. Albertini, Commissaire Central à Monsieur le Secrétaire Général de la Cochinchine," September 8, 1891, GOUCOCH IB.38/172, TTLTQG-II.

40. "Le Gouverneur Général de l'Indo-Chine à Monsieur le Lieutenant-Gouverneur à Saïgon," March 28,1893, GOUCOCH IB.37/257(5), TTLTQG-II.

41. *Police des Mœurs: Règlement et instructions* (Saigon: Imprimerie Commerciale Rey, Curiol & Cie, 1893), GOUCOCH IB.37/257(5), TTLTQG-II.

42. For more details, see Sachiko Sone, "The Karayuki-San of Asia, 1868–1938: The Role of Prostitutes Overseas in Japanese Economic and Social Development," *Review of Indonesian and Malaysian Affairs* 25, no. 2 (1992): 44–62; James Francis Warren, *Ah-Ku and Karayuki-san: Prostitution in Singapore, 1870–1940,* 2nd ed. (Singapore: Singapore University Press, 2002).

43. "Monsieur F. Drouhet, Secrétaire Général des Colonies, Maire de la Ville de Chợ Lớn, à Monsieur le Lieutenant-Gouverneur," June 24, 1904, GOUCOCH IB.38/172, TTLTQG-II. Despite the bureaucratic documentation, information about prostitutes in colonial Saigon remains remarkably elusive. It is impossible to say with any certainty how many women worked as prostitutes in the city. Neither the municipal authorities nor the colonial government systematically compiled statistics on prostitution. And those numbers that were gathered are probably underestimates since brothel owners and prostitutes both wanted to avoid being counted and regulated. The fragmentary statistics that are available indicate the unsteady growth of prostitution in Saigon. The earliest figures appear in letters from one colonial administrator to another. A letter from the central commissioner of police to the secretary general of Cochinchina in 1888 states that there were ninety-five prostitutes registered that year. By 1893, that number had grown to 114, according to a letter from the governor general of Indochina to the lieutenant governor of Cochinchina. In 1932, the League of Nations published a report on the traffic of women and children in the Far East. That report stated that there were more than 200 prostitutes in Saigon and a further 270 in Chợ Lớn in 1930. A study published by a Vietnamese doctor in 1935 listed 314 registered prostitutes in Saigon and 92 in Chợ Lớn. "Monsieur Girard, Commissaire central de police, à Monsieur le Secrétaire Général de la Cochinchine," January 24,

1888, GOUCOCH IB.38/171; "Le Gouverneur Général de l'Indo-Chine à Monsieur le Lieutenant-Gouverneur à Saïgon," March 28, 1893, GOUCOCH IB.37/237(5), TTLTQG-II; League of Nations, *Commission of Enquiry into Traffic in Women and Children in the Far East* (Geneva: League of Nations, 1932), 215; Dr. Tung, "La Prostitution: Etude Locale," *Bulletin d'Aide Mutuelle et Assistance Sociale* 40 (January 1935): 1175.

44. A. Landes, "Rapport sur la prostitution," *Excursions et Reconnaissances* 4 (1880): 145–147.

45. "Le Commissaire de police de la ville de Chợ Lớn à Monsieur le Commissaire Central de Police à Saïgon," April 23, 1908, GOUCOCH IB.37/357(7), TTLITQG-II.

46. "Chanteuses inscrites en 1908 dans les maisons de tolérance chinoises de la Ville de Chợ Lớn," GOUCOCH IB.37/357(7), TTLITQG-II.

47. "Le Chef de Service de l'Immigration et du Contrôle de la Main d'Oeuvre Engagée à Monsieur le Chef du Service des Affaires Administratives et Economiques," September 15, 1930, GOUCOCH VIA.8/286(17), TTLTQG-II; League of Nations, *Commission of Enquiry,* 57.

48. "Le Commissaire de police de la ville de Chợ Lớn à Monsieur le Commissaire Central de Police à Saïgon," April 23, 1908, GOUCOCH IB.37/357(7), TTLTQG-II.

49. Unfortunately, this letter was not preserved in the dossier with the other materials on Lương Thị Lắm.

50. André Baudrit, "Contribution à l'histoire de Saïgon: Extraits des registres de délibérations de la Ville de Saïgon (Indochine Française), 1867–1916," II, *Bulletin de la Société des Etudes Indochinoises,* New Series 10, nos. 1–3 (1935): 136. See also Baudrit, *Guide historique,* 162–164.

51. Dang Van Chin, *La Prostitution à Saïgon en 1952* (Saigon: Imprimerie Française d'Outre-Mer, 1953), 49.

52. Clavel, *L'Assistance médicale indigène,* 256.

53. For an example of this usage, see the letter from Nguyễn Văn Đông and Huỳnh Thị Kiều, June 17, 1905, GOUCOCH IB.38/172, TTLTQG-II. For the explanation of this reference, see Dang Van Chin, *Prostitution à Saigon,* 49.

54. Malarney, "Introduction," 7–8.

55. Letter, January 16, 1915, GOUCOCH VIA.8/286(19), TTLTQG-II. This letter documents practices that took place in the municipal dispensary in Chợ Lớn eight years later. It is possible, however, that many of the same practices went on in the municipal dispensary in Saigon in 1906–1907. It appears that many prostitutes worked in both places at different times (they were less than two kilometers apart). They were subject to the same legal constraints and had the same resources available. They doubtless also gossiped among themselves about how to fool the doctor.

56. "Minute," September 28, 1889, GOUCOCH IB.38/171, TTLTQG-II.

57. "M. Marquis à Monsieur le Secrétaire Général de la Cochinchine," November 25, 1889, GOUCOCH IB.38/171, TTLTQG-II.

58. "M. Forestier, Administrateur de l'arrondissement de Cho-Lon à Monsieur le Secrétaire Général," November 5, 1889, GOUCOCH IB.38/171, TTLTQG-II.

59. "Minute," December 6, 1889, GOUCOCH IB.38/171, TTLTQG-II.

60. M. L. R. Montel, *Rapport sur l'état sanitaire de la Ville de Saïgon et sur l'Assistance médicale urbaine* (Saigon: Coudurier & Montégout, 1908), 33–37, 43–44.

61. "Note pour Monsieur le Gouverneur de la Cochinchine," May 13, 1912, GOUCOCH VIA.8/286(14), TTLTQG-II.

62. Each ride cost $0.08. See Baudrit, "Contribution à l'histoire de Saigon," II, 275.

63. See the letters exchanged between the administrator of Biên Hòa, the mayor of Saigon, and the Lieutenant Governor of Cochinchina in GOUCOCH IB.37/257(7), TTLTQG-II.

64. Personal details about Đỗ Thị Tư and the circumstances surrounding her arrest can be found in the record of her interrogation. "Procès Verbal," November 9, 1905, GOU-COCH IB.38/172, TTLTQG-II.

65. The first letter is dated February 12, 1906, the second letter is undated. GOUCOCH IB.38/172, TTLTQG-II.

66. "M. Bos, Administrateur, à Monsieur le Lieutenant-Gouverneur de la Cochinchine (3ème Bureau)," July 4, 1906, GOUCOCH IB.38/172, TTLTQG-II.

67. "Procès Verbal," April 6, 1905, GOUCOCH IB.38/172, TTLTQG-II.

68. Letter from Nguyen Van Dong and Huynh Thi Kieu, June 17, 1905, GOUCOCH IB.38/172, TTLTQG-II.

69. "M. Doceul, Administrateur, à Monsieur le Lieutenant-Gouverneur de la Cochin-chine," August 7, 1906, GOUCOCH IB.38/172, TTLTQG-II.

70. "Etat nominatif des filles soumises de diverses maisons de tolérances ou clandes-tines existantes en traitement au Dispensaire Municipale," GOUCOCH IB.37/257(5), TTLTQG-II.

71. "Rapport de la Commission chargée d'examiner les incurables au dispensaire munici-pal," GOUCOCH IB.37/257(5), TTLTQG-II.

72. "Note pour Monsieur le Lieutenant Gouverneur," April 4, 1907, GOUCOCH IB.37/257(5), TTLTQG-II.

73. John F. Cady, *The Roots of French Imperialism in Eastern Asia* (Ithaca, N.Y.: Cornell University Press, 1954), 272–274; Mark McLeod, *The Vietnamese Response to French Interven-tion, 1862-1874* (New York: Praeger, 1991), 57–59.

74. Letter, April 4, 1899, GOUCOCH IB.38/172, TTLTQG-II; "Le Maire de la Ville de Saï-gon à Monsieur le Gouverneur de la Cochinchine," February 8, 1917, GOUCOCH VIA.8/286(17), TTLTQG-II.

75. November 21, 1934, GOUCOCH VIA.6/311(2), TTLTQG-II.

76. Dr. Tung, "La Prostitution," 1176–1179; Dang Van Chin, *Prostitution à Saigon,* 23–38.

77. "Règlement de Police conformément aux ordres du Vice-Amiral, Gouverneur et Com-mandant en chef," January 22, 1867, SL 4518, TTLTQG-II.

78. *Recueillies des arrêtés sur la police des mœurs* (Saigon: Imprimerie F.-H. Schneider, 1908), 7, GOUCOCH IB.37/257(5), TTLTQG-II.

79. "Commission Municipale: Séance extraordinaire du 2 août 1907. Procès verbal," GOUCOCH IB.37/257(5), TTLTQG-II.
80. "Commission Municipale: Séance extraordinaire du 2 août 1907. Procès verbal," GOUCOCH IB.37/257(5), TTLTQG-II.
81. "Conseil Municipal: Extrait du régistre des délibérations. Séance du 26 Novembre 1905. Procès Verbal," GOUCOCH IB.38/174, TTLTQG-II.

Chapter 3. Between Heaven and Earth

1. Huỳnh Sanh Thông, ed. and trans., *An Anthology of Vietnamese Poems: From the Eleventh through the Twentieth Centuries* (New Haven, Conn.: Yale University Press, 1996), 41.
2. On Quách Đàm, see Nguyễn Phú Xuân, "Quách Đàm: Người Xây Chợ Bình Tây" [Quách Đàm: The man who built Bình Tây Market], *Xưa Và Nay* [Past and present] 214 (2004): 29–30.
3. "A Monsieur le Gouverneur de la Cochinchine à Saïgon," April 17, 1916; "Le Chef du Service de l'Immigration et de l'Identité à Monsieur le Gouverneur de la Cochinchine (Ier Bureau) à Saïgon," August 7, 1916; "Le Commissaire de police de la ville de Cholon, à Monsieur le Président de la Commission municipale, Cholon," September 12, 1916; "Le Chef du Service de l'Immigration et de l'Identité à Monsieur le Gouverneur de la Cochinchine à Saïgon," September 14, 1916; "Expulsion du Chinois Quan-Thanh," GOUCOCH V/10/06.06, TTLTQG-II.
4. Calculated from data in Albert Coquerel, *Paddys et riz de Cochinchine* (Lyon: A. Rey, 1911), Appendix (Table VI).
5. Gouvernement Général de l'Indochine, *Rapports au Conseil Colonial (Session Ordinaire de 1902* (Saigon: Imprimerie Coloniale, 1902), 13.
6. Frederic E. Wakeman, *Strangers at the Gate: Social Disorder in South China, 1839–1861* (Berkeley: University of California Press, 1966), 139–156.
7. For an absorbing study of the mind of Hong Xiuquan, see Jonathan D. Spence, *God's Chinese Son: The Taiping Heavenly Kingdom of Hong Xiuquan* (New York: Norton, 1996). On the nature of the civil war, see Stephen Platt, *Autumn in the Heavenly Kingdom: China, the West, and the Epic Story of the Taiping Civil War* (New York: Alfred A. Knopf, 2012). On the aftermath of the civil war, see Tobie Meyer-Fong, *What Remains: Coming to Terms with Civil War in 19th Century China* (Stanford: Stanford University Press, 2013).
8. Alfred H. Y. Lin, *The Rural Economy of Guangdong, 1870–1937: A Study of the Agrarian Crisis and its Origins in Southernmost China* (London: Macmillan, 1997), 51.
9. Kaoru Sugihara, *Japan, China, and the Growth of the Asian International Economy, 1850–1949* (Oxford: Oxford University Press, 2005), 247.
10. The main biographical details on Trần Dưỡng can be found in a letter written by his wife, Khưu Thị Tâm, to the acting governor of Cochinchina. See Letter. September 24, 1916. GOUCOCH V/10/06.06, TTLTQG-II. In 1916, Khưu Thị Tâm reported that her husband had been in the colony for 13 years, implying that he arrived in 1903.

This is contradicted by "Note pour le chef du Ier Bureau," August 21, 1916, GOUCOCH V/10/06.06, TTLTQG-II, which states that Trần Dưỡng arrived in 1908. The latter is likely to be a transcription error since 3 and 8 often look very similar. Khưu Thị Tâm is unlikely to have been mistaken about how long her husband had been in Cochinchina and all of the other details in her letter can be verified in other documents.

11. Philip A. Kuhn, *Chinese Among Others: Emigration in Modern Times* (Singapore: NUS Press, 2008), 31-32.

12. Đào Trinh Nhất, *Thế Lực Khách Trú Và Vấn Đề Di Dân Vào Nam Kỳ* [Chinese influence and the issue of immigration in Cochinchina] (Hà Nội: Thuỵ Ký, 1924), 19.

13. Sow-Theng Leong, *Migration and Ethnicity in Chinese History: Hakkas, Pengmin, and Their Neighbors* (Stanford: Stanford University Press, 1997), 19, 32-33, 35-36, 65-66.

14. Đào Trinh Nhất, *Thế Lực Khách Trú*, 21.

15. Mary Somers Heidhues, *Golddiggers, Farmers, and Traders in the "Chinese Districts" of West Kalimantan, Indonesia* (Ithaca, N.Y.: Cornell Southeast Asia Program, 2003), 31-43; Daniel Chew, *Chinese Pioneers on the Sarawak Frontier, 1841-1941* (Singapore: Oxford University Press, 1990), 18-24.

16. Wong Lin-Ken, *The Malayan Tin Industry to 1914* (Tucson: University of Arizona Press, 1965), 17-43.

17. Đào Trinh Nhất, *Thế Lực Khách Trú*, 21; "Notice sur la situation des Chinois en Indochine," *Revue Indochinoise* 11 (1909): 1072.

18. Đào Trinh Nhất, *Thế Lực Khách Trú*, 20-21; "Notice sur la situation des Chinois en Indochine," 1071-1073.

19. "Monographie de la Province de Bienhoa en 1930," unpublished typescript, National Library of Vietnam, Hanoi, 19.

20. "Monographie de Biên Hòa," 184; Société des Etudes Indochinoises, *Monographie de la Province de Biên Hòa* (Saigon: Imprimerie L. Ménard, 1901), 43.

21. Distance calculated using figures in Gouvernement Général de l'Indochine, *Rapports au Conseil Colonial (Session Ordinaire de 1914)* (Saigon: Imprimerie Commerciale C. Ardin, 1914), 11; Gouvernement Général de l'Indochine, *Rapports au Conseil Colonial (Session Ordinaire de 1915)* (Saigon: Imprimerie Commerciale C. Ardin, 1915), 12; Gouvernement Général de l'Indochine, *Rapports au Conseil Colonial (Session Ordinaire de 1916)* (Saigon: Imprimerie Commerciale C. Ardin, 1916), 11.

22. Nguyen Quoc Dinh, *Les congrégations Chinoises en Indochine française* (Paris: Recueil Sirey, 1941), 96-121.

23. Letter, September 22, 1916, GOUCOCH V/10/06.06, TTLTQG-II.

24. "L'agitation antifrançaise dans les pays Annamites de 1905 à 1918," GGI 65514, ANOM.

25. "L'Administrateur de Bienhoa à Monsieur le Gouverneur de la Cochinchine," September 9, 1916, GOUCOCH V/10/06.06, TTLTQG-II.

26. E. A. F. Garrigues, "La Cochinchine," in *La Justice en Indochine: Organisation Générale—La Justice Indigène*, ed. H. Morché (Hanoi: Imprimerie d'Extrême-Orient, 1931), 47, 53-54.

27. "L'Administrateur de Bienhoa à Monsieur le Gouverneur de la Cochinchine," September 9, 1916, GOUCOCH V/10/06.06, TTLTQG-II.

28. Garrigues, "La Cochinchine," 46–47.

29. Garrigues, "La Cochinchine," 50–51.

30. Letter, September 9, 1916 and letter, July 18, 1916, GOUCOCH V/10/06.06, TTLTQG-II.

31. Letter, July 31, 1916, GOUCOCH V/10/06.06, TTLTQG-II.

32. Nguyễn Thị Nguyệt, "Thiên Hậu Cổ Miếu" [Ancient temple to the Empress of Heaven], in Đồng Nai Di Tích Lịch Sử Văn Hóa [Cultural historical relics of Đồng Nai], ed. Trần Quang Toại (Đồng Nai: Tổng Hợp Đồng Nai, 2004), 219–220, 225.

33. Letter, September 22, 1916, GOUCOCH V/10/06.06, TTLTQG-II.

34. James L. Watson, "Standardizing the Gods: The Promotion of T'ien Hou ("Empress of Heaven") Along the South China Coast, 960–1960," in Popular Culture in Late Imperial China, ed. David Johnson, Andrew Nathan, and Evelyn Rawski (Berkeley: University of California Press, 1985), 293, 295, 299. See also Valerie Hansen, Changing Gods in Medieval China, 1127–1276 (Princeton, N.J.: Princeton University Press, 1990), 144–148.

35. Tsai Maw-Kuey, Les Chinois au Sud-Vietnam (Paris: Bibliothèque Nationale, 1968), 220–223.

36. Lê Văn Lưu, Pagodes Chinoises et Annamites de Cholon (Hanoi: Imprimerie Tonkinois, 1931), 41–58.

37. Mark Ravinder Frost, "Emporium in Imperio: Nanyang Networks and the Straits Chinese in Singapore, 1819–1914," Journal of Southeast Asian Studies 36, no. 1 (2005): 45–46.

38. "L'Administrateur de Bienhoa à Monsieur le Gouverneur de la Cochinchine," August 5, 1915, GOUCOCH V/10/06.06, TTLTQG-II.

39. "Note pour Monsieur le Chef du Ier Bureau," August 21, 1916, GOUCOCH V/10/06.06, TTLTQG-II.

40. Jean-Baptiste Duvergier, Collection complète des lois, décrets, ordonnances, règlements, vol. 49 (Paris: 1849), 418–419.

41. Journal Officiel de la République française, June 10, 1874, 3873. On the powers of the Governor of Cochinchina, see Journal Officiel de l'Indochinese française, no. 12 (1911): 1383–1403.

42. "Arrêté," August 23, 1916, GOUCOCH V/10/06.06, TTLTQG-II.

43. A. Brebion and Antoine Cabaton, Dictionnaire de bio-bibliographie générale, ancienne et moderne de l'Indochine française (Paris: Société d'Editions, 1935), 328–329.

44. "Note," September 11, 1916, GOUCOCH V/10/06.06, TTLTQG-II.

45. "Letter," August 28, 1916; "Letter," August 29, 1916; "H. de Mérona, Avocat-Défenseur à Monsieur le Gouverneur de Cochinchine," August 31, 1916, GOUCOCH V/10/06.06, TTLTQG-II.

46. "L'Administrateur de Bienhoa à Monsieur le Gouverneur de la Cochinchine," September 9, 1916, GOUCOCH V/10/06.06, TTLTQG-II.

47. Yves Henry, Economie agricole de l'Indochine (Hanoi: Imprimerie d'Extrême-Orient, 1932), 273; Coquerel, Paddys et riz, Appendix (Table VI).

48. Annuaire Statistique de l'Indochine, 1913–1922 (Hanoi: Imprimerie d'Extrême-Orient, 1927), 218.

49. André Baudrit, *Guide historique des rues de Saigon* (Saigon: S.I.L.I., 1945), table after 80.

50. Gouvernement Général de l'Indochine, *Rapports au Conseil Colonial (Session ordinaire de 1917)* (Saigon: C. Ardin et fils, 1917), 14–15.

51. "Rapport sur la situation politique de la Cochinchine pendant le 2ème trimestre 1914," GGI 64335, ANOM. On the stalls in the market and their economic role during the colonial period more generally, see Lebon, "L'importance économique des Halles Centrales de Saïgon," *Bulletin économique de l'Indochine* 42 (1939): 125–134.

52. Gouvernement Général de l'Indochine, *Rapports au Conseil Colonial (Session ordinaire de 1917)* (Saïgon: C. Ardin et fils, 1917), 14–15.

53. "Extrait du rapport sur la situation politique de la Cochinchine pendant le 4ème trimestre 1915," INDO NF 28(2), ANOM.

54. On the floods at the beginning of 1914, for example, see "Rapport sur la situation générale du Tonkin 1914," GGI 64188, ANOM.

55. See Luo Zhitian, "National Humiliation and National Assertion: The Chinese Response to the Twenty-One Demands," *Modern Asian Studies* 27, no. 2 (1993): 297–319.

56. "Extrait du rapport sur la situation politique de la Cochinchine pendant le 1er trimestre 1915," INDO NF 28(2), ANOM.

57. Gouvernement Général de l'Indochine, *Rapports au Conseil Colonial (Session Ordinaire de 1916)* (Saigon: Imprimerie Commerciale C. Ardin, 1916), 49.

58. "Extrait du rapport sur la situation politique de la Cochinchine pendant le 2ème trimestre 1915," INDO NF 28(2), ANOM.

59. "Gouverneur Général Roume à M. le Ministre de Colonies," March 31, 1916, INDO NF 570, ANOM; "Résident Supérieur Baudoin à M. le Gouverneur Général Roume," January 29, 1916, INDO NF 28(3), ANOM. On this episode, see also Alain Forest, "Les manifestations de 1916 au Cambodge," in *Histoire de l'Asie du Sud-Est: révoltes, réformes, révolutions,* ed. Pierre Brocheux (Lille: Presses universitaires de Lille, 1981), 63–82; Milton Osborne, "Peasant Politics in Cambodia: The 1916 Affair," *Modern Asian Studies* 12, no. 2 (1978): 217–243.

60. "L'agitation antifrançaise dans les pays Annamites de 1905 à 1918," GGI 65514, ANOM; "Le Gouverneur de la Cochinchine à Monsieur le Gouverneur Général de l'Indochine," March 3, 1916, INDO NF 28(2), ANOM; Coulet, *Les sociétés secrètes,* 20; Lương Văn Lựu, *Biên Hòa Sử Lược,* vol. 2 [A brief history of Biên Hòa] (n.p., 1972), 195; Georges Coulet, *Les sociétés secrètes en terres d'Annam* (Saigon: C. Ardin, 1926), 19–20.

61. "Le Gouverneur Général de l'Indochine à Monsieur le Ministre de Colonies," March 29, 1916, INDO NF 28(2), ANOM.

62. E. Alexander Powell, *Where the Strange Trails Go Down* (New York: Charles Scribner's Sons, 1921), 276.

63. Dian H. Murray and Qin Baoqi, *The Origins of the Tiandihui: The Chinese Triads in Legend and History* (Stanford: Stanford University Press, 1994), 16–20.

64. Murray and Qin, *Origins of the Tiandihui,* 189. The translation is by Murray and Qin.

65. On the Tây Sơn rebellion, see Li Tana, *Nguyễn Cochinchina: Southern Vietnam in the Seventeenth and Eighteenth Centuries* (Ithaca, N.Y.: Southeast Asia Program, Cornell

University, 1998), 139–154; George Dutton, *The Tây Sơn Uprising: Society and Rebellion in Eighteenth-Century Vietnam* (Honolulu: University of Hawaiʻi Press, 2006).

66. Quốc Sử Quán Triều Nguyễn, *Đại Nam Liệt Truyện* [Biographies of Đại Nam], Tập 1–2, trans. Đỗ Mộng Khương (Huế: Thuận Hóa, 2013), 516–517.

67. On this incident, see Nguyen The Anh, "Secret Societies: Some Reflections on the Court of Huế and the Government of Cochinchina on the Eve of Tự Đức's Death (1882–1883)," *Asian Affairs* 65, no. 2 (1978): 179–185; Nola Cooke, "The Heaven and Earth Society Upsurge in Early 1880s French Cochinchina," *Chinese Southern Diaspora Studies* 4 (2010): 42–73.

68. "L'agitation antifrançaise dans les pays Annamites de 1905 à 1918," GGI 65514, ANOM.

69. For seven different accounts of this origin story, see Murray and Qin, *Origins of the Tiandihui*, 197–228. For an extended analysis of the story, see Barend ter Haar, *Ritual and Mythology of the Chinese Triads: Creating an Identity* (Leiden: Brill, 1998), 365–416. Although the most famous Shaolin monastery is in Henan province, the origin story refers to a Shaolin monastery in Gansu.

70. Henri Dusson, *Les sociétés secrètes en Chine et en terre d'Annam: réquisitoire* (Saigon: Imprimerie Phat Toan, 1911), 46–48. On the ceremony, see ter Haar, *Ritual and Mythology of the Chinese Triads,* 101–136.

71. "L'agitation antifrançaise dans les pays Annamites de 1905 à 1918," GGI 65514, ANOM. On the decomposition of characters important to the Heaven and Earth Society, see Barend ter Haar, "Messianism and the Heaven and Earth Society: Approaches to Heaven and Earth Society Texts," in *"Secret Societies" Reconsidered: Perspectives on the Social History of Modern South China and Southeast Asia,* ed. David Ownby (Armonk, N.Y.: M.E. Sharpe, 1993), 156–157.

72. Đào Trinh Nhất, *Thế Lực Khách Trú,* 63. The first tattoo is from Book XV, Chapter 8 of *The Analects* by Confucius.

73. Dusson, *Les sociétés secrètes,* 42–43.

74. "L'agitation antifrançaise dans les pays Annamites de 1905 à 1918," GGI 65514, ANOM.

75. Dusson, *Les sociétés secrètes,* 55–56.

76. Letter, September 24, 1916, GOUCOCH V/10/06.06, TTLTQG-II.

77. Letter, September 22, 1916, GOUCOCH V/10/06.06, TTLTQG-II.

78. Letter, September 20, 2016, GOUCOCH V/10/06.06, TTLTQG-II.

79. Letter, September 22, 1916, GOUCOCH V/10/06.06, TTLTQG-II.

80. Letter, September 24, 1916, GOUCOCH V/10/06.06, TTLTQG-II.

Chapter 4. A Human Horse

1. Huỳnh Sanh Thông, ed. and trans., *An Anthology of Vietnamese Poems: From the Eleventh through the Twentieth Centuries* (New Haven, Conn.: Yale University Press, 1996), 121.

2. "Gendarmerie Nationale," December 3, 1914, GOUCOCH V.10/07.06, TTLTQG-II.

3. "Le Commissaire Spécial, Monnier, à Monsieur le Chef du Service de la Sûreté, Saïgon," September 18, 1922, GOUCOCH V.10/07.07, TTLTQG-II.

4. On the Cham towers and Vijaya, see Trần Kỳ Phương, "The Architecture of the Temple-Towers of Ancient Champa (Central Vietnam)," in *Champa and the Archaeology of Mỹ Sơn (Vietnam)*, ed. Andrew Hardy, Mauro Cucarzi, and Patrizia Zolese (Singapore: NUS Press, 2009); Michael Vickery, "Champa Revised," in *The Cham of Vietnam: History, Society and Art,* ed. Trần Kỳ Phương and Bruce M. Lockhart (Singapore: NUS Press, 2011), 363–420.

5. On Nguyễn Hoàng, see Keith W. Taylor, "Nguyen Hoang and the Beginning of Vietnam's Southward Expansion," in *Southeast Asia in the Early Modern Era: Trade, Power, and Belief,* ed. Anthony Reid (Ithaca, N.Y.: Cornell University Press, 1993), 42–65.

6. On the Save the King Movement, see David G. Marr, *Vietnamese Anticolonialism, 1885–1925* (Berkeley: University of California Press, 1971), 44–76; For details on the death of Phan Đình Phùng, see "Rapport à M. le Gouverneur Général. Situation générale de l'Annam pendant la période de Janvier 1896," GGI 64209, ANOM.

7. "Rapport à M. le Gouverneur Général sur la situation générale de l'Annam en février 1896"; "Rapport à M. le Gouverneur Général. Rapport politique de Mai-Juin 1896," GGI 64209, ANOM.

8. "Rapport à M. le Gouverneur Général. Rapport politique d'Octobre 1896," GGI 64209, ANOM.

9. An astonishing number of people questioned by the police said that they did not know who their parents were. See various reports in GOUCOCH VIA.6/076(6); SL 1706; GOUCOCH VIA.8/1812(5); GOUCOCH VIA.8/325(1); GOUCOCH VIA.8/201(1); GOUCOCH VIA.8/282(2), TTLTQG-II.

10. See Direction Générale de l'Instruction Publique, *L'Annam scolaire: de l'enseignement traditionnel annamite à l'enseignement moderne franco-indigène* (Hanoi: Imprimerie d'Extrême-Orient, 1931), 7–10.

11. "Rapport d'Inspection de la province de Binh Dinh," August 1913, INDO NF 206, ANOM.

12. For the population figure from the Gia Long reign, see Quốc Sử Quán Triều Nguyễn, *Đại Nam Nhất Thống Chí* [Gazetteer of Đại Nam], vol. 3, trans. Phạm Trọng Điềm (Huế: Thuận Hóa, 2006), 18. For later figures, see Đinh Văn Liên, *Bình Định: Đất Võ Trời Văn* [Bình Định: Martial land, civilian sky] (Hồ Chí Minh City: Trẻ, 2008), 14–15.

13. "Rapport d'Inspection de la province de Binh Dinh," August 1913, INDO NF 206, ANOM.

14. "Rapport de mission présenté par Camille Devilar, Publiciste, à Monsieur le Gouverneur Générale. Petites Industries, et Industries Familiales en Indochine et au Japon," 1913, INDO NF 966, ANOM.

15. "Rapport d'Inspection de la province de Binh Dinh," August 1913, INDO NF 206, ANOM.

16. "L'Agitation Antifrançaise dans les Pays Annamites de 1905 à 1918," vol. 2, GGI 65514, ANOM.

17. "Le Résident Supérieur p.i. en Annam à Monsieur le Gouverneur Général de l'Indochine," October 16, 1913, GGI 64222, ANOM.

18. "Rapport d'Inspection de la province de Binh Dinh," August 1913, INDO NF 206, ANOM.

19. "Rapport politique du 1er trimestre 1913," March 20, 1913; "Rapport à Monsieur le Gouverneur Général: Rapport politique du 2e trimestre 1913"; "Rapport politique au 2e trimestre 1913 à M. le Résident Supérieur en Annam," June 19, 1913, GGI 64222, ANOM.

20. "Interrogation du nommé Trần Văn Lang, objet de la lettre n°2171 en date du 4 Décembre 1914 de M. l'Administrateur de Vinh Long," GOUCOCH V.10/07.06, TTLTQG-II.

21. On the role of rail in colonial Vietnamese history, see David del Testa, "Paint the Trains Red: Labor, Nationalism, and the Railroads in French Colonial Indochina, 1898–1945," (Ph.D. diss., University of California at Davis, 2001). For a study of public works in the Mekong delta during the colonial period, see David Biggs, *Quagmire: Nation-Building and Nature in the Mekong Delta* (Seattle: University of Washington Press, 2010), 23–125.

22. Société des Etudes Indochinoises, *Monographie de la Province de Vinh Long* (Saigon: Imprimerie Commerciale M. Rey, 1911) refers to "two colonial routes" traversing the province, numbered four and seven, 8. These were not, however, the two "Colonial Routes," numbered four and seven. Colonial Route Four extended from the frontier with China through Tonkin and Laos. Colonial Route Seven linked the coast of Annam with the Mekong River Valley through Laos. See A. A. Pouyane, *Les Travaux Publics de l'Indochine* (Hanoi: Imprimerie d'Extrême-Orient, 1926), 69–70. For a later discussion of these roads, see Huynh Minh, *Vĩnh Long Xưa* [Vĩnh Long in the past] (Saigon: Thanh Niên, 2002), 52.

23. "Rapport sur la situation politique de la Cochinchine pendant le 2ème trimestre 1914," GGI 64335, ANOM.

24. See Pouyane, *Travaux Publics de l'Indochine,* 196, 205.

25. On Đồng Tháp Mười, see Victor Delahaye, *La Plaine des Joncs et sa mise en valeur: étude géographique* (Rennes, France: Imprimerie de l'Ouest-Eclair, 1928).

26. *Monographie de la Province de Vinh Long,* 5, 6, 19.

27. Henri Brenier, *Essai d'atlas statistique de l'Indochine française* (Hanoi-Haiphong: Imprimerie d'Extrême-Orient, 1914), 149–151. The information in the *Essai d'atlas* varies a little from other sources. The *Monographie de la Province de Vinhlong* gives an area of 115,000 hectares, of which 88,000 had been cultivated in 1910. Coquerel reports a cultivated area of 90,000 hectares for 1910. See Albert Coquerel, *Paddys et riz de Cochinchine* (Lyons: Imprimerie A. Rey, 1911), Appendices (Table V). Nguyễn Đình Đầu gives the area of the province as 1,087 square kilometers, or 108,700 hectares. See Nguyễn Đình Đầu, *Nghiên Cứu Địa Bạ Triều Nguyễn: Vĩnh Long* [Research on the cadastral registers of the Nguyễn Dynasty: Vĩnh Long] (Hồ Chí Minh City: Thành Phố Hồ Chí Minh, 1994), 102. The *Annuaire Statistique* for 1913–1922 gives an area of 1,000 square kilome-

ters or 100,000 hectares. See *Annuaire Statistique de l'Indochine, vol. 1: 1913-1922* (Hanoi: Imprimerie d'Extrême-Orient, 1927), 31.

28. *Statistique Commerciale de la Cochinchine pour l'année 1938* (Saigon: Société des Imprimeries et Librairies Indochinoises, 1939), 455.

29. "Rapport sur la situation politique de la Cochinchine pendant le 1er trimestre 1914," GGI 64335, ANOM.

30. *Statistique Commerciale*, 452.

31. *Monographie de la Province de Vinh Long*, 23-24.

32. Brenier, *Essai d'atlas*, 69.

33. *Annuaire Statistique de l'Indochine, vol. 1, 1913-1922*, 274.

34. Vu Van Hien, "Les institutions annamites depuis l'arrivée des français: l'impôt personnel et les corvées de 1862 à 1936," *Revue Indochinoise Juridique et Economique* 13 (1940): 92-93, 103-104.

35. See Masaya Shiraishi, "State, Villagers, and Vagabonds: Vietnamese Rural Society and the Phan Bá Vành Rebellion," *Senri Ethnological Studies* 13 (1984): 345-400.

36. *Etat de la Cochinchine Française* (1879): 75-76; *Etat de la Cochinchine Française* (1880): 113-115; *Etat de la Cochinchine Française* (1881): 123-125; *Etat de la Cochinchine Française* (1882): 121-123; *Etat de la Cochinchine Française* (1885): 87-88; *Etat de la Cochinchine Française* (1895): 141-142; *Etat de la Cochinchine Française* (1900): 210; *Annuaire Statistique de l'Indochine, vol. 1, 1913-1922*, 94. Contemporary observers also documented a significant increase in vagrancy at the turn of the twentieth century. See Maurice Chautemps, *Le Vagabondage en pays annamite* (Paris: Paris: Librairie Nouvelle de Droit et de Jurisprudence, 1908). The Vietnamese journalist and Trotskyist Phan Văn Hùm commented in his memoirs on the number of vagrants in the Saigon Central Prison. Convicts were constantly being imprisoned and freed. "Sitting in prison," he wrote, "one sees people come in every day, so that each week one sees the whole population reborn twice." The convicts had committed many different offences: "burglary, robbery, disorderly behavior, homicide, etc. But," Phan Văn Hùm observed, "there are also people sentenced for a single month for the crime of having 'no livelihood' as they say in prison (vagrancy), or for a couple of days for failure to pay the head tax." Phan Văn Hùm explained that "to have 'no livelihood' is to say that they are unemployed, and because they are unemployed, they lack official documents, then because they lack official documents, they are thrown into prison." See Phan Văn Hùm, *Ngồi Tù Khám Lớn* [Sitting in the big jail] (Sài Gòn: Dân Tộc, 1957), 135. For a discussion of the place of vagrants in Vietnamese prisons, see Peter Zinoman, *The Colonial Bastille: A History of Imprisonment in Vietnam, 1862-1940* (Berkeley: University of California Press, 2001), 101-102.

37. Letter, February 25, 1899; letter, October 1901, SL 223, TTLTQG-II.

38. "M. Debernardi administrateur, à Monsieur le Lieutenant Gouverneur," October 16, 1901, SL 223, TTLTQG-II.

39. "Notes de Sûreté concernant la situation politique indigène au 25 Mai 1923," GGI 65474, ANOM.

40. "M. Pétillet, Administrateur de Vinhlong à Monsieur, le Commissaire Central de police à Saigon," December 4, 1914; "Interrogation du nommé Trần Văn Lang, objet de la lettre n°2171 en date du 4 Décembre 1914 de M. l'Administrateur de Vinh Long"; Arrêté, December 11, 1914, GOUCOCH V.10/07.06, TTLTQG-II.

41. M. Robert, *Monographie de la Province de Biênhoa* (Saigon: Imprimerie du Centre, 1924), 101–117; *Annuaire statistique de l'Indochine, vol. 1, 1913–1922* (Hanoi: Imprimerie d'Extrême-Orient, 1927), 116; *Annuaire statistique de l'Indochine, vol. 2, 1923–1929* (Hanoi: Imprimerie d'Extrême-Orient, 1931), 148.

42. Robequain, *Economic Development,* 202.

43. Fernand de Montaigut, *La colonisation française dans l'est de la Cochinchine* (Limoges: Imprimerie Commerciale Perrette, 1929), 20–21.

44. For detailed migration figures from 1919 until 1930, see E. Delamarre, *L'émigration et l'immigration ouvrière en Indochine* (Hanoi: Imprimerie d'Extrême-Orient, 1931), 34ff. See also International Labour Office, *Labour Conditions in Indochina* (Geneva: League of Nations, 1938), 292.

45. Robert, *Monographie,* 89–91. The same area, number of trees, and production figures for Suzannah are reported in *Annales des planteurs de caoutchouc de l'Indochine* (1922).

46. The best-known account of life on a rubber plantation is Trần Tử Bình, *Phú Riềng Đỏ* [The red earth] (Hà Nội: Lao Động, 1971). For an English translation, see Tran Tu Binh, *The Red Earth: A Vietnamese Memoir of Life on a Colonial Rubber Plantation,* trans. John Spragens, Jr., ed. and intro. David G. Marr (Athens: Ohio University Center for International Studies, 1985).

47. Delamarre, *L'émigration et l'immigration,* 34ff. Of the 366 deserters each year, the authorities located 89, on average, and returned them to the plantations.

48. See César N. Caviedes, *El Niño in History: Storming Through the Ages* (Gainesville: University of Florida Press, 2001). On the interaction between El Niño and European colonial rule, see Mike Davis, *Late Victorian Holocausts: El Niño Famines and the Making of the Third World* (London: Verso, 2001).

49. "Rapport sur la situation politique de la Cochinchine pendant le 1er trimestre 1919"; "Rapport sur la situation politique de la Cochinchine pendant le 2ème trimestre 1919," GGI 64336, ANOM; "Rapport économique de Cochinchine," 1919. INDO NF 800, ANOM. On the surge in prosecutions for vagrancy and begging, see *Annuaire Statistique de l'Indochine, vol. 1, 1913–1922,* 94. There were 1,583 prosecutions for vagrancy and begging in Cochinchina in 1919, more than there had been in the whole of Indochina in five of the previous six years.

50. *Statistique Commerciale,* 455. The fall in rice exports in 1919 was the largest year-on-year drop during the colonial period.

51. See V. D. Wickizer and M. K. Bennett, *The Rice Economy of Monsoon Asia* (Stanford: Stanford University Press, 1941), 326. See also Paul H. Kratoska, "The British Empire and the Southeast Asian Rice Crisis of 1919–1921," *Modern Asian Studies* 24, no. 1 (1990): 115–146.

52. Calculated from figures in *Statistique Commerciale de la Cochinchine pour l'année 1935* (Saigon: Société des Imprimeries et Librairies Indochinoises, 1936), 462–463.

53. Direction des Services Economiques, *Résumé statistique relatif aux années 1913 à 1940* (Hanoi: Imprimerie d'Extrême-Orient, 1941), 30.

54. "Les Chinois font fortune," *Tribune Indigène*, March 20, 1919.

55. Đắc Văn, "Lettres aux compatriotes: La solidarité. La solidarité entre producteurs. Une féderation des syndicats agricoles," *Tribune Indigène*, April 29, 1919.

56. On this boycott campaign, see Micheline Lessard, "'Organisons-nous!' Racial Antagonism and Vietnamese Economic Nationalism in the Early Twentieth Century," *French Colonial History* 8 (2007): 171–201; Christopher E. Goscha, "Widening the Colonial Encounter: Asian Connections inside French Indochina during the Interwar Period," *Modern Asian Studies* 43 (2009): 1200–1209. Both Lessard and Goscha are more concerned with the antagonism between the Vietnamese and Chinese in Cochinchina than they are with the economic situation that underlay that antagonism.

57. *Annuaire économique de l'Indochine, 1926–1927, Deuxième Partie,* 631–13.

58. Direction des Services Economiques, *Résumé statistique,* 11.

59. "Rapport sur le fonctionnement des monts-de-piété de Saïgon pendant l'année 1920," GGI 3107, ANOM.

60. "Rapport économique annuel de l'année 1920," GOUCOCH DIVERS 3155, TTLTQG-II.

61. "Rapport politique du 4e trimestre 1920," SL 365, TTLTQG-II.

62. "Rapport économique annuel de l'année 1920," GOUCOCH DIVERS 3155, TTLTQG-II.

63. André Baudrit, *Guide historique des rues de Saïgon* (Saigon: S.I.L.I, 1943), table after 80.

64. On administrative aspects of the rickshaw trade in French Indochina, see Hazel Hahn, "The Rickshaw Trade in Colonial Vietnam, 1883–1940," *Journal of Vietnamese Studies* 8, no. 4 (2014): 47–85. On the rickshaw in Singapore, see James Francis Warren, *Rickshaw Coolie: A People's History of Singapore, 1880–1940* (Singapore: Singapore University Press, 2003), 14, 33–50, 282; idem, "The Singapore Rickshaw Pullers: The Social Organization of a Coolie Occupation, 1880–1940," *Journal of Southeast Asian Studies* 16, no. 1 (1985): 1–15; on the rickshaw in Beijing, see David Strand, *Rickshaw Beijing: City People and Politics in the 1920s* (Berkeley: University of California Press, 1989).

65. André Masson, *Hanoï pendant la période héroïque (1873–1888)* (Paris: Librairie Orientaliste Paul Geuthner, 1929), 168; Trần Huy Liệu, *Lịch Sử Thủ Đô Hà Nội* [History of the capital Hà Nội] (Hà Nội: Sử Học, 1960), 118.

66. Paul Bourde, *De Paris au Tonkin* (Paris: Calmann Lévy, 1885), 342–343.

67. Masson, *Hanoï,* 169.

68. André Baudrit, "Contribution à l'histoire de Saïgon: Extraits des registres de délibérations de la Ville de Saïgon (Indochine Française), 1867–1916," II, *Bulletin de la Société des Etudes Indochinoises,* New Series 10, nos. 1–3 (1933): 222–247.

69. Baudrit, "Contribution à l'histoire de Saïgon," II, 273–274.

70. Baudrit, "Contribution à l'histoire de Saïgon," II, 229.

71. "Arrêté concernant la règlementation de la circulation des voitures japonaises dites pousse-pousse," GOUCOCH III59/N81(1), TTLTQG-II. Earlier regulations make no mention of different classes of vehicles. See "Arrêté. Le Maire de la Ville de Saïgon. Règlementation des pousse-pousse," January 4, 1896, GOUCOCH III.59/N94(4), TTLTQG-II.
72. "Arrêté: Le Maire de la Ville de Saïgon," GOUCOCH IA.20/277(5), TTLTQG-II.
73. The city of Saigon seems to have kept no systematic record of the number of rickshaws on its streets or the number of pullers in the profession. In 1916, there were 1,362 rickshaws registered in the city. See "Ville de Saïgon: Situation Trimestrielle. Santé, Hygiène et Salubrité publiques. Etat-Civil européen et indigène. Assistance publique et médicale. Situation économique. Travau. 4ème trimestre 1916," GOU-COCH IA.8/232, TTLTQG-II. By 1935, there were 2,984. See "Nombre de pousse-pousse circulant sur le territoire de la région de Saigon-Cholon," GOUCOCH VIA.7/192(14), TTLTQG-II. Each rickshaw usually had two pullers who rented it from a proprietor in shifts, which meant that there were roughly 6,000 rickshaw pullers in Saigon. If each puller had a spouse and only a single child, as many as eighteen thousand people in Saigon would have relied on rickshaw pulling for their livelihood. This would have constituted nearly a sixth of the population. A member of the Colonial Council made a similar calculation when Saigon and Chợ Lớn considered abolishing rickshaws two years later: "If one considers that there are more than 4,000 rickshaws in circulation, that each rickshaw occupies two pullers, that it is necessary to have foremen in these enterprises, and that the great majority of these workers are married and the fathers of a family," the councilor reasoned, then if the rickshaw was abolished "one can evaluate from 40,000 to 50,000 the number of people who will be deprived of their current means of existence." See "Procès Verbal," July 5, 1937, GOUCOCH VIA.8/186(16), TTLTQG-II. See also a very similar calculation by a French proprietor of a rickshaw firm in "M. Poggi, Président du Sydicat des Entrepreneurs de pousse-pousse de la Ville de Saigon, à Monsieur le Gouverneur de la Cochinchine à Saigon," GOUCOCH VIA.7/192(14).
74. Baudrit, "Contribution à l'histoire de Saïgon," II, 359.
75. Baudrit, "Contribution à l'histoire de Saïgon," II, 363.
76. *Rapports au Conseil Colonial sur les fonctionnement des services locaux (session ordinaire de 1920)* (Saigon: C. Ardin, 1920), 11; *Rapports au Conseil Colonial sur le fonctionnement des services locaux (session ordinaire de 1921)* (Saigon: Imprimerie Commerciale, 1921), 10.
77. These remained in force until the end of the 1930s. For a mention establishing that the bylaws of 1913 remained in force in 1934, see "M. Poggi, Président du Sydicat des Entrepreneurs de pousse-pousse de la Ville de Saïgon, à Monsieur le Gouverneur de la Cochinchine à Saigon," GOUCOCH VIA.7/192(14); and in 1937, see "Arrêté," GOUCOCH VIA.8/186(16), TTLTQG-II.
78. "Arrêté: Le Maire de la Ville de Saïgon," GOUCOCH IA.20/277(5), TTLTQG-II.
79. "Arrêté: Le Maire de la Ville de Saïgon," GOUCOCH IA.20/277(5), TTLTQG-II.

80. "Arrêté: Le Maire de la Ville de Saïgon," GOUCOCH IA.20/277(5), TTLTQG-II.

81. See *Guide pratique: Renseignements & Adresses. Saïgon* (Saigon: J. Aspar, n.d.), 13; See also the advice on rickshaw travel in L.I., *Saïgon-Souvenir, petit guide saïgonnais à l'usage des passagers des débutants dans la colonie* (Saigon: Imprimerie et Librairie Nouvelles, 1906); Cl. Madrolle, *Guide du Voyageur: Indo-Chine canal de Suez, Djibouti et Harrar. Indes, Ceylan, Siam, Chine Méridionale* (Paris: Librairie Africaine et Coloniale, 1902); idem, *Vers Angkor* (Paris: Librairie Hachette, 1925); *Indochine du Nord: Tonkin, Annam, Laos, Yunnan, Kouang-Tcheou Wan* (Paris: Librairie Hachette, 1932).

82. "Indices du coût de la vie à Hanoï et à Saïgon," *Bulletin économique de l'Indochine* 34 (1931): 15–21. See also the weighting assigned to rickshaw travel in Jean-Dominique Giacometti, "Wages and Consumer Price for Urban and Industrial Workers in Vietnam under French Rule (1910–1954)," in *Quantitative Economic History of Vietnam, 1900–1990: An International Workshop*, ed. Jean-Pascal Bassino, Jean-Dominique Giacometti, and Konosuke Odaka (Tokyo: Institute of Economic Research, Hitotsubashi University, 1999), 172.

83. For this observation, see "M. Poggi, Président du Sydicat des Entrepreneurs de pousse-pousse de la Ville de Saïgon, à Monsieur le Gouverneur de la Cochinchine à Saïgon," GOUCOCH VIA.7/192(14), TTLTQG-II; "Procès Verbal," July 5, 1937, GOUCOCH VIA.8/186(16), TTLTQG-II.

84. The travel guides discussed above indicate the relative costs of different forms of public transport.

85. For uses of this phrase in Vietnamese-language journalism, see Tam Lang, "Tôi Kéo Xe" [I pulled a rickshaw], in *Phóng Sự Việt Nam, 1932–1945* [Vietnamese reportage, 1932–1945], vol. 1, comp. Phan Trọng Thưởng (Hà Nội: Văn Học, 2000), 17–71. See also the fine translation in Greg Lockhart and Monique Lockhart, trans., *The Light of the Capital: Three Modern Vietnamese Classics* (Kuala Lumpur: Oxford in Asia, 1996), 51–120. Another important, later, example of this phrase in Vietnamese literature can be found in Nguyễn Công Hoan, "Người Ngựa Và Ngựa Người" [Horse men and men horses] in *Nguyễn Công Hoan Toàn Tập: Truyện Ngắn* [The collected works of Nguyễn Công Hoan: Short stories], vol. 1 (Hà Nội: Văn Học, 2003), 163–174. Both of these prominent examples come from Hà Nội and date from 1932 and 1930, respectively. There was, however, an active newspaper campaign against rickshaw pulling in the Saigon newspaper *Công Giáo Đồng Thinh* (Catholic voice) in 1928 that also referred to "người ngựa."

86. See "Note," June 11, 1935, GOUCOCH VIA.7/192(14), TTLTQG-II. Although this observation dates from thirteen years later, it very likely applied in 1922 as well.

87. International Labour Office, *Opium and Labour: Being a Report on a Documentary Investigation into the Extent and Effects of Opium-Smoking among Workers* (Geneva: League of Nations, 1935), 35.

88. "Arrêté: Le Maire de la Ville de Saïgon," GOUCOCH IA.20/277(5), TTLTQG-II.

89. "Procès Verbal: Examen d'un projet d'arrêté portant modification à l'arrêté réglementant la circulation et les conditions de fabrication des pousse-pousse," November 16, 1910, GOUCOCH IA.20/277(5); "Procès Verbal," July 5, 1937, GOUCOCH VIA.8/186(16), TTLTQG-II.

90. Laurent Gaide and Pierre Dorolle, *La Tuberculose et sa prophylaxie en Indochine française* (Hanoi: Imprimerie d'Extrême-Orient, 1930), 10, 24.

91. On tuberculosis, see Thomas M. Daniel, *Captain of Death: The Story of Tuberculosis* (Rochester, N.Y.: University of Rochester Press, 1997).

92. International Labour Office, *Opium and Labour*, 35–36.

93. Jacques Dumarest, *Les monopoles de l'opium et du sel en Indochine* (Lyon: Bosc Frères M. & L. Riou, 1938), 15–16, 22–27; League of Nations, *Commission of Enquiry into the Control of Opium-Smoking in the Far East: Report to the Council*, vol. 2, *Detailed Memoranda on Each Territory Visited by the Commission* (Geneva: League of Nations, 1931), 297–299. Cochinchina had the largest number of such licensed opium vendors—some 903 in 1928. See League of Nations, *Commission of Enquiry*, 301.

94. International Labour Office, *Opium and Labour*, 35.

95. On *écorce d'opium* and dross, see League of Nations, *Commission of Enquiry*, 298, 306–307.

96. The contribution that the opium monopoly made to the finances of the colonial government is discussed in Chantal Descours-Gatan, *Quand l'opium finançait la colonisation en Indochine: l'élaboration de la régie générale de l'opium* (Paris: L'Harmattan, 1992), esp. 191–226; Philippe Le Failler, *Monopole et prohibition de l'opium en Indochine: le pilori des chimères* (Paris: L'Harmattan, 2001), esp. 81–118. The importance of opium to the budget of the colonial government declined after World War I as a consequence of the international movement to suppress the smoking of opium and the decrease in disposable income after the Great Depression. In 1920 opium accounted for 19% of the colonial government's budget. It provided only 10.5% of the budget in 1925, 9.5% in 1930, and 4.7% in 1932. See Dumarest, *Les monopoles de l'opium*, 122–123.

97. "Procès Verbal," July 5, 1937, GOUCOCH VIA.8/186(16), TTLTQG-II.

98. "Note," September 7, 1922, GOUCOCH V.10/07.06, TTLTQG-II.

99. J. Obrecht, "Le problème de l'identification et l'organisation des Services d'Identité en Indochine," *Revue Indochinoise Juridique et Economique* 17 (1942): 2–3. For an absorbing discussion of criminal identification and criminal tribes in South Asia, see Clare Anderson, *Legible Bodies: Race, Criminality, and Colonialism in South Asia* (Oxford: Berg, 2004).

100. Obrecht, "Le problème de l'identification," 8.

101. Obrecht, "Le problème de l'identification," 14–16.

102. Obrecht, "Le problème de l'identification," 18–20.

103. "Fiche pour recherches sur la voie publique," GOUCOCH V.10/07.06, TTLTQG-II.

104. "Le Chef du Service de la Sûreté à Monsieur le Gouverneur de la Cochinchine (Cabinet)," December 14, 1922, GOUCOCH V.10/07.06, TTLTQG-II.

Chapter 5. A Holy Childhood

1. Huỳnh Sanh Thông, ed. and trans., *An Anthology of Vietnamese Poems: From the Eleventh through the Twentieth Centuries* (New Haven, Conn.: Yale University Press, 1996), 154.

2. Jacques Daurelle, *Vence et ses monuments d'après les archives* (Vence, France: Éditions de la "Vieille Provence," 1934), 151, 57–95, 35–41.

3. For further details, see Maurice Block, *Dictionnaire de l'administration française,* 5th ed. (Paris: Berger-Levraut and Company, 1905), 531.

4. "Certificate of Indigence," October 5, 1923, GOUCOCH IA.22/0520, TTLTQG-II.

5. Georges Castellan, *Histoire de Vence et du Pays Vençois* (Aix-en-Provence: Édisud, 1992), 251, 254–255. The last census in Vence before the war was in 1911. No census was conducted during World War I.

6. Castellan, *Histoire de Vence,* 253.

7. Hue-Tam Ho Tai, *Millenarianism and Peasant Politics in Vietnam* (Cambridge, Mass.: Harvard University Press, 1983), 57–58. See also Cochinchine Française, *Rapports au Conseil Colonial 1887* (Saigon: Imprimerie Coloniale, 1887), 5; "Cochinchine, 1887," INDO AF A20(21), ANOM; "Rapports mensuels du Gouverneur Filipini," 1887, INDO AF A20(22), ANOM; "Rapports mensuels," 1887, GGI 64313, ANOM.

8. Pierre Brocheux and Daniel Hémery, *Indochine: La colonisation ambiguë, 1858–1954* (Paris: Editions la découverte, 2001), 81–82. The protectorate of Annam-Tonkin was divided into two separate residencies by a decree on May 9, 1889.

9. Nguyen P. J. B. Trong Quan, *Truyện Thầy Lazaro Phiền của Nguyễn Trọng Quản* [The story of Master Lazaro Phiền by Nguyễn Trọng Quản], 2nd ed. (Saigon: Impr. de J. Viet, 1919). See also Nguyễn Q. Thắng. *Tiến Trình Văn Nghệ Miền Nam: Văn Học Việt Nam Nơi Miền Đất Mới* [The progress of southern arts and letters: Vietnamese literature in a new region] (Hồ Chí Minh City: Văn Hiến, 1994), 265–268. Nguyễn Trọng Quản was the student and son-in-law of Trương Vĩnh Ký, one of the most important Vietnamese officials in the early French administration. See Nguyễn Q. Thắng and Nguyễn Bá Thế, *Từ Điển Nhân Vật Lịch Sử* [Dictionary of historical personages], (Hồ Chí Minh City: Tổng Hợp Thành Phố Hồ Chí Minh, 2006), 985–986.

10. "Special Commissioner Monnier to Head of the Security Service," March 24, 1924, GOUCOCH IA.22/0520, TTLTQG-II.

11. M. Lahaye, "Rapport sur le régime forestier de la Cochinchine," *Bulletin de la société des études indochinoises* 1 (1883): 132–141.

12. Alfred Schreiner, *Abrégé de l'histoire d'Annam,* 2nd ed. (Saigon: L'auteur, 1906), 440.

13. The Chinese *Compendium of Materia Medica* (*Bản thảo cương mục* in Vietnamese) by Li Shizhen discusses a number of different herbal, animal, and mineral substances that can allegedly be used to cause abortions. On this text, see Carla Nappi, *The Monkey and the Inkpot: Natural History and Its Transformations in Early Modern China* (Cambridge, Mass.: Harvard University Press, 2009).

14. Vietnamese parents seldom seem to have abandoned their children anonymously and in public, as was frequently the case in France and in China. On this point, see

Etat de la Cochinchine Française (1882): 93. For the situation in France, see Rachel Fuchs, *Abandoned Children: Foundlings and Child Welfare in Nineteenth-Century France* (Albany, N.Y.: State University of New York Press, 1984). On child abandonment in China, see Henrietta Harrison, "'A Penny for the Little Chinese': The French Holy Childhood Association in China, 1843–1951," *American Historical Review* 113 (2008): 73, 76–78. For the comparison with Vietnam, see "Lettre de M. Lizé, de la Société des Missions Etrangères, Missionnaire apostolique de Mitho (Cochinchine), à M. le Directeur de l'Œuvre du diocèse de Fréjus et Toulon, 16 Juin 1867," *Annales* 20 (1868): 322.

15. C. E. Bouillevaux, *Voyage dans l'Indo-Chine 1848–1856, avec carte du Camboge et d'une partie des royaumes limitrophes* (Paris: Victor Palmé, 1858), 115; "Extrait d'une lettre de Sœur Benjamin, Supérieur des Sœurs de Saint-Paul de Chartres à Saigon, à M. le Directeur de l'Œuvre, 23 Mars, 1864," *Annales* 16 (1864): 383; Charles Lemire, *Cochinchine Française et Royaume de Cambodge* (Paris: Librairie Coloniale, 1889), 235–236; Anonymous, "Note sur l'esclavage," *Revue maritime et coloniale* 7 (1863): 78–80; Jules Silvestre, "Rapport sur l'esclavage," *Excursions et Reconnaissances* 4 (1880): 96–144; A. Landes, "Rapport sur la prostitution," *Excursions et Reconnaissances* 4 (1880): 145–147. Child trafficking lasted well into the twentieth century. Eugène Teston and Maurice Percheron wrote in their encyclopaedia *L'Indochine moderne* that the "custom of selling children, quite common amongst the poor, though it shocks our European sensibility with good reason, is not so unusual or so revolting as may often be believed." See Teston and Percheron, *L'Indochine moderne: encylopédie administrative, touristique, aritistique et économique* (Paris: Librairie de France, 1931), 352. See also League of Nations, *Commission of Enquiry into Traffic in Women and Children in the East, Report to Council* (Geneva: League of Nations, 1932), 79, 212–238; René Bunout, *La Main-d'œuvre et la législation du travail en Indochine* (Bordeaux: Imprimerie-Librairie Delmas, 1936), 36–39. There is also a growing body of contemporary scholarship on the traffic in women and children in French Indochina. See Karine Delaye, "Slavery and Colonial Representations in Indochina from the Second Half of the Nineteenth to the Early Twentieth Century," *Slavery and Abolition* 24 (2003): 129–142; David Pomfret, "'Child Slavery' in British and French Far-Eastern Colonies, 1880–1945," *Past and Present* 201 (2008): 175–213; Micheline Lessard, "'Cet ignoble trafic': The Kidnapping and Sale of Vietnamese Women and Children in French Colonial Indochina, 1873–1935," *French Colonial History* 10 (2009): 1–34. The most important recent study is Micheline Lessard, *Human Trafficking in Colonial Vietnam* (New York: Routledge, 2015).

16. Harrison, "'A Penny for the Little Chinese,'" 73.

17. Chanoine Jean Vaudon, *Les filles de Saint-Paul en Indo-Chine* (Chartres: Procure des Sœurs de Saint-Paul, 1931), 2; "Le Maire de la Ville de Saïgon à Monsieur le Gouverneur de la Cochinchine," May 13, 1930, GOUCOCH VIA.8/323(1), TTLTQG-II.

18. See Christina Elizabeth Firpo, *The Uprooted: Race, Children, and Imperialism in French Indochina, 1890–1980* (Honolulu: University of Hawai'i Press, 2016), 21.

19. Cl. Chivas-Baron, *La femme française aux colonies* (Paris: Editions Larose, 1929), 90; Vaudon, *Les filles de Saint-Paul*, 2. Both works seem to have relied on L.-E. Louvet, *La Cochinchine réligieuse*, vol. 2 (Paris: Ernest Leroux, 1885), 238ff.

20. "Extrait d'une lettre de Mgr Lefebvre, Vicaire Apostolique de la Cochinchine occidentale, à M. le Directeur de l'Œuvre, 29 Janvier, 1861," *Annales* 13 (1861): 249.

21. See André Baudrit, *Guide historique des rues de Saïgon* (Saigon: S.I.L.I., 1945), 211.

22. Vaudon, *Les filles de Saint-Paul,* 17.

23. For mention of the different parts of the orphanage, see "Extraits relatifs à l'orphelinat de la Sainte-Enfance de Saïgon, d'un Rapport au Directeur de l'assistance publique par M. Turc, président de la Commission de l'assistance publique. *Courrier de Saïgon, journal officiel de la Cochinchine française,* n° du 30 Octobre 1868," *Annales* 21 (1869): 26. For a more detailed description, though from a later period, see "Rapport de surveillance sanitaire des établissements privés de bienfaisance de la Ville de Saïgon," March 20–21, 1925, GOUCOCH VA.8/327(1), TTLTQG-II. This report mentions that the dormitory was located beneath the roof and that it lacked a ceiling, which would have left the rafters exposed.

24. "Extrait d'une lettre de Sœur Benjamin, Supérieur des Sœurs de Saint-Paul de Chartres à Saigon, à M. le Directeur de l'Œuvre, 23 Mars, 1864," *Annales* 16 (1864): 382.

25. "À Monsieur le Procureur Impérial, chef de la justice en Cochinchine," March 23, 1867, INDO AF 28bis, ANOM.

26. "À Monsieur le Procureur Impérial, chef de la justice en Cochinchine," March 19, 1868, INDO AF 28bis, ANOM.

27. "Monsieur d'Espinassous, président du tribunal de 1ère Instance ffons de juge de paix," November 6, 1867, INDO AF 28bis, ANOM.

28. "Monsieur le président du tribunal de 1ère Instance," November 6, 1867, INDO AF 28bis, ANOM.

29. P. Vial, *Les Premières Années de la Cochinchine: colonie française,* vol. 2 (Paris, 1874), 254. Silvestre also described this "panic"; see Silvestre, "Rapport sur l'esclavage," 48.

30. "Lettre de Mgr Lefebvre, Vicaire Apostolique de la Cochinchine-Occidentale à M. le Directeur de l'Œuvre, 31 Mars 1863," and "Lettre de Sœur Benjamin, Supérieur des Sœurs de Saint-Paul de Chartres à Saïgon, à M. le Directeur de l'Œuvre, 22 Février, 1863," *Annales* 15 (1863): 189; Vaudon, *Les filles de Saint-Paul,* 17; "Extrait d'une lettre de Sœur Benjamin, Supérieur des Sœurs de Saint-Paul de Chartres à Saïgon, à M. le Directeur de l'Œuvre, 23 Mars, 1864," *Annales* 15 (1864): 385, 383; "Extrait d'une lettre de Sœur Benjamin, Supérieur des Sœurs de Saint-Paul de Chartres à Saïgon, à M. le Directeur de l'Œuvre, 24 août, 1864," *Annales* 16 (1865): 117; "Au sujet des mésures à prendre pour faire connaître à la population que les malheureux sont sécourus et réçus dans des maisons de bienfaisance," October 7, 1868, GOUCOCH IA.8/155(11), TTLTQG-II.

31. On payments for children, see "Lettre de M. Lizé, de la Societé des Missions Etrangères, Missionnaire apostolique de Mitho (Cochinchine), à M. le Directeur de l'Œuvre du diocèse de Fréjus et Toulon, 16 Juin 1867," *Annales* 20 (1868): 322. For the broader details on admission, see "Extraits rélatifs à l'orphelinat de la Sainte-Enfance de Saïgon, d'un Rapport au Directeur de l'assistance publique par M. Turc, président de la Commission de l'assistance publique. *Courrier de Saïgon, journal officiel de la Cochinchine française,* n° du 30 Octobre 1868," *Annales* 21 (1869): 27.

32. Some evidence suggests that at least some Eurasian children were forcibly removed from their Vietnamese mothers and placed into institutional care. See Christina Firpo, "Crisis of Whiteness and Empire in Colonial Indochina: The Removal of Abandoned Eurasian Children from the Vietnamese Milieu, 1890-1956," *Journal of Social History* 43, no. 3 (2010): 587-613.

33. "Extraits rélatifs à l'orphelinat," 28.

34. "Extraits rélatifs à l'orphelinat," 28.

35. "Extraits rélatifs à l'orphelinat," 26-32.

36. Valuable earlier studies of children of ethnically mixed ancestry in Vietnam include Ann Laura Stoler, *Carnal Knowledge and Imperial Power: Race and the Intimate Colonial Rule* (Berkele: University of California Press, 2002). Emmanuelle Saada, *Les enfants de la colonie: les métis de l'empire français entre sujétion et citoyenneté* (Paris: Découverte, 2007); Firpo, *The Uprooted*; David Pomfret, "Raising Eurasia: Race, Class, and Age in French and British Colonies," *Comparative Studies in Society and History* 51, no. 2 (2009): 314-343; idem, *Youth and Empire: Trans-Colonial Childhoods in British and French Asia* (Stanford: Stanford University Press, 2016). These studies often tend to be concerned with the judicial and legal status of *métis* children, rather than with the actual conditions under which they lived. The marginal status of *métis* children persisted throughout the colonial period. For an example of derogatory views from the twentieth century, see P. Douchet, *Métis et congaies d'Indochine* (Hanoi: n.p., 1928). For testimony of the deplorable social situation of these children, see Auguste Bonifacy, "Les métis Franco-Tonkinois," *Bulletins et Mémoires de la Société d'Anthropologie* 1, no. 1 (1910): 607-642; Henri Bonvicini, *Enfants de la Colonie* (Saigon: Editions Orient-Occident, 1938); Justin Godart, *Rapport de mission en Indochine, 1er Janvier-14 Mars 1937*, ed. François Bilange, Charles Fourniau, and Alain Ruscio (Paris: L'Harmattan, 1994); M. Bonnio, *L'enfance métisse malheureuse* (Saigon: Imprimerie de l'Union, 1940).

37. Louvet, *Cochinchine réligieuse*, vol. 2, 374-375.

38. Schreiner, *Abrégé de l'histoire d'Annam*, 338; A. Brebion and A. Cabaton, *Dictionnaire de bio-bibliographie générale de l'Indochine française* (Paris: Société des Editions Géographiques, Maritimes et Coloniales, 1935), 211.

39. Vaudon, *Les filles de Saint-Paul*, 56; Louvet, *Cochinchine réligieuse*, 375.

40. *Etat de la Cochinchine française* (1887): 69.

41. In 1887, the Colonial Council allocated twenty thousand francs for this purpose. See Colonial Council, Meeting of February 10, 1887, GOUCOCH IA.8/084, TTLTQG-II.

42. On Eulalie Boyer, see "Subvention de 250$ à Melle Eulalie Boya pour son trousseau," March 31, 1882; on Josephine Larrieu, see "Madame la Supérieure de la Sainte Enfance à Monsieur le Gouverneur Général de l'Indo-Chine," October 16, 1887, and "Conseil Colonial: Session ordinaire 1887-1888. Extrait de la Séance du 21 Janvier 1888"; on Emélie Blanc, see "La Supérieure Principale des Sœurs de St Paul à Monsieur le Lieutenant Gouverneur," February 26, 1895; on Bathilde Silvestre, see "Monsieur Belland, Commissaire Central à Monsieur le Lieutenant Gouverneur de la Cochinchine fran-

çaise," March 30, 1904; "Acte de Mariage entre M. Blaise Léon, Nicolas et Mlle Silvestre Bathilde Léontine Cécile, Nanette," GOUCOCH IA.8/084, TTLTQG-II.

43. André Baudrit, "Contribution à l'histoire de Saïgon: Extraits des registres de délibéra-tions de la Ville de Saïgon (Indochine Française), 1867–1916," II, *Bulletin de la Société des Etudes Indochinoises,* New Series 10, nos. 1–3 (1933): 275.

44. One in Chợ Lớn in 1870, one in Vĩnh Long in 1871, one in Biên Hòa and another at Thị Nghè in 1876, and the last in Tân Định in 1877. See Louvet, *Cochinchine réligieuse,* 377–378.

45. "Etat de la mission de Cochinchine Occidentale: Au 1er septembre 1887," 756.741, ASMEP.

46. "Etat de la mission de Cochinchine Occidentale: Au 1er septembre 1888," 756.742, ASMEP.

47. Edouard Marquis, *L'œuvre humaine de la France en Cochinchine* (Saigon: Imprimarie de Théatre, 1936), 38.

48. "Lettre de Mgr Lefebvre, Vicaire Apostolique de la Cochinchine-Occidentale, à M. le Directeur de l'Œuvre, 31 Mars 1863," *Annales* 15 (1863): 375.

49. "Lettre de M. H. Lemée, de la Société des Missions Etrangères, Mission apost. en Cochinchine, à M. le Directeur de l'Œuvre," *Annales* 19 (1867): 248–249.

50. "Extraits relatifs à l'orphelinat," 25.

51. "Etat de la mission de Cochinchine Occidentale: Au 1er Septembre 1887," 756.740, ASMEP.

52. Direction Générale de la Santé, Gouvernement Général de l'Indochine, "Fonc-tionnement des Services de la Direction Générale de la Santé pendant l'année 1907," GGI 65324, ANOM.

53. "Procès verbal des opérations de la Commission de surveillance administrative des établissements privés de bienfaisance de la province de Giadinh," GOUCOCH VA.8/327(1), TTLTQG-II.

54. M. Montel, "Sur la mortalité infantile en Cochinchine," *Bulletin de la Société Médico-Chirurgicale de l'Indochine* 6 (November 1926): 573.

55. "La Supérieure Principale des Sœurs de Saint Paul à Monsieur Rodier, Lieutenant-Gouverneur de la Cochinchine," November 27, 1902; "Congrégations réligieuses," SL 1704, TTLTQG-II.

56. For a discussion of the application of the *lois laïques* of July 1, 1901, July 7, 1904, De-cember 9, 1905, in French Indochina, see Patrick J. N. Tuck, *French Catholic Missionaries and the Politics of Imperialism in Vietnam, 1857-1914: A Documentary Survey* (Liverpool: Liv-erpool University Press, 1987), 255–284; Charles P. Keith, "Catholicisme, bouddhisme, et lois laïques au Tonkin (1899–1914)," *Vingtième Siècle: Revue d'histoire* 87 (2005), 113–128.

57. For those other measures, see Tuck, *French Catholic Missionaries,* 257; Vaudon, *Filles de Saint-Paul,* 351–352.

58. "La Supérieure Principale des Sœurs de Saint Paul à Monsieur Rodier"; "Le Commis-saire Central à Monsieur le Gouverneur de la Cochinchine," April 12, 1912, SL1706, TTLTQGII; "Etat du vicariat apostolique de la Cochinchine Occidentale, au 1er Octobre

1900," 757.77, ASMEP; "Société des Missions Etrangères, Mission de la Cochinchine Occidentale, Exercice 1904–1905," 757.113, ASMEP.

59. "Le Maire de la Ville de Saïgon, à Monsieur le Gouverneur de la Cochinchine," May 13, 1930, GOUCOCH VIA.8/325(1), TTLTQGII.

60. "Société de protection et d'éducation des jeunes métis français de la Cochinchine et du Cambodge," GGI 7701, ANOM.

61. "Notice sur la Société de Protection de l'Enfance en Cochinchine," GOUCOCH VIA.8/282(23), TTLTQG-II; M. Mathieu, "La Société de la Protection de l'Enfance en Cochinchine: Son œuvre—Sa portée sociale," *Bulletin Mensuel des Associations d'Aide Mutuelle et Assistance Sociale* 35–36 (1934): 782–784.

62. "La Protection de l'Enfance en Cochinchine," 785.

63. "Notice sur la Société de Protection de l'Enfance"; "La Protection de l'Enfance en Cochinchine," 786–787. The society had removed the word *métis* from its name in 1897 but returned it in 1900. It considered removing the word again in 1903 but decided not to do so. The society's revised statutes from 1927 removed the words "by race or religion." See "Statuts," GOUCOCH VIA.8/325(2), TTLTQG-II.

64. "Le Président de la Société de Protection de l'Enfance à Monsieur le Gouverneur de la Cochinchine à Saïgon," August 25, 1921, GOUCOCH DIVERS 2981, TTLTQG-II.

65. See the photographs in "Les nouveaux aménagements de l'orphelinat de Cholon, 6, Boulevard Frédéric-Drouhet," GOUCOCH VIA.8/325(1), TTLTQG-II.

66. "L'Inspecteur des affaires politiques et administratives de la Cochinchine Bary, à Monsieur le Gouverneur de la Cochinchine," October 2, 1935, GOUCOCH VIA.8/282(2), TTLTQG-II.

67. See the comments to this effect in, for example, "Le Président de la Société de Protection de l'Enfance à Monsieur le Gouverneur de la Cochinchine à Saïgon," August 25, 1921, GOUCOCH DIVERS 2981, TTLTQG-II.

68. "Le Président de la Société de Protection de l'Enfance à Monsieur le Gouverneur de la Cochinchine," August 25, 1921, GOUCOCH DIVERS 2981, TTLTQGII. "Société de Protection de l'enfance de Cochinchine: Projet de budget 1909," GOUCOCH IA.8/207(2), TTLTQGII; "Société de la Protection de l'Enfance de la Cochinchine à Monsieur le Lieutenant-Gouverneur de la Cochinchine," July 6, 1909, GOUCOCH IA.8/207(2), TTLTQG-II.

69. "Orphelinat de Cholon: Règlement intérieur," GOUGOCH VIA.8/325(1), TTLTQG-II.

70. "Procès-Verbal de l'Assemblée Générale du 29 Mars 1935," GOUCOCH VIA.8/282(23). This report states that almost all the orphans put on weight during the year, the majority gaining between one and three kilograms.

71. "Orphelinat de Cholon: Règlement intérieur," GOUGOCH VIA.8/325(1), TTLTQG-II.

72. "L'Inspecteur des affaires politiques et administratives de la Cochinchine Bary, à Monsieur le Gouverneur de la Cochinchine," October 2, 1935, GOUCOCH VIA.8/282(2), TTLTQG-II.

73. "Orphelinat de Cholon: Règlement intérieur," GOUGOCH VIA.8/325(1), TTLTQG-II.

74. "Procès-Verbal de l'Assemblée Générale du 26 Mars 1929," GOUCOCH VIA.8/325(2), TTLTQG-II; "Procès-Verbal de l'Assemblée Générale du 26 Mars 1930," GOUCOCH VIA.8/325(2), TTLTQG-II.

75. See the complaints in "Procès-verbal de l'Assemblée Générale du 5 Mars 1931," 5–6, GOUCOCH VIA.8/325(1), TTLTQG-II; and "Procès-verbal de l'Assemblée Générale du 29 Mars 1935," 6. GOUCOCH VIA.8/282(23), TTLTQG-II.

76. "Orphelinat de Cholon: Règlement intérieur," GOUGOCH VIA.8/325(1), TTLTQG-II.

77. "Procès-Verbal de l'Assemblée Générale du 11 Avril 1928," GOUCOCH VIA.8/323(1), TTLTQG-II.

78. "Orphelinat de Cholon: Règlement intérieur," GOUGOCH VIA.8/325(1), TTLTQG-II.

79. "Le Maire de la Ville de Saïgon à Monsieur le Gouverneur de la Cochinchine," May 13, 1930, GOUCOCH VIA.8/323(1), TTLTQG-II; "L'Inspecteur des affaires politiques et administratives."

80. "Rapport du Conseil d'Administration à l'Assemblée générale ordinaire du 6 Mars 1923," GOUCOCH VIA.8/325(2), TTLTQG-II; "Procès-Verbal de l'Assemblée Générale du 5 Mars 1931," GOUCOCH VIA.8/325(2), TTLTQG-II.

81. On the danger to public health posed by the area, see Dr. M. L. R. Montel, *Rapport sur l'état sanitaire de la Ville de Saïgon et sur l'Assistance médicale urbaine* (Saigon: Goudurier et Montégout, 1908), 14ff. For complaints about prostitution in Tân Định, see GOUCOCH IB.37/257(7), TTLTQG-II.

82. Certificate, May 30, 1916, GOUCOCH IA.22/0520, TTLTQG-II.

83. Most of the documents relating to the French military hospital, also known as the Hôpital Grall, were lost after the Japanese coup de force on March 9, 1945. The oldest documents in the Ministry of Colonies collection have been badly damaged by humidity. Others, evacuated to France after 1954, have been destroyed. Henri Mianet, a doctor who worked at the hospital in the 1960s, published a commemorative volume to mark its centenary. See Henri Mianet, *Un siècle d'évolution hospitalière en pays tropical, histoire de l'hôpital Grall de Saïgon* (Paris: impr. R. Foulon et Cie, 1962), dates of the commencement, completion, and eventual demolition of the hospital's buildings, 32; map of the hospital, 95; an account of the impressive qualities of the hospital's buildings and grounds, 33; description of the gardens, see 61 (Paul Doumer quotation). Mianet also mentions on 61 that patients walked in the garden.

84. Certificate, January 31, 1921, GOUCOCH IA.22/0520, TTLTQG-II.

85. Certificate. May 29, 1921, GOUCOCH IA.22/0520, TTLTQG-II.

86. Eric T. Jennings, *Curing the Colonizers: Hydrotherapy, Climatology, and French Colonial Spas* (Durham, N.C.: Duke University Press, 2006), 8–39.

87. Known as the Banque Industrielle de Chine in French or Zhongfa Shiye Yinhang/中法實業銀行 in Chinese.

88. Patrice Morlat, *Le Krach de la Banque Industrielle de Chine: La rivalité des banques françaises en Extrême-Orient (1912-1928)* (Paris: Les Indes Savantes, 2012), 38, 44. On loans to the Rizeries d'Extrême-Orient rice mill, see 45–56.

89. Jean-Noël Jeanneney, "Finances, presse et politique: l'affaire de la Banque industrielle de Chine (1921–1923)," *Revue historique* 253, no. 2 (1975): 382.

90. Morlat, *Le Krach,* 49–55. See also André Bureau, *La crise bancaire en 1921-1923: Etude juridique et politique de l'intervention de l'état* (Paris: Société Anonyme de Publications Périodiques, 1923), 1–5, 14–17; Frank H. H. King, "Patriotic Banking and the Modernization of China; The Banque Industrielle de Chine, 1900–1922," in *Finance and Modernization: A Transnational and Transcontinental Perspective for the 19th and 20th Centuries,* ed. Gerald Feldman and Peter Hertner (Burlington, Vt.: Ashgate, 2008), 236.

91. "Mlle A. Hennion, Surveillante à l'Orphelinat de Cholon (Cochinchine) en congé en France rue tarbé des Sablons à Eaubonne, Seine et Oise à Monsieur le Gouverneur Général de l'Indochine à Hanoï, Tonkin," November 14, 1921, GOUCOCH IA.22/0519(1), TTLTQG-II.

92. "Mademoiselle Lahaye Aimée, à Vence (Alpes Maritimes) à Monsieur le Ministre de Colonies," December 17, 1923, GOUCOCH IA.22/0520, TTLTQG-II.

93. For a critical assessment of Sarraut's time as governor general, see Joseph Buttinger, *Vietnam: A Political History* (New York: Praeger, 1968), 137–144. For a discussion of the complicated impact of Sarraut's policy of "collaboration" in Vietnam, see Agathe Larcher, "La voie étroite des réformes coloniales et la 'collaboration Franco-Annamite' (1917–1928)," *Revue française d'histoire d'outre-mer* 82, no. 309 (1995), 387–420.

94. See Albert Sarraut, *La mise en valeur des colonies françaises* (Paris: Payot & Cie, 1923).

95. Quoted in Morlat, *Le Krach,* 57–58.

96. "Le Commissaire Spécial Monnier à Monsieur le Chef du Service de la Sûreté," March 24, 1924, GOUCOCH IA.22/0520, TTLTQG-II.

97. "Gouverneur Général de l'Indochine à Résident Supérior de Cambodge," March 6, 1928, GGI B 221 101, ANOM.

98. For a complaint about child beggars in Saigon, see "Le Gouverneur p.i. de la Cochinchine à Monsieur l'Administrateur de la Région de Saïgon-Cholon," November 21, 1938; "*Le Populaire d'Indochine* du 30 Novembre 1938," GOUCOCH VIA.8/282(4), TTLTQG-II.

Chapter 6. Tristes Tropiques

1. Huỳnh Sanh Thông, ed. and trans., *An Anthology of Vietnamese Poems: From the Eleventh through the Twentieth Centuries* (New Haven, Conn.: Yale University Press, 1996), 346.

2. Jasper Whiting, *The Journal of Jasper Whiting* (Boston: Napoleon Tennyson Hobbs, Jr., 1902), excerpted in *Saigon: Mistress of the Mekong,* ed. Anastasia Edwards (Oxford: Oxford University Press, 2003), 91.

3. Jules Janin, *Un hiver à Paris,* 2nd ed. (Paris: L. Curmer, 1844), 201–202. For an admirable discussion of Janin's impressions of nineteenth-century Paris, see Louis Chevalier,

Classes laborieuses et classes dangereuses à Paris pendant la première moitié du XIXe siècle (Paris: Plon, 1958), 50–57.

4. On the history of medicine and public health in French Indochina, see Laurence Monnais-Rousselot, *Médecine et colonisation: l'aventure indochinoise, 1860-1939* (Paris: CNRS Editions, 1999).

5. "NOTE," November 21, 1930, GOUCOCH VIA.6/076(6), TTLTQG-II.

6. *Chuyên Khảo Về Tỉnh Gia Định* [Monograph on Gia Định province], introduction and notes by Nguyễn Đình Đầu (Hồ Chí Minh City: Trẻ, 1997), 21–23. This work is a reprint of Société des Etudes Indochinoises, *Monographie de la province de Gia Định* (Saigon: L. Ménard, 1902). See also Huỳnh Minh, *Gia Định Xưa* [Gia Định in the past] (Hồ Chí Minh City: Văn Hóa-Thông Tin, 2006); Sơn Nam, *Đất Gia Định-Bến Nghé Xưa & Người Sài Gòn* [The lands of Gia Định and Bến Nghé in the past & the people of Saigon] (Hồ Chí Minh City: Trẻ, 2004) appears to rely on the same source.

7. *Chuyên Khảo Về Tỉnh Gia Định*, 58–80.

8. *Chuyên Khảo Về Tỉnh Gia Định*, 81–90.

9. *Chuyên Khảo Về Tỉnh Gia Định*, 95–101.

10. *Chuyên Khảo Về Tỉnh Gia Định*, 44–46, 101–103.

11. *Chuyên Khảo Về Tỉnh Gia Định*, 133–135.

12. In the following year, Nguyễn Văn Của bought the printing presses of the Imprimerie de l'Union. In 1921, he bought the popular newspaper *Lục Tỉnh Tân Văn* (*News of the Six Provinces*), which he merged with *Nam Trung Nhựt Báo*. The new *Lục Tỉnh Tân Văn* had a daily print run of 3,500 copies and sold for $0.05 per issue. It soon became the most widely read Vietnamese-language newspaper in Saigon. Civil servants, business proprietors, and other notables all subscribed to it. *Lục Tỉnh Tân Văn* supported the colonial government, which bought subscriptions of the newspaper for every commune in Cochinchina. In 1923, Nguyễn Văn Của began to print a new newspaper called *Đông Pháp Thời Báo* (*The Indochina Courier*), which sold for $0.10 per issue, or the cost of a rickshaw ride. He also took over the printing of *Nông Cổ Mín Đàm* (*Agricultural and Commercial Affairs*), the longest-running newspaper in Saigon. In addition, Nguyễn Văn Của printed the French-language Vietnamese newspaper *Echo Annamite*. On Nguyễn Văn Của and the newspapers he printed, see "Notes de Sûreté concernant la situation politique indigène au 25 mai 1923," GGI 65474, ANOM. See also Nguyễn Công Khanh, *Lịch Sử Báo Chí Sài Gòn-Thành phố Hồ Chí Minh* [The history of newspapers and magazines in Saigon-Hồ Chí Minh City] (Hồ Chí Minh City: Tổng Hợp Thành Phố Hồ Chí Minh: 2006), 32–42.

13. For rice export figures from Saigon, see *Statistique commerciale de la Cochinchine* (Saigon: Chambre de Commerce, 1938), table after 452.

14. For rice prices, see Direction des Services Economiques, *Résumé statistique relatif aux années 1913 à 1940* (Hanoi: Imprimerie d'Extrême-Orient, 1941), 30.

15. See André Baudrit, *Guide historique des rues de Saïgon* (Saigon: S.I.L.I, 1943), table after 80.

16. On the founding of these companies, see Huỳnh Ngọc Tráng et al, *Sài Gòn-Gia Định Xưa* [Saigon-Gia Định in the Past] (Hồ Chí Minh City: Thành Phố Hồ Chí Minh, 1996),

91–97. For further information on these and other enterprises during this period, see Direction des Services Economiques, *Répertoire des sociétés anonymes Indochinois* (Hanoi: Imprimerie d'Extrême-Orient, 1944).

17. The figure for 1930 was 1,008. See "Service central de renseignements et de Sûreté Générale à Chef du service de legislation et d'administration au Gouverneur Général," GGI 4838, TTLTQG-I.

18. As discussed in chapter 4, there are no exact figures for the number of beggars and vagrants in Saigon during this period. Their number does seem to have increased significantly, however, since in 1926 the colonial administration began to search for a suitable site to locate a *dépôt de mendicité* or poorhouse to house those arrested for vagrancy and begging in Saigon and Chợ Lớn. See the correspondence attached to "Gouverneur Général à Monsieur le Procureur général près la Cour d'Appel, Saïgon," December 21, 1927, GOUCOCH VIA.8/325(6), TTLTQG-II.

19. Edouard Marquis, *L'oeuvre humaine de la France en Cochinchine* (Saigon: Imprimerie de Théatre, 1936), 121.

20. Jonathan Andrews et al., *The History of Bethlem* (London: Routledge, 1997), 51.

21. Guenter Risse, *Mending Bodies, Saving Souls: A History of Hospitals* (Oxford: Oxford University Press, 1999), 295.

22. "Gouverneur Général à Monsieur le Procureur general près la Cour d'Appel, Saïgon," December 21, 1927, GOUCOCH VIA.8/325(6), TTLTQG-II; *Rapport au Conseil Colonial sur l'état de la Cochinchine pendant la période 1929-1930* (Saigon: Imprimerie Nouvelle A. Portail, 1930), 50.

23. Marquis, *L'oeuvre humaine*, 121.

24. Marquis, *L'oeuvre humaine*, 122–125.

25. On the progress of the disease, see Cyril William Dixon, *Smallpox* (London: J. & A. Churchill, 1962); F. Fenner et al., *Smallpox and its Eradication* (Geneva: World Health Organisation, 1988).

26. See C. Michele Thompson, *Vietnamese Traditional Medicine: A Social History* (Singapore: NUS Press, 2015), 25–57.

27. See the figures reported annually in *Rapports au Conseil Colonial*.

28. See Laurent Gaide and Bodet, *La variole et les vaccinations jennériennes en Indochine* (Hanoi: Imprimerie d'Extrême-Orient, 1930), 5–6. The figures in this study for earlier years do not always agree with those in extant contemporary documents, which have been used instead.

29. Georges Montel, *La ville de Saïgon: Etude de démographie et d'hygiène coloniales* (Bordeaux: Imprimerie Moderne, 1911), 55. On the outbreak in Khánh Hội, see "Rapport sur la situation politique de la Cochinchine pendant le mois de Novembre 1908," GGI 64329, ANOM. See also *Rapports au Conseil Colonial (Session Ordinaire de 1909)* (Saigon: Imprimerie Commerciale Marcellin Rey, 1909), xxvi.

30. "M.L.R. Montel: Ville de Saïgon. Rapport Médical annuel (1916)," GOUCOCH IA.8/232, TTLTQG-II.

31. See Gouvernement Général de l'Indochine, *Rapports au Conseil Colonial (Session Ordinaire de 1919)* (Saigon: C. Ardin Imprimeur-Editeur, 1919), 191.

32. For figures for 1917 and discussion of the origins of the outbreak, see "Rapport médical annuel sur les services municipaux de la ville de Saigon. Année 1917," GOUCOCH IA.8/234(1), TTLTQG-II. For 1918, see Gouvernement Général de l'Indochine, *Rapports au Conseil Colonial (Session Ordinaire de 1919)* (Saigon: C. Ardin Imprimeur-Editeur, 1919), 192.

33. For figures for Cochinchina, see *Rapport au Conseil Colonial sur l'état de la Cochinchine pendant la période 1930-1931* (Saigon: Imprimerie Nouvelle A. Portail, 1931), 381.

34. See *Rapport au Conseil Colonial sur l'état de la Cochinchine pendant la période 1929-1930* (Saigon: Imprimerie Nouvelle A. Portail, 1930), 415.

35. For figures for Saigon, see "Rapport annuel sur le fonctionnement du Service d'hygiène de la Région de Saigon-Cholon pour l'année 1934," GOUCOCH III.59/N130(4), TTLTQG-II. For figures for Cochinchina, see "Gouvernement de la Cochinchine: Direction Locale de la Santé. Rapport Annuel de l'Assistance Médicale. Année 1938," GOUCOCH III.59/N130(2), TTLTQG-II.

36. See *Rapport au Conseil Colonial* (1930–1931), 381.

37. "Rapport annuel sur le fonctionnement du Service d'hygiène de la Région de Saïgon-Cholon pour l'année 1934," GOUCOCH III.59/N130(4), TTLTQG-II.

38. For smallpox figures for Cochinchina for the rest of the decade, see "Gouvernement de la Cochinchine: Rapport sur le fonctionnement de l'Assistance en 1940," III.59/N130(2).

39. M. L. R. Montel, *Rapport sur l'état sanitaire de la Ville de Saigon et sur l'Assistance médicale urbaine* (Saigon: Coudurier & Montégout, 1908), 14.

40. "Ville de Saïgon: Rapport annuel sur la protection de la santé publique. Année 1910," GOUCOCH IA.8/153(11), TTLTQG-II.

41. See Robert Pollitzer, *Cholera* (Geneva: World Health Organization, 1959), 684–737.

42. Pollitzer, *Cholera,* 97–201, 820–892.

43. Laurent Gaide and Bodet, *Choléra en Indochine* (Hà Nội: Imprimerie d'Extrême-Orient, 1930), 7.

44. Montel, *Etude de démographie,* 66.

45. Gaide and Bodet, *Choléra en Indochine,* 7.

46. For the total figure, see Gaide and Bodet, *Choléra en Indochine,* 7. For the number in Saigon and commentary, see "Ville de Saigon: Service de l'assistance médicale. Rapport annuel. Année 1915," GOUCOCH IA.8/232, TTLTQG-II.

47. See "Ville de Saigon: Service de l'assistance médicale. Rapport annuel. Année 1915," GOUCOCH IA.8/232, TTLTQG-II.

48. Gaide and Bodet, *Choléra en Indochine,* 7; and *Rapport au Conseil Colonial* (1930–1931), 379.

49. Gaide and Bodet, *Choléra en Indochine,* 7.

50. For the figure from 1930, see *Rapport au Conseil Colonial* (1930–1931), 379. For the number in Saigon in that year, see "Rapport annuel sur le fonctionnement du Service

d'hygiène de la Région de Saïgon-Cholon pour l'année 1934," GOUCOCH III.59/N130(4), TTLTQG-II.

51. For figures for Saigon and the quotation, see "Rapport annuel sur le fonctionnement du Service d'hygiène de la Région de Saïgon-Cholon pour l'année 1934," GOUCOCH III.59/N130(4), TTLTQG-II. For figures for Cochinchina, see "Gouvernement de la Cochinchine: Direction Locale de la Santé. Rapport Annuel de l'Assistance Médicale. Année 1938," GOUCOCH III.59/N130(2), TTLTQG-II. For figures for the rest of the decade, see "Gouvernement de la Cochinchine: Rapport sur le fonctionnement de l'Assistance en 1940," GOUCOCH III.59/N130(2), TTLTQG-II.

52. See "Rapport annuel sur le fonctionnement du Service d'hygiène de la Région de Saïgon-Cholon pour l'année 1934," GOUCOCH III.59/N130(4), TTLTQG-II.

53. Montel, *Rapport sur l'état sanitaire,* 14. For the location of the print shop, see *Vade mecum annamite* (Saigon: n.p., 1928), 10.

54. Montel, *Rapport sur l'état sanitaire,* 15–16. See also André Baudrit, "Contribution à l'histoire de Saïgon: Extraits des registres de délibérations de la Ville de Saigon (Indochine Française), 1867–1916," II, *Bulletin de la Société des Etudes Indochinoises,* New Series 10, nos. 1–3 (1933): 160–163.

55. "Ville de Saigon: Rapport annuel sur la protection de la santé publique. Année 1910," GOUCOCH IA.8/153(11), TTLTQG-II.

56. Gaide and Bodet, *La peste en Indochine* (Hanoi: Imprimerie d'Extrême-Orient, 1930), 20.

57. See Myron Echenberg, *Plague Ports: The Global Urban Impact of Bubonic Plague, 1894-1901* (New York: New York University Press, 2007).

58. Montel, *Etude de démographie,* 66.

59. Robert Pollitzer, *Plague* (Geneva: World Health Organization, 1954), 343–355, 483–486.

60. Gaide and Bodet, *La peste en Indochine,* 21.

61. Pollitzer, *Plague,* 420.

62. Montel, *Rapport sur l'état sanitaire,* 11.

63. Montel, *Rapport sur l'état sanitaire,* 11.

64. Montel, *Etude de démographie,* 66.

65. Gaide and Bodet, *La peste en Indochine,* table after 20.

66. This number is the sum of the cases recorded in the lieutenant governor's reports for the year. See "Rapport sur la situation politique de la Cochinchine pendant le 4me Trimestre 1911"; "Rapport sur la situation politique de la Cochinchine pendant le troisième Trimestre 1911"; "Rapport sur la situation politique de la Cochinchine pendant le 2me Trimestre 1911"; "Rapport sur la situation politique de la Cochinchine pendant le 1e Trimestre 1911," GGI 64332, ANOM.

67. Gaide and Bodet, *La peste en Indochine,* 21.

68. "M.L.R. Montel: Ville de Saigon. Rapport Médical annuel 1914," GOUCOCH IA.8/232, TTLTQG-II.

69. "M.L.R. Montel: Ville de Saigon. Rapport Médical annuel (1916)," GOUCOCH IA.8/232, TTLTQG-II.

70. See "Rapport annuel sur le fonctionnement du Service d'hygiène de la Région de Saïgon-Cholon pour l'année 1934," GOUCOCH III.59/N130(4), TTLTQG-II.

71. See "Gouvernement de la Cochinchine: Rapport sur le fonctionnement de l'Assistance en 1940," GOUCOCH III.59/N130(2), TTLTQG-II.

72. For observations of this nature, see "Ville de Saïgon: Rapport annuel sur la protection de la santé publique. Année 1910," GOUCOCH IA.8/153(11), TTLTQG-II; "M.L.R. Montel: Ville de Saigon. Rapport Médical annuel 1914," GOUCOCH IA.8/232, TTLTQG-II; "Rapport annuel sur le fonctionnement du Service d'hygiène de la Région de Saïgon-Cholon pour l'année 1934," GOUCOCH III.59/N130(4), TTLTQG-II.

73. Frank M. Snowden, *The Conquest of Malaria: Italy, 1900–1962* (New Haven, Conn.: Yale University Press, 2006), 11–12.

74. Pierre Brocheux, *The Mekong Delta: Ecology, Economy, and Revolution, 1860–1960* (Madison: Center for Southeast Asian Studies, University of Wisconsin-Madison, 1995), 225n17.

75. Snowden, *The Conquest of Malaria*, 13–15.

76. Montel, *Etude de démographie*, 31.

77. "M.L.R. Montel: Ville de Saïgon. Rapport Médical annuel (1916)," GOUCOCH IA.8/232, TTLTQG-II. The population in 1916 is from Baudrit, *Guide historique*, table after 80.

78. "Rapport annuel sur le fonctionnement du Service d'hygiène de la Région de Saïgon-Cholon pour l'année 1934," GOUCOCH III.59/N130(4), TTLTQG-II.

79. "Ville de Saïgon: Rapport annuel sur la protection de la santé publique. Année 1910," GOUCOCH IA.8/153(11), TTLTQG-II.

80. "M.L.R. Montel: Ville de Saïgon. Rapport Médical annuel 1914," GOUCOCH IA.8/232, TTLTQG-II.

81. "Gouvernement de la Cochinchine: Direction Locale de la Santé. Rapport Annuel de l'Assistance Médicale. Année 1937," GOUCOCH III.59/N130(2), TTLTQG-II.

82. For this observation, see Montel, *Etude de démographie*, 31; see also "Ville de Saigon: Rapport annuel sur la protection de la santé publique. Année 1910," GOUCOCH IA.8/153(11), TTLTQG-II; "M.L.R. Montel: Ville de Saïgon. Rapport Médical annuel 1914," GOUCOCH IA.8/232, TTLTQG-II; "Rapport annuel sur le fonctionnement du Service d'hygiène de la Région de Saigon-Cholon pour l'année 1934," GOUCOCH III.59/N130(4), TTLTQG-II.

83. Montel, *Rapport sur l'état sanitaire*, 11. Colonial doctors repeated the same view twenty years later. See Gaide and Dorolle, *La tuberculose et sa prophylaxie en Indochine française* (Hà Nội: Imprimerie d'Extrême-Orient, 1930), 26.

84. "Ville de Saïgon: Rapport annuel sur la protection de la santé publique. Année 1910," GOUCOCH IA.8/153(11), TTLTQG-II.

85. "M.L.R. Montel: Ville de Saigon. Rapport Médical annuel (1916)," GOUCOCH IA.8/232, TTLTQG-II.

86. "Gouvernement de la Cochinchine: Direction Locale de la Santé. Rapport Annuel de l'Assistance Médicale. Année 1937," GOUCOCH III.59/N130(2), TTLTQG-II.

87. Thomas M. Daniel, *Captain of Death: The Story of Tuberculosis* (Rochester, N.Y.: University of Rochester Press, 1997), 93.

88. "Ville de Saïgon: Rapport annuel sur la protection de la santé publique. Année 1910," GOUCOCH IA.8/153(11), TTLTQG-II.

89. "Ville de Saïgon: Rapport annuel sur la protection de la santé publique. Année 1910," GOUCOCH IA.8/153(11), TTLTQG-II.

90. On the use of the BCG tuberculosis vaccine in French Indochina, see Laurent Gaide and Pierre Dorolle, *La Tuberculose et sa prophylaxie en Indochine française* (Hanoi: Imprimerie d'Extrême-Orient, 1930), 43–45.

91. See the figures reported in "M.L.R. Montel: Ville de Saigon. Rapport Médical annuel 1914," GOUCOCH IA.8/232, TTLTQG-II.

92. See the estimate in "M.L.R. Montel: Ville de Saïgon. Rapport Médical annuel (1916)," GOUCOCH IA.8/232, TTLTQG-II.

93. These rough calculations are based on mortality figures in "Rapport annuel sur le fonctionnement du Service d'hygiène de la Région de Saigon-Cholon pour l'année 1934," GOUCOCH III.59/N130(4), TTLTQG-II, and population figures in Baudrit, *Guide historique,* table after 80. The population figure for "Asians" has been derived from summing the figures for "Vietnamese" and "Chinese" in Baudrit's table. If the category of "Others" is included among "Asians," the crude death rate becomes 25.0 for 1930, 25.3 for 1931, 28.0 for 1932, 25.1 for 1933, and 22.8 for 1934.

94. In 1940, it was 25.97. Estimate based on figures in "Gouvernement de la Cochinchine: Rapport Annuel 1940," GOUCOCH III.59/N130(2), TTLTQG-II.

95. For the complaint about the number of poor dying in the streets and the cost to the municipality of Chợ Lớn, see "Monsieur F. Drouhet, Secrétaire Général des Colonies, Maire de la Ville de Cholon à Monsieur le Lieutenant Gouverneur, à Saïgon," September 12, 1903 and "Note pour Monsieur le Lieutenant Gouverneur de la Cochinchine, Saigon," September 17, 1903, GOUCOCH IA.8/155(17), TTLTQG-II.

96. See the entries for "Cadavres" and "Décès" in A. Belland, *Guide des agents de police de la ville de Saïgon* (Saigon: Impr. Claude, 1897); A. Mouchonière, *Guide des agents de police de la ville de Cholon* (Saigon: Impr. Nguyen-Van-Cua, 1921).

97. M. L. R. Montel, *Rapport sur l'état sanitaire de la Ville de Saïgon et sur l'Assistance médicale urbaine* (Saigon: Coudurier & Montégout, 1908), 6.

98. "Le Gouverneur p.i. De la Cochinchine à Monsieur le Maire de la Ville de Saïgon," April 21, 1914, GOUCOCH IA.8/038(4), TTLTQG-II.

99. The procedure is outlined in "Ville de Saïgon: Rapport annuel sur la protection de la santé publique. Année 1910," GOUCOCH, IA.8/153(11), TTLTQG-II.

100. "Rapport au Conseil Colonial: Au sujet de la création de cimetières indigènes," SL 4510, TTLTQG-II.

101. "Arrêté," September 28, 1903, GOUCOCH IA.8/155(17), TTLTQG-II.

102. André Baudrit, "Contribution à l'histoire de Saïgon: Extraits des registres de délibérations de la Ville de Saïgon (Indochine Française), 1867–1916, Deuxieme Partie," *Bulletin de la Société des Etudes Indochinoises,* New Series 10, nos. 1–3 (1933): 147.

103. Montel, *Rapport sur l'état sanitaire,* 20.

104. Baudrit, "Contribution à l'histoire de Saïgon: Deuxième Partie," 147.

105. On the European cemetery, see Hilda Arnold, *Promenades dans Saïgon* (Saigon: S.I.L.I., 1948), 101–106.

106. On these mutual aid associations, see *Amicale de la pagode de Thiên Hậu Chí Phước Hưng Hội* (Saigon: Imprimerie J. Nguyen Van Viet, 1937); La Tandinh Chrétienne, *Association Mutuelle des Employés Catholiques* (Saigon, n.d.); La Tandinh Chrétienne, *Association mutuelle des employés Catholiques: Statuts* (Saigon: Imprimerie J. Viet, 1923); *Association mutuelle Catholique de Caukho* (Saigon, 1935); *Association Mutuelle Catholique de Caukho: Statuts* (Saigon, n.d.); Association mutuelle de la pagode Namchon, *Liste des Membres de l'Association* (Saigon, n.d.); Association d'aides-mutuelles pour l'administration de la pagode de Co-Hon, *Statuts* (Saigon: Imprimerie Thanh-Tân, 1940); Association mutuelle des employés indigènes de commerce et d'industrie de Cochinchine, *Statuts* (Saigon: Imp. J. Nguyen-Van-Viet, 1941).

107. Pagode de Ngu-Hanh, *Société de Thai-Hoa Nam-Ky Nghia-Dia dite Cimetière Annamite de la Cochinchine* (Saigon: Imprimerie de l'Union, 1940).

Chapter 7. A Prodigal Son

1. Huỳnh Sanh Thông, ed. and trans., *An Anthology of Vietnamese Poems: From the Eleventh through the Twentieth Centuries* (New Haven, Conn.: Yale University Press, 1996), 132.

2. "Morin Edouard François, Bar de la Joiliette, Saïgon à Monsieur le Gouverneur de la Cochinchine Française à Saïgon," December 19, 1921; "Le Commissaire Spécial Etievant à Monsieur l'Administrateur Chef de la Sûreté," December 12, 1921; "Le Commissaire Spécial Etievant à Monsieur l'Administrateur Chef de la Sûreté," December 15, 1921, GOUCOCH IA.10/196(4), TTLTQG-II.

3. W. Somerset Maugham, *The Gentleman in the Parlour: A Record of a Journey from Rangoon to Haiphong* (Garden City, N.Y.: Doubleday, Doran & Company, 1930), 245. See also Jeffrey Meyers, *Somerset Maugham: A Life* (New York: Alfred A. Knopf, 2004), 254.

4. Gwendolyn Wright, *The Politics of Design in French Colonial Urbanism* (Chicago: University of Chicago Press, 1991), 161–234.

5. Osbert Sitwell, *Escape with Me: An Oriental Sketchbook* (London: Macmillan & Co., 1939), 51. See also Philip Ziegler, *Osbert Sitwell* (London: Chatto & Windus, 1998), 206.

6. "Le Commissaire Central de Police à Monsieur le Résident Supérieur au Tonkin," September 29, 1919, GGI 15726, ANOM.

7. David Arnold, "European Orphans and Vagrants in India in the Nineteenth Century," *Journal of Imperial and Commonwealth History* 7, no. 2 (1979): 104–127, quotations 114.

8. On poor whites in colonial Malaya, see John Butcher, *The British in Malaya, 1880–1941: The Social History of a European Community in Colonial Southeast Asia* (Kuala Lumpur: Oxford University Press, 1979), 26, 95, 133, 140, 224, quotations 95.

9. Ann Laura Stoler, *Carnal Knowledge and Imperial Power: Race and the Intimate Colonial Rule* (Berkeley: University of California Press, 2002), 22–40.

10. For an absorbing study of the life of a poor Frenchman in colonial Cambodia, see Gregor Müller, *Colonial Cambodia's "Bad Frenchmen": The Rise of French Rule and the Life of Thomas Caraman, 1840-1887* (London: Routledge, 2006).

11. The reports were collated and filed in GOUCOCH VIA.8/282(14), TTLTQG-II.

12. "Notice de renseignements concernant M. Colonna D'Istria Charles André Félix," July 16, 1937, GOUCOCH VIA.8/282(14), TTLTQG-II. Unless otherwise noted, this source forms the basis for the main events in Félix's life.

13. "Acte de naissance, Charles André Félix Colonna d'Istria," October 29, 1878, 1B85, Archives Municipales d'Avignon. Monsieur Antoine Colonna d'Istria made available copies of the birth certificates for Félix and his father. On the marriage of Félix's parents, see "Acte de marriage, Ignace Alexandre Antoine Colonna d'Istria et Laurence Emélie Knoll," March 6, 1880, Archives Municipales de Troyes.

14. Jacques Sicard and François Vauvillier, *Les Chasseurs d'Afrique* (Paris: Histoire et Collections, 1999), 8–13.

15. On fin-de-siècle Hanoi, see William S. Logan, *Hanoi: Biography of a City* (Seattle: University of Washington Press, 2000), 67–113; Philippe Papin, *Histoire de Hanoï* (Paris: Fayard, 2001), 225–250.

16. See Direction des Douanes et Régies, *Administration des Douanes et Régies en Indochine* (Hanoi: Imprimerie d'Extrême-Orient, 1930). The colonial government taxed salt because of its widespread use in Vietnamese cookery as a condiment and preservative.

17. For 1899 and 1913, see Henri Brenier, *Essai d'atlas statistique de l'Indochine Française* (Hanoi-Haiphong: Imprimerie d'Extrême-Orient, 1914), 21–41, 88–89, 115. For the size of the service relative to other departments in subsequent years, see *Annuaire statistique de l'Indochine, vol. 1, 1913-1922* (Hanoi: Imprimerie d'Extrême-Orient, 1927), 247; *Annuaire statistique de l'Indochine, vol. 2, 1923-1929* (Hanoi: Imprimerie d'Extrême-Orient, 1931), 284.

18. See the vivid accounts in Ngo Vinh Long, *Before the Revolution: The Vietnamese Peasants Under the French* (New York: Columbia University Press, 1991), 64–67; Truong Buu Lam, *Colonialism Experienced: Vietnamese Writings on Colonialism, 1900-1931* (Ann Arbor: University of Michigan Press, 2000), 48.

19. For correspondence concerning the prolongation of Félix's leave, see the letters and certificates in EE II 2425, ANOM. On the subject of entitlement to administrative and convalescent leaves and the abuse of such leave, see Jean Suignard, *Une grande administration Indochinoise: les services civils de l'Indochine* (Rennes, France: Faculté de droit, 1931), 117.

20. The police report in GOUCOCH VIA.8/282(14), TTLTQG-II states that Félix left the Customs and Excise Service in 1919. Correspondence in EE II 2425, ANOM, including letters from Félix himself, indicate that he left the service in 1915. Given that these documents are contemporaneous, this latter date is used here.

21. For an excellent study of the colonial alcohol monopoly, see Gerard Sasges, *Imperial Intoxication: Alcohol and the Making of Colonial Indochina* (Honolulu: University of Hawai'i Press, 2017).

22. Direction des Douanes et Régies, *Administration des douanes et régies,* 23–24; Société des Etudes Indochinoises, *Monographie de la Province de Bien-Hoa* (Saigon: Imprimerie L. Ménard, 1901), 44; M. Robert, *Monographie de la Province de Biênhoa* (Saigon: Imprimerie du Centre, 1924), 120; and "Monographie de la Province de Bienhoa en 1930," unpublished typescript, National Library of Vietnam, Hanoi, 233–234.

23. On Liu Bowen, see L. Carrington Goodrich and Chaoying Fang, eds., *Dictionary of Ming Biography, 1368-1644,* vol. 1 (New York: Columbia University Press, 1976), 932–938.

24. "Rapport politique mensuel," August 1928, GGI 64340, ANOM. These predictions may have been related to similar prognostications in the countryside emanating from the Cao Đài sect. See Hue-Tam Ho Tai, *Millenarianism and Peasant Politics in Vietnam* (Cambridge, Mass.: Harvard University Press, 1983), 100.

25. Baudrit, *Guide historique,* table after 80.

26. F. Leurence, "Les variations du coût de la vie pour les Européens à Saigon de 1910 à 1925," *Bulletin économique de l'Indochine* 28 (1925): 435–448; Direction des Services Economiques, *Résumé statistique,* 32.

27. "Dossier concernant les renseignements sur le coût de la vie de Saigon," 1927, GOUCOCH VIA.8/284(4), TTLTQG-II.

28. This periodical is available at the National Library of Vietnam in Hanoi and at the Bibliothèque Nationale de France in Paris.

29. For a discussion of colonial censorship, see Shawn Frederick McHale, *Print and Power: Confucianism, Communism, and Buddhism in the Making of Modern Vietnam* (Honolulu: University of Hawai'i Press, 2004), 39–60.

30. On the growth of print culture in colonial Vietnam, see David G. Marr, *Vietnamese Tradition on Trial, 1920-1945* (Berkeley: University of California Press, 1981); McHale, *Print and Power;* Philippe M. F. Peycam, *The Birth of Vietnamese Political Journalism: Sài Gòn, 1916-1930* (New York: Columbia University Press, 2013). On the development of a "Grub Street" in early modern France, see Robert Darnton, *The Literary Underground of the Old Regime* (Cambridge, Mass.: Harvard University Press, 1982). The circulation figures are from Marr, *Tradition on Trial,* 46–47.

31. *L'Express du Commerce et de l'Industrie,* June 1924.

32. On Béziat and Ardin, see Walter Langlois, *André Malraux: The Indochina Adventure* (New York: Praeger, 1966), 49, 62, 81–83.

33. F. Colonna d'Istria, "Lettre ouverte au collège électoral du 5 mai 1929," *L'Express du Commerce et de l'Industrie,* April 4, 1929.

34. "Rapport Annuel du 1er Juin 1928 au 31 Mai 1929," GGI 65476, ANOM.

35. F. Colonna d'Istria, "Aux affaires sérieuses," *L'Express du Commerce et de l'Industrie,* May 25, 1929.

36. On the origins of the Great Depression, see Charles P. Kindleberger, *The World in Depression, 1929-1939,* rev. ed. (Berkeley: University of California Press, 1986); Barry Eichengreen, *Golden Fetters: The Gold Standard and the Great Depression, 1919-1939* (New York: Oxford University Press, 1992). On the historiography of the Great Depression in Southeast Asia, see Peter Boomgaard and Ian Brown, "The Economies of Southeast

Asia in the 1930s Depression: An Introduction," in *Weathering the Storm: The Economies of Southeast Asia in the 1930s Depression,* ed. Peter Boomgaard and Ian Brown (Singapore: ISEAS, 2000), 1–19.

37. Charles Robequain, *The Economic Development of French Indo-China,* trans. Isabel A. Ward (London: Oxford University Press, 1944), 132–133. For a more detailed discussion of these tariffs, see Paul Reny, *Le problème des relations commerciales entre l'Indochine et la France* (Nancy: Georges Thomas, 1938), 21–28.

38. For the changing mix of rice exports to France, Hong Kong, and China during the Great Depression, see *Statistique commerciale de la Cochinchine* (Saigon: Chambre de Commerce, 1938), 461, 464–465. On the effects of the Depression in China, see Tomoko Shiroyama, *China during the Great Depression: Market, State, and the World Economy, 1929–1937* (Cambridge, Mass.: Harvard University Asia Center, Harvard University Press, 2008).

39. On the price of rice in this period, see Direction des Services Economiques, *Résumé statistique,* 30. Others agree that the Depression manifested itself most significantly through a drop in the price of rice in Indochina. Paul Bernard wrote that the crisis "has thus manifested itself in Indochina mainly by the sharp fall in the price of rice. . . . The Indochinese crisis is thus mainly a crisis of riziculture." See Paul Bernard, *Le problème économique indochinois* (Paris: Nouvelles éditions latines, 1934), 123–124. See also Irene Nørlund, "Rice and the Colonial Lobby: The Economic Crisis in French Indo-China in the 1920s and 1930s," in *Weathering the Storm: The Economies of Southeast Asia in the 1930s Depression,* ed. Peter Boomgaard and Ian Brown (Singapore: ISEAS, 2000), 198–226.

40. While several studies have examined the effects of the Great Depression on rural parts of Southeast Asia, few studies have examined its effects on the cities of the region. The notable exception is the work of Daniel Doeppers on Manila. See Daniel F. Doeppers, "Metropolitan Manila in the Great Depression: Crisis for Whom?" *Journal of Asian Studies* 50, no. 3 (1991): 511–535.

41. Statistique Générale de l'Indochine, *Indices économiques Indochinois* (Hanoi: n.p., 1933), 99.

42. Statistique Générale, *Indices économiques,* 93–94.

43. *Rapport au Conseil Colonial sur l'état de la Cochinchine pendant la période 1930-1931* (Saigon: A. Portail, 1931), 169.

44. *Rapport au Conseil Colonial sur l'état de la Cochinchine pendant la période 1932-1933* (Saigon: Joseph Viêt et Fils, 1933), 144.

45. These calculations and the figures they are based on are in *Rapport No. 14 du 9 Mars 1937 de M. Tupinier, Inspecteur de 1ère classe des Colonies concernant les conflits sociaux et la rémunération du Travail en Cochinchine,* Direction du Contrôle 701, ANOM.

46. The average wage of male workers during this period was $0.62. These averages are based on figures in Statistique Générale de l'Indochine, *Indices économiques Indochinois,* Second Series (Hanoi: n.p., 1937), 52.

47. Statistique Générale de l'Indochine, *Indices économiques Indochinois* (Hanoi: n.p., 1933), 26; Statistique Générale de l'Indochine, *Indices économiques Indochinois,* Second Series (Hanoi: n.p., 1937), 52.

48. "Rapport Politique: Mois de Février 1931," GGI 64343, ANOM.

49. For an indication of the reduced income from indirect taxation on these goods between 1931 and 1935 in Cochinchina, see "Recettes détaillées des Douanes et Régies de Cochinchine," GOUCOCH DIVERS 3607, TTLTQG-II. For an indication of the increased consumption of these goods after the Depression, see "L'année 1938 dans l'évolution économique de l'Indochine," *Bulletin économique de l'Indochine* 42 (1939): 29.

50. Dr. Lebon, "Fonctionnement du service vétérinaire dans la Région Saïgon-Cholon pendant l'année 1938," *Bulletin économique de l'Indochine* 42 (1939): 568.

51. In 1935, Saigon and Chợ Lớn consumed 46% of all the electricity in French Indochina and 88% of the electricity used in Cochinchina. Saigon and Chợ Lớn used more than one and a half times the amount of electricity used in the whole of Tonkin and five times the amount used in Annam. While the domestic consumption of electricity in the city declined, the industrial consumption declined even further. See G. Chevry, "Production et consommation d'énergie électrique en Indochine," *Bulletin économique de l'Indochine* (1936): 787; André Touzet, *L'économie Indochinoise et la grande crise universelle* (Paris: Marcel Giard, 1934), 184.

52. Statistique Générale de l'Indochine, *Indices économiques Indochinois,* Second Series (Hanoi: n.p., 1937), 133.

53. Statistique Générale de l'Indochine, *Indices économiques,* Second Series, 143, 168.

54. *Rapport au Conseil Colonial sur l'état de la Cochinchine pendant la période 1930–1931* (Saigon: A. Portail, 1931), 58.

55. *Rapport au Conseil Colonial sur l'état de la Cochinchine pendant la période 1932–1933* (Saigon: Joseph Viêt et Fils, 1933), 147.

56. See *Rapport No. 14 du 9 Mars 1937 de M. Tupinier, Inspecteur de 1ère classe des Colonies concernant les conflits sociaux et la rémunération du Travail en Cochinchine,* Direction du Contrôle 701, ANOM.

57. See *Rapport au Conseil Colonial sur l'état de la Cochinchine pendant la période 1930–1931* (Saigon: A. Portail, 1931), 52.

58. Calculations based on figures in International Labour Office, *Labour Conditions in Indochina* (Geneva: League of Nations, 1938), 292.

59. The populations of Saigon and Chợ Lớn began to grow again only in 1934 as the economy started to recover. See Baudrit, *Guide historique,* table after 80. A sharp drop in the population of Chợ Lớn during the Depression is also noted in Jean Rondepierre, *Le Port de Saïgon* (Paris: Les Presses Modernes, 1934), 92. In 1937, the Chinese population of Saigon and Chợ Lớn surged to 209,000 after the incident at Marco Polo Bridge, dwarfing the number of Vietnamese in those cities. This figure is confirmed in P. Huard, "Chinois, Japonais et Hindoues en Indochine," *Bulletin économique de l'Indochine* 42 (1939): 482.

60. "Charles André Félix Colonna d'Istria chez M. Diep ngoc Huong, Commerçant à Govap (Giadinh) à Monsieur le Gouverneur Général de l'Indochine à Hanoï," December 19, 1932; "Commandeur de la Légion d'Honneur, Monsieur le Ministre des Colonies," January 20, 1933; Monsieur Colonna d'Istria, Félix ex-préposé des Douanes & Régies de l'Indochine à Saïgon, à Monsieur le Directeur Général des Douanes & Régies de l'Indochine à Hanoï," February 20, 1930, GGI 51698, ANOM.

61. On problems with recruitment to the civil service, see Jean Suignard, *Une grande administration indochinoise: les services civils de l'Indochine* (Rennes, France: Faculté de droit, 1931), 51–56.

62. The figures on education in Cochinchina are taken from Gail Paradise Kelly, "Franco-Vietnamese Schools, 1918–1938" (Ph.D. diss., University of Wisconsin, Madison, 1975), 76–77, 88. On improvements in Vietnamese education in Cochinchina more generally, see Direction Générale de L'Instruction Publique, *La Cochinchine scolaire: l'enseignement dans le pays le plus évolué de l'Union Française* (Hanoi: Imprimerie d'Extrême-Orient, 1931).

63. Suignard, *Une grande administration,* 49–50.

64. These percentages are calculated from figures on the number of French and colonized in the colonial administration in *Annuaire statistique de l'Indochine, vol. 1, 1913–1922* (Hanoi: Imprimerie d'Extrême-Orient, 1927), 247; *Annuaire statistique de l'Indochine, vol. 2, 1923–1929* (Hanoi: Imprimerie d'Extrême-Orient, 1931), 284; *Annuaire statistique de l'Indochine, vol. 3, 1930–1931* (Hanoi: Imprimerie d'Extrême-Orient, 1932), 196–197; *Annuaire statistique de l'Indochine, vol. 4, 1931–1932* (Hanoi: Imprimerie d'Extrême-Orient, 1933), 216–217; *Annuaire statistique de l'Indochine, vol. 5, 1932–1933* (Hanoi: Imprimerie d'Extrême-Orient, 1934), 265–266; *Annuaire statistique de l'Indochine, vol. 6, 1934–1936* (Hanoi: Imprimerie d'Extrême-Orient, 1937), 259–260; *Annuaire statistique de l'Indochine, vol. 7, 1936–1937* (Hanoi: Imprimerie d'Extrême-Orient, 1938), 240–241. For a guide to these changes, see Directions des Services Economiques, *Résumé statistique,* 34. For an observation on the reduction of French personnel in the colonial workforce, see Charles Robequain, *Economic Development,* 29. The figures in the body text are the official published figures on the number of administrative personnel rather than the figures that Robequain provides and for which he does not give sources. Robequain also concludes that the number of French in the colonial administration decreased by approximately 20% during the Great Depression.

65. Jacques Dumarest, *Les monopoles de l'opium et du sel en Indochine* (Lyon: Bosc Frères M. & L. Riou, 1938), 99–101. Of the eighty-five thousand smokers in Cochinchina in 1938, 38% lived in Saigon-Chợ Lớn, most of them Vietnamese.

66. "Extrait du registre des actes de reconnaissance de l'année 1929," April 4, 1929. This document is in the possession of Mlle. Cécile Colonna d'Istria, granddaughter of Jean André Colonna d'Istria, and great-granddaughter of Félix Colonna d'Istria. I am grateful to her for answering questions about her grandfather and great-grandfather. Jean André Colonna d'Istria left Saigon for France after the city fell to communist forces in 1975. Personal communications, September 7, 2010, and August 3, 2011.

67. Vũ Trọng Phụng, "Kỹ Nghệ Lấy Tây" [The industry of marrying foreigners] in *Phóng Sự Việt Nam, 1932–1945* [Vietnamese reportage, 1932–1945], vol. 3, comp. Phan Trọng Thưởng (Hà Nội: Văn Học, 2000), 678–679. Concerning the Sacred Tiger, Vũ Trọng Phụng writes, "Nếu họ phải lấy một người vợ đất Nam Việt thì đó là Hùm thiêng khi đã sa cơ" (679). This is a reference to the classic Vietnamese poem *The Tale of Kiều* by Nguyễn Du. Nguyễn Du writes "Đang khi bất ý chẳng ngờ, Hùm thiêng khi đã sa cơ cũng hèn." See Nguyễn Du, *Truyện Kiều* [The tale of Kiều] (Hà Nội: Văn Học, 1979), 149.

68. Vũ Trọng Phụng, "Kỹ Nghệ Lấy Tây," 680–681.

69. On the life of François Gevin, see "Notice de renseignements concernant M. Gevin François Marius," July 16, 1937, GOUCOCH VIA.8/282(14), TTLTQG-II.

70. On French Indians in Indochina, see Natasha Pairaudeau, *Mobile Citizens: French Indians in Indochina, 1858–1954* (Copenhagen: Nordic Institute of Asian Studies, 2016). The estimate is based on figures in *annuaire Statistique d'Indochine: Recueil des statistiques relatives aux années 1913–1922* (Hanoi: Imprimerie d'Extrême-Orient, 1922), 33, 36–37; *Cahier des voeux annamites* (Saigon: Imprimerie de l'Echo Annamite, 1926), 40; P. Huard, "Chinois, Japonais et Hindous en Indochine," *Bulletin économique de l'Indochine* 3 (1939): 485.

71. Robequain, *Economic Development*, 23.

72. See Pairaudeau, *Mobile Citizens*, 71–118.

73. "Notice des renseignements concernant Mr. Aroule André," July 22, 1937; "Notice des renseignements concernant Mr. Condjandassamy Paquiry," July 22, 1937; "Notice des renseignements concernant Mr. Hilaire Marie, Joseph," July 22, 1937; "Notice des renseignements concernant Mr. Samou Sandanassamy," July 22, 1937, GOUCOCH VIA.8/282(14), TTLTQG-II.

74. "Aide aux nécessiteux," *Bulletin Mensuel des Associations d'Aide Mutuelle et d'Assistance Sociale* 8 (August 1938), 583; "Rapport du président du Comité d'assistance aux chômeurs," GOUCOCH VIA.8/094(10), TTLTQG-II.

75. "Statuts du Comité d'assistance aux chômeurs," September 13, 1939, GOUCOCH VIA.8/094(10), TTLTQG-II.

76. "Statuts du Comité d'assistance aux chômeurs," September 13, 1939, GOUCOCH VIA.8/094(10), TTLTQG-II.

77. "Aide aux nécessiteux," *Bulletin Mensuel des Associations d'Aide Mutuelle et d'Assistance Sociale* 8 (August 1938), 583; "Rapport du président du Comité d'assistance aux chômeurs," GOUCOCH VIA.8/094(10), TTLTQG-II. In 1938, the committee budgeted 1,800 piasters.

78. "Notice des renseignements concernant M. Durand Pierre," July 24, 1937; "Notices des renseignements concernant M. de Boyer d'Eguilles," July 24, 1937; "Notice des renseignements concernant Mr. Trang Joseph," July 22, 1937; "Notice des renseignements concernant Mr. Ponnou Souvakime, Ponnoussamy," July 22, 1937, GOUCOCH VIA.8/282(14), TTLTQG-II.

79. *Etat de la Cochinchine* (1904), 3; (1905), 4; (1906), 4; (1907), 3; (1908), 4; "Rapport du Gardien Chef Aujard de la Maison Centrale de Saigon à Monsieur le Directeur du dit

établissement," October 1, 1907; "M. de Lavigne, Sainte Suzanne, Directeur de la Maison Centrale de Saigon, à Monsieur le Lieutenant Gouverneur de la Cochinchine à Saïgon," October 12, 1907; "Monsieur Duranton, Président de la Commission Municipale, à Monsieur le Lieutenant Gouverneur de la Cochinchine," November 23, 1907, GOUCOCH IA.8/155(22), TTLTQG-II.

80. "Note de Service," March 5, 1907, GOUCOCH IA.10/193, TTLTQG-II.

81. The quote is from "Monsieur Duranton, Président de la Commission Municipale, à Monsieur le Lieutenant Gouverneur de la Cochinchine," October 31, 1907, GOUCOCH IA.8/155(22), TTLTQG-II. In 1906, 68 indigent Europeans received 2,519 days of treatment at the municipal dispensary. See Clavel, *L'assistance médicale indigène en Indo-Chine: organisation et fonctionnement* (Paris: Librairie Maritime et Coloniale, 1908), 256.

82. Before 1910, the colony paid for the cost of repatriating poor Europeans. From that year, the cities of Saigon and Chợ Lớn met the cost of repatriating them. See "Le Ministre des Colonies à Monsieur le Gouverneur Général de l'Indo-Chine," November 3, 1897; "Ville de Saïgon: Conseil Municipal. Session Ordinaire de Juillet 1910. Séance du 27 Juillet 1910. Procès-Verbal," GOUCOCH IA.10/193, TTLTQG-II.

83. Bureau de Bienfaisance de la Ville de Saigon, *Origine de la fondation décret du 9 avril 1914: Arrêté reglementaire du 28 décembre 1914* (Saigon: Imprimerie de l'Union, 1915), 2–7, GOUCOCH VIA.8/244(6), TTLTQG-II.

84. Bureau de Bienfaisance de la Ville de Saigon, *Origine de la fondation décret du 9 avril 1914: Arrêté réglementaire du 28 décembre 1914* (Saigon: Imprimerie de l'Union, 1915), 22–24, GOUCOCH VIA.8/244(6), TTLTQG-II.

85. "Bureau de Bienfaisance de la Ville de Saïgon: Extrait du Registre des Délibérations de la Commission Administrative," June 15, 1916; "Bureau de Bienfaisance de Saïgon: Extrait du Registre des Délibérations de la Commission Administrative," June 22, 1917; "Bureau de Bienfaisance de Saïgon: Procès-Verbal de la Réunion du 20 juillet 1921 de la Commission Administrative," July 20, 1921; "Bureau de Bienfaisance de Saïgon: Procès Verbal de la Réunion du 22 Juin 1923 de la Commission Administrative," June 22, 1923, COUCOCH IA.8/286, TTLTQG-II; "Bureau de Bienfaisance de Saïgon: Procès Verbal de la Réunion du 27 Mai 1928 de la Commission Administrative," May 27, 1928, GOUCOCH VIA.8/244(6); "Bureau de Bienfaisance de Saïgon: Extrait du Procès-Verbal de la Réunion du 22 Mai 1940 de la Commission Administrative," May 22, 1940, GOUCOCH VA.8/055(9), TTLTQG-II.

86. For this phrase and a penetrating discussion of the sociology of colonial society, see Georges Balandier, "La situation coloniale: Approche théorique," *Cahiers internationaux de sociologie* 11 (1951): 44–79.

87. Mlle. Cécile Colonna d'Istria reports that the year of his death is unknown but is presumed to be during World War II. Personal communication, August 3, 2011.

88. The calculation for the proportion of the population uses figures taken from Baudrit, *Guide historique*, table after 80.

89. On the fractured nature of European colonial communities, especially in Indonesia, see Stoler, *Carnal Knowledge and Imperial Power*; and in Cambodia, see Gregor Müller, *Colonial Cambodia's "Bad Frenchmen."*

90. On the fruitless efforts of Mlle. Marcelle Fix to find work and the perilous health of Ernest Costa, see the correspondence in GOUCOCH IA.10/196(2), TTLTQG-II. For correspondence concerning the declining condition of Monsieur Lacquement, see GOUCOCH IIA.10/196(1), TTLTQG-II.

Epilogue

1. Huỳnh Sanh Thông, ed. and trans., *An Anthology of Vietnamese Poems: From the Eleventh through the Twentieth Centuries* (New Haven, Conn.: Yale University Press, 1996), 125. According to Huỳnh Sanh Thông, "lines 5 and 6 allude pejoratively to foreign men who use their money and power to seduce and debauch Vietnamese women. *Bushmen* refers to coarse, brutish Frenchmen." Tản Đà was the pen name of the poet Nguyễn Khắc Hiếu (1889–1939).

2. Vũ Xuân Tự, *Túi Bạc Saigon* (Hà Nội: Trung Bắc Thư Xã, 1941), 3.

3. Vũ Xuân Tự repeats the then well-known ditty "Nhất Sĩ, nhì Phương, tam Xường, tứ Trạch," which alludes to the careers of these four wealthy individuals.

4. Phạm Quỳnh, *Một Tháng ở Nam Kỳ* [One month in Cochinchina] (Hà Nội: n.p., 1919); Đào Trinh Nhất, *Thế Lực Khách Trú Và Vấn Đề Di Dân Vào Nam Kỳ* [Chinese influence and the issue of immigration in Cochinchina] (Hà Nội: Thuỵ Ký, 1924).

5. Vũ Xuân Tự, *Túi Bạc Saigon*, 7.

6. Vũ Xuân Tự, *Túi Bạc Saigon*, 58–61.

7. Vũ Xuân Tự, *Túi Bạc Saigon*, 62–63.

8. Vũ Xuân Tự, *Túi Bạc Saigon*, 66–80.

9. Vũ Xuân Tự, *Túi Bạc Saigon*, 23–28.

10. Vũ Xuân Tự, *Túi Bạc Saigon*, 29–31, 34–55.

11. Vũ Xuân Tự, *Túi Bạc Saigon*, 9.

12. Vũ Xuân Tự, *Túi Bạc Saigon*, 9–11.

13. Vũ Xuân Tự, *Túi Bạc Saigon*, 8.

14. J. Décaudin, "Un essai d'économie dirigée: le marché du paddy et le marché du riz en Cochinchine, 1941–1944," *Bulletin économique de l'Indochine* 47, no. 3–4 (1944): 161.

15. Décaudin, "Un essai d'économie dirigée," 161.

16. André Baudrit, *Guide historique des rues de Saïgon* (Saigon: S.I.L.I., 1945), table after 79; Bộ Quốc Gia Kinh Tế, *Thống Kê Niên Giám Việt Nam* [Statistical annual of Vietnam], vol. 1 (Saigon: Viện Thống Kê Và Khảo Cứu Kinh Tế Việt Nam, 1951), 23.

17. On the economic history of Vietnam during World War II, see Le Manh Hung, *The Impact of World War II on the Economy of Vietnam* (Singapore: Eastern Universities Press, 2004). For a good discussion of the overall economic situation in French Indochina during World War II, see David G. Marr, *Vietnam 1945: The Quest for Power* (Berkeley:

University of California Press, 1995), 13–69. On the First Indochina War, see Hugues Tertrais, *Piastre et le fusil: le coût de la guerre d'Indochine, 1945–1954* (Paris: Ministère de l'économie, des finances et de l'industrie, Comité pour l'histoire économique et financière de la France, 2002); on the Second Indochina War, see Đặng Phong, *Lịch Sử Kinh Tế Việt Nam, 1945–2000* [Economic history of Vietnam, 1945–2000], vol. 2 (Hà Nội: Khoa Học Xã Hội, 2002).

18. For this understanding of the ordering of historical time, see Clifford Geertz, *After the Fact: Two Countries, Four Decades, One Anthropologist* (Cambridge, Mass.: Harvard University Press, 1995), 2.

INDEX

Page numbers in *italics* refer to figures.